How to Write for Class: A Student's Guide to Grammar, Punctuation, and Style

Erica L. Meltzer

 THE CRITICAL READER

New York

ALSO BY ERICA MELTZER

. . . .

Table of Contents

Introduction

For more than a decade, I tutored writing in one capacity or another. My students ranged from seventh graders to college seniors, but all of them struggled with the same essential question: how to take the mass of thoughts swirling around in their heads and put them down on paper in a comprehensible way. Over time, I came to realize that many students' ability to grapple with complex ideas outpaced their grasp of English usage and mechanics. While their insights could be compelling, their ability to convey their thoughts in writing was at times so compromised that it was hard to understand what they were literally trying to say. More than once, students also announced that they had learned more grammar in a session or two of SAT prep than they had learned in all their years of school. I knew I was a good teacher, but I also wasn't deluded enough to think I was *that* good! Something was very clearly amiss.

When I thought back to my own high school experience, however, this state of affairs wasn't particularly shocking. I will never forget how utterly baffled I was when my freshman English class began studying gerunds and different types of sentences. I'd acquired a general understanding of what nouns and verbs and adjectives were in elementary school, and my eighth-grade class had done a brief unit on prepositions, but otherwise, I received no systematic instruction in grammar at any point in my K-8 career. I did not know what a clause was, or how to identify the subject of anything beyond the simplest sentence, or what the heck was meant by "predicate nominative" (a term that, for the record, does not appear in this book). In addition, I had only the most tenuous grasp of just what sort of information belonged in a formal paper. I was an avid reader and had intuited the rules of written English well enough to compose a reasonably engaging personal narrative, but literary analysis—the only kind of writing I was now assigned—was largely a mystery to me. Alas, I do not have any samples of my ninth-grade writing, but I am sure that much of it was positively cringeworthy. I struggled the entire year, and for my efforts earned a B-.

It was not until I was asked to tutor a high school sophomore for a grammar test more than a decade later that I went back and, armed with a degree in French and several years of foreign-language tutoring, finally figured out what comma splices and compound-complex sentences actually were. And it was not for five more years that I learned enough about the history of the American school system to understand how such an extraordinary curricular gap between my pre-high school and ninth-grade experiences could have occurred. I also became aware of the fundamental unfairness of asking students to master advanced concepts when they have never been given a real foundation. There is helpful rigor, and there is unhelpful rigor, and throwing students into the proverbial deep end of a subject without ensuring they know the basics first is a recipe for confusion and frustration. In fact, I only learned grammar at all because of my foreign-language classes, where it was understood that everything needed to be taught logically and sequentially, from the ground up. When I began to teach English, I approached it more or less as I would have approached a foreign language. The success of that method prompted me to write my first book—the original version of *The Ultimate Guide to SAT Grammar*, on which this guide is based.

A few key points I'd like to emphasize:

First, my goal here is not to present a set of dry, abstract principles (or a set of ironclad regulations handed down from the grammar gods on high), but rather to show how the various concepts can be applied to improve the clarity and effectiveness of your writing. While grammatical terminology is used insofar as it is necessary to explain particular concepts, it is not treated as an end in itself. Knowing about compound and complex sentences is not really about learning to label clauses on a worksheet; rather it's about knowing how to construct long sentences that are grammatically coherent vs. ones that are—not to put too fine a spin on it—a big, honking mess. As much as possible, I have sought to strike a balance between prescriptiveness and flexibility. I have also done my best to indicate exceptions when appropriate, and to present errors in contexts in which they often appear. For the sake of authenticity, I have also adapted numerous examples from actual student papers. If you have used other grammar books, you may find some of the sentences in the examples and exercises significantly more challenging. This was a deliberate choice on my part: statements such as *Tom and his cousin moved the sofa* or *The sun is shining brightly today* may be useful for learning fundamentals, but most students cannot automatically apply what they've learned studying simple sentences to the project of composing vastly more complex statements about literature, history, biology, etc. If you can't understand how high-level sentences dealing with these types of topics are put together, there's a good chance you won't be able to construct solid ones of your own. This book is designed in part to bridge that gap.

Next, a key theme of this book is that grammar is about logic, not just memorization. (Note that it is, for the most part, unconcerned with the sort of "artificial," persnickety rules, e.g., the prohibition against splitting infinitives or ending sentences with prepositions, that are commonly trotted out to give the study of grammar a bad name.) One common misconception is that studying grammar is primarily about learning to correct errors. In reality, however, learning about grammar means learning about the underlying structures that govern language—and in turn, thought. In fact, good writing is not really separable from good thinking; grammar informs meaning and vice-versa. Knowing how the building blocks of language can be combined in different ways, to produce different effects in different situations, will help you form more complex—and more interesting—statements, without getting lost in them.

About those readers… remember that you're writing for *them*. When people speak, they have access to a broad range of communication strategies: gestures, movements, intonation, and facial expressions can all be used to convey meaning when words fall short. Statements can be fragmentary and disjointed in ways that would render them incomprehensible on paper. In writing, however, none of those supporting strategies are available; the reader is entirely reliant on the text. As a result, you must explain your ideas as clearly and precisely as possible, and grammar plays a central role in your ability to do so. For example, pronoun agreement errors should be avoided not because someone made the arbitrary decision that they were "bad," but rather because they can make it difficult for readers to figure out what the heck you're talking about! Ideally, grammar and meaning should work together seamlessly, allowing readers to focus on what you are saying as opposed to worrying about how you are saying it. However, the fact that good writing often gives the *appearance* of being effortless should not be taken as evidence that learning to write well actually *is* effortless. No one would watch an accomplished athlete perform a hair-raising move without breaking a sweat and believe that a beginner could quickly learn to do the same. Mastery requires effort and practice, and that is as true for writing as it is for anything else.

While reasonably comprehensive, this book is best treated as a jumping-off point rather than a permanent solution to anyone's grammar woes. Although the exercises are designed to make you continually apply concepts in slightly new ways rather than merely plug in the same thing ten times by rote (a common pitfall that makes so much grammar study ineffective), the reality is that answering a single set of questions is probably not sufficient to imprint a new way of thinking on your brain for good, regardless of how well you understand it in the moment. Skills must be applied on a regular basis if they are to become automatic—and if the majority of the writing you do involves texting or posting on social media, you might have to make more of an effort to switch into school mode than you realize. It's one thing to know how you're *expected* to write in a paper; it's another thing to actually do it. The good news is that mastering the skills in this book can make you immeasurably more secure as a writer. Really understanding how English works, as opposed to just doing what you think sounds right, is the difference between being in control of your writing and being at its mercy. And it's a big difference.

~Erica Meltzer

Chapter One

Parts of Speech and Basic Conventions

1. Noun

Nouns indicate people, places, objects, and ideas.

Common nouns refer to **general** categories, e.g., *girl, city, house, father, doctor, author, school*, and are **not capitalized**.

Proper nouns refer to **specific** people, places, and things, e.g., *Jake, Hawaii, Toyota*, and are **capitalized**.

Collective nouns refer to groups and organizations, e.g., *family, team, country, school, society, company*.

Concrete nouns refer to objects that can be touched and felt, e.g., *book, table, dog*. These nouns are often derived from Germanic (Anglo-Saxon) words and tend to be associated with everyday language.

Abstract nouns refer to ideas and things that cannot be touched. These nouns are usually derived from Greek, Latin, or French and are associated with more formal language. They often have the following endings:

- –ISM, e.g., *realism*
- –ITY, e.g., *unity*
- –LOGY, e.g., *ideology*
- –MENT, e.g., *movement*
- –TUDE, e.g., *solitude*
- –SION, e.g., *exclusion*
- –NESS, e.g., *happiness*
- –TION, e.g., *notion*
- –TUDE, e.g., *solitude*

With the exception of some proper nouns, most nouns can be preceded by **articles**. The **definite article** *the* refers to specific nouns, and the **indefinite articles** *a* and *an* are used to refer to nouns in general.

- Nouns beginning with consonants should be preceded by *a*.

- Nouns beginning with vowels or vowel sounds should be preceded by *an*.

Consonant	Vowel
A pencil A leader A reaction	An object An idea An hour

As a general rule, if you are not sure whether a word can be a noun, try placing *a(n)* or *the* before it. For example, *report* can be a noun because you can say *a report* or *the report*, but *relate* cannot be a noun because it is incorrect to say *a relate* or *the relate*.

2. Pronoun

Pronouns replace nouns.

Examples: *it, they, them, which, s/he, this, that*

- <u>Samantha</u> loves <u>basketball</u>. **She** plays **it** every day after school.

- <u>Marco</u> walks to school with <u>Sherri and Ann</u>. **He** meets **them** at the corner.

Personal pronouns refer to people. They are often referred to in the following way:

	Singular	Plural
1st Person	I	We
2nd Person	You	You (pl.)
3rd Person	S/he, It, One	They

Indefinite pronouns refer to unspecified quantities.

(N)either No one None Any Anybody Anyone	One Each Everybody Everyone Few Both	Some Something Several Many Others All

3. Verb

There are two main types of verbs:

1) Action verbs

Action verbs indicate specific activities, although not necessarily physical actions.

> **Examples:** *talk, write, travel, speak, jump, go, believe, think*

2) Being verbs

Being verbs, also known as **linking verbs**, indicate states of being, seeming, and feeling.

> **Examples:** *be, become, seem, appear, feel, stay, remain, taste*

The "to" form of a verb is known as the **infinitive**. If you are uncertain whether a word can be used as a verb, try placing *to* in front of it to form an infinitive. For example, *clean* can be a verb because you can say *to clean*, but *door* cannot be a verb because you cannot say *to door*.

Verbs are not always used as infinitives, however. In order to indicate who is performing an action, it is necessary to **conjugate** the verb and provide its **subject** (noun or pronoun).

Most conjugations simply involve removing *to* from the infinitive (e.g., *to read* → *I read*); however, third-person singular verbs also add *–s* at the end (e.g., *to work* → *it works*).

To be and *to have*, the most common English verbs, are **irregular**: their conjugated forms differ from their infinitives.

To Be

Sing. (pres.)	Pl. (pres.)
I am	We are
You are	You (pl.) are
S/he, It is	They are

Sing. (past)	Pl. (past)
I was	We were
You were	You (pl.) were
S/he, It was	They were

To Have

Sing. (pres.)	Pl. (pres.)
I have	We have
You have	You (pl.) have
S/he, It has	They have

Note: When an individual's gender is not specified, *they* can also be used as a singular pronoun. This construction tends to be more common in informal writing, so you may want to check with your instructor before using it in a paper.

The **tense** of a verb indicates when an action occurred.

It is = Present	It would be = Conditional
It has been = Present Perfect	It would have been = Past Conditional
It was = Simple Past	It will be = Future
It had been = Past Perfect	It will have been = Future Perfect

4. Preposition

Prepositions are **location** and **time** words: they indicate where things are, where they're going, or when they occurred. They are usually followed by nouns.

> **Example:**   The dog ran **under** the fence and jumped **into** the neighboring yard **in** only a matter **of** seconds.

Common prepositions include the following:

About	Along	Behind	Beyond	From	Off	To
Above	Among	Below	By	In(side)	On	Toward
Across	Around	Beneath	Despite	Near	Over	Underneath
After	At	Beside	During	Next to	Since	Until
Against	Before	Between	For	Of	Through(out)	With(out)

5. Adjective

Adjectives modify nouns, pronouns, and other adjectives.

> **Examples:** *large, pretty, interesting, solid, wide, exceptional, smart, complicated, blue*

- <u>The class</u> was so **boring** that I thought I would fall asleep.

- The **beautiful** <u>view</u> left them at a loss for words.

- We agreed to meet in front of the **light blue** <u>house</u>.

6. Adverb

Adverbs modify verbs, adjectives, and other adverbs. They can also modify phrases and clauses. Adverbs often—but not always—end in *-ly*.

> **Examples:** *rapidly, calmly, strikingly, mildly, boldly, sharply, well, fast, very*

- She <u>smiled</u> **warmly** at him when he entered the room.

- He did **exceedingly** <u>well</u> on the test.

- The professors <u>spoke</u> so **rapidly** that I could **hardly** keep up.

A number of common adverbs involve **time**. Note that the majority of them do <u>not</u> end in *–ly*.

Almost	Before	Just	Next	Soon
Already	Even	Last	Now	Still
Also	First	Later	Often	Tomorrow
Always	Forever	Never	Sometimes	Yesterday

Conjunctive adverbs are transition words: they indicate relationships between clauses.

> **Examples:** *however, therefore, thus, moreover, consequently, nevertheless, indeed, instead, otherwise*

- The game was canceled because of the rain; it was, **however**, rescheduled for Tuesday.

- I overslept by an hour this morning. **Therefore**, I was late for my first class.

7. Conjunction

Conjunctions are **transition words** that indicate relationships between words, phrases, and clauses. There are two main types of conjunctions:

1) Coordinating conjunctions

These conjunctions join two independent clauses (complete sentences). There are seven coordinating conjunctions, known by the acronym FANBOYS: **F**or, **A**nd, **N**or, **B**ut, **O**r, **Y**et, **S**o.

- Emma went to the dentist, **but** she later went to the candy store.

- We watched the movie until midnight, **and** then we went to bed.

Note that some coordinating conjunctions can also be placed between nouns or adjectives.

- Wolves **and** dogs are closely related. (Between nouns)

- Silk is a delicate **yet** strong material. (Between adjectives)

2) Subordinating conjunctions

These conjunctions join dependent clauses (fragments) and independent clauses.

After	Before	Though	Whenever
Although	Despite	Unless	Whereas
As	If	Until	Whether
Because	Since	When	While

- **Because** I stayed up too late, I overslept this morning.
- The book is interesting, **although** it is also very challenging to read.

8. Interjection

Interjections are exclamation words and are often punctuated with exclamation points. They are associated with informal writing and should generally be avoided in academic work.

- Right!
- Crazy!
- LOL!

Multipurpose Parts of Speech

Some words can act as more than one part of speech.

Nouns vs. Verbs

Nouns are typically preceded by *a(n)* or *the*; verbs are preceded by subjects (nouns or pronouns).

Noun: The waiter handed me **the drink**.

Verb: **I drink** at least 16 oz. of water every day.

Nouns vs. Adjectives

Some nouns can also act as modifiers (adjectives), in which case they are known as **adjectival nouns**. Often, these words involve nationalities and/or professions. They are placed **right before proper names**.

Noun: Frank Gehry <u>is</u> **an American** and **an architect** who has designed some of the most famous buildings in the world.

Adjective: **American architect** <u>Frank Gehry</u> has designed some of the most famous buildings in the world.

Verbs vs. Adjectives

Certain phrasal verbs (verbs followed by specific prepositions) also have noun or adjective forms.

As a rule, these **verbs** are written as **two words**, whereas these **nouns** are written as **one word**.

Verb	Noun/Adjective
To work out	A workout
To sign up	A signup sheet
To log in	A login

Incorrect: Students can **signup** for a variety of clubs at the activities fair this afternoon.

Correct: Students can **sign up** for a variety of clubs at the activities fair this afternoon.

Incorrect: Students who want to join a club should write their names on the **sign up** sheet.

Correct: Students who want to join a club should write their names on the **signup** sheet.

Prepositions vs. Conjunctions

"Time" words such as *before*, *after*, and *until* can act as either prepositions or conjunctions.

When these words act as prepositions, they precede nouns.

Preposition: We stopped for dinner **before** the movie.

When these words act as conjunctions, they precede subjects and verbs.

Conjunction: **Before** we went to the movie, we stopped for dinner.

Exercise: Identifying Parts of Speech

For each underlined word below, identify the part of speech: noun, pronoun, verb, adjective, adverb, preposition, or conjunction. (Answers p. 269)

Example:

Although cheerleading is the fastest growing form of
   A   B

physical activity for girls, more than half of Americans do
               C   D

not believe that it should be considered a sport.
              E

A. __Conjunction__

B. __Noun__

C. __Preposition__

D. __Verb__

E. __Pronoun__

1. A large stash of books that once belonged to Thomas
     A   B   C

Jefferson was recently discovered.
         D   E

A. _____

B. _____

C. _____

D. _____

E. _____

2. Although the center of Los Angeles has long been
    A

famous for its traffic jams, the city's center is becoming
 B   C

increasingly accessible to pedestrians.
     D   E

A. _____

B. _____

C. _____

D. _____

E. _____

3. The presence of the Olympic stadium has transformed
     A   B

the formerly run-down area of the city.
    C   D   E

A. _____

B. _____

C. _____

D. _____

E. _____

4. The author's first novel has received <u>generally</u>
                                            A

favorable reviews, <u>but</u> <u>it</u> has thus far failed to <u>become</u>
                    B C   D

an <u>overwhelming</u> success.
       E

A. _____

B. _____

C. _____

D. _____

E. _____

5. The <u>increasing</u> emphasis <u>on</u> test scores <u>has</u> some
        A   B   C

education experts concerned that young children's ability

<u>to learn</u> through play <u>is</u> being compromised.
  D   E

A. _____

B. _____

C. _____

D. _____

E. _____

6. The <u>discovery</u> that both Lewis Carroll and Chopin <u>had</u>
       A   B

epilepsy <u>is</u> threatening to redefine the <u>concept</u> <u>of</u> genius.
      C   D E

A. _____

B. _____

C. _____

D. _____

E. _____

7. Drum languages, once <u>common</u> throughout Africa as a
                           A

<u>means</u> of sending messages, <u>began</u> to disappear almost as
 B   C

soon as <u>they</u> <u>were</u> documented.
      D   E

A. _____

B. _____

C. _____

D. _____

E. _____

8. <u>British</u> scientist J.D. Bernal <u>believed</u> that people would

    A   B

<u>eventually</u> be replaced <u>by</u> creatures that <u>were</u> half-human

    C   D   E

and half-machine.

A. _____

B. _____

C. _____

D. _____

E. _____

9. New research <u>shows</u> that <u>those</u> <u>who</u> live on islands are

                A   B   C

far more likely to suffer <u>from</u> obesity than those who live

                          D

in other <u>environments</u>.

        E

A. _____

B. _____

C. _____

D. _____

E. _____

10. The <u>book</u> *Cane*, written by poet and <u>author</u> Jean

      A   B

Toomer, <u>contains</u> a mix <u>of</u> fiction, poetry, and <u>drama</u>.

          C   D   E

A. _____

B. _____

C. _____

D. _____

E. _____

11. Protests <u>against</u> the country's government <u>have</u> been

            A   B

growing in <u>recent</u> days, and observers <u>fear</u> that they may

              C   D

<u>explode</u> into utter chaos.

  E

A. _____

B. _____

C. _____

D. _____

E. _____

12. Painted by Paul Cézanne, *The Card Players* <u>depicts</u>
                                              A

three men seated <u>around</u> a table, <u>with</u> a fourth gazing
                  B   C

<u>watchfully</u> <u>in</u> the background.
   D   E

A. _____

B. _____

C. _____

D. _____

E. _____

13. <u>It</u> is arguable whether Mark Augustus Landis,
    A

responsible <u>for</u> perpetrating one <u>of</u> the <u>largest</u> art-forgery
            B   C   D

sprees, ever actually <u>broke</u> the law.
                      E

A. _____

B. _____

C. _____

D. _____

E. _____

14. <u>Activities</u> such as bird-watching <u>evolved</u> from people's
    A   B

desire to observe the <u>natural</u> world without <u>actively</u>
                      C   D

participating in <u>it</u>.
                 E

A. _____

B. _____

C. _____

D. _____

E. _____

15. <u>Australian</u> geography is <u>remarkably</u> varied; although
    A   B

Australia <u>is</u> the world's <u>smallest</u> continent, <u>it</u> is the sixth
          C   D   E

largest country.

A. _____

B. _____

C. _____

D. _____

E. _____

Basic Conventions: Capitalization and Punctuation

Please note: although the rules laid out here are generally consistent with MLA style, this book is not intended to be strictly aligned with any particular style guide. If your instructor requires you to adhere to a specific set of punctuation and/or citation formats, those should obviously take precedence.

Capitalization

The first letter of the first word of a sentence is always capitalized.

Incorrect: **more** than ever, companies are looking to expand internationally.

Correct: **More** than ever, companies are looking to expand internationally.

The word *I* is always capitalized.

Incorrect: The company where **i** worked last summer is looking to expand internationally.

Correct: The company where **I** worked last summer is looking to expand internationally.

Proper nouns—names of specific people, places, and things— are always capitalized.

Incorrect: More than ever, companies in the **united states** are looking to expand internationally.

Correct: More than ever, companies in the **United States** are looking to expand internationally.

Proper nouns include:

- Names of individuals and organizations, e.g., *Jane Austen, Microsoft, Harvard University, Labour*

- Titles of books, movies, paintings, e.g., *Pride and Prejudice, Gone with the Wind, The Mona Lisa*

- Political figures and heads of state, e.g., *Queen Elizabeth II, The Prime Minister of India*

- States, cities, provinces, countries, and languages, e.g., *Los Angeles, Nebraska, Thailand, Spanish*

- Days, months, time periods, e.g., *Friday, July 4th, The Renaissance*

- Holidays, e.g., *Thanksgiving, Bastille Day, Diwali*

- Acronyms and initialisms, e.g., *NASA, CEO, USA, SAT*

Capitalization and Titles

As a general rule, the first word of a title and any nouns, verbs, adjectives, or pronouns are capitalized.

Internal articles (e.g., *the*, *an*) and prepositions (e.g., *in*, *of*, *with*) are lower case.

Incorrect: When it was published in 1859, Charles Darwin's ***On The Origin Of The Species*** quickly became an immensely controversial work.

Correct: When it was published in 1859, Charles Darwin's ***On the Origin of the Species*** quickly became an immensely controversial work.

Do **NOT** capitalize:

Non-proper nouns

Incorrect: The **Company** where I worked last summer is expanding internationally.

Correct: The **company** where I worked last summer is expanding internationally.

Seasons

Incorrect: The company where I worked last **Summer** is expanding internationally.

Correct: The company where I worked last **summer** is expanding internationally.

Occupations and political offices when not part of a specific individual's title

Incorrect: The sole avenue to becoming a fully licensed **Doctor** in the United States involves submitting to what is known as "the match."

Correct: The sole avenue to becoming a fully licensed **doctor** in the United States involves submitting to what is known as "the match."

Incorrect: Although **Kings and Queens** were once true heads of state across Europe, today their roles are largely symbolic.

Correct: Although **kings and queens** were once true heads of state across Europe, today their roles are largely symbolic.

Correct: **Queen Victoria**, who sat on the British throne from 1837 to 1901, was England's longest-reigning monarch.

Family members

Incorrect: When I worked in New York, my **Dad** came to visit me for a week.

Correct: When I worked in New York, my **dad** came to visit me for a week.

Note: when the title of a family member is treated as a proper name—that is, when it is not preceded by a pronoun—then it should be capitalized, e.g., *I went out to lunch with Dad last week.*

Academic subjects

Incorrect: I'm looking forward to taking an **Economics** class next semester.

Correct: I'm looking forward to taking an **economics** class next semester.

If a subject is included as part of a course title, however, it should be capitalized.

Correct: With over 600 students typically enrolled, **Economics 101** is among the university's most popular undergraduate classes.

Note: the exception to this rule is *English*, which, as a language, is always capitalized.

Punctuation

A period is always placed at the end of a sentence.

Incorrect: More than ever, companies are looking to grow **internationally**

Correct: More than ever, companies are looking to grow **internationally.**

A question mark is always placed at the end of a question.

Incorrect: <u>When</u> is the company's new office in China expected to **open.**

Correct: <u>When</u> is the company's new office in China expected to **open?**

When parentheses are attached to a sentence, place ending punctuation <u>outside</u> the close parenthesis.

Incorrect: More than ever, companies are looking to grow internationally (particularly in **Asia.)**

Correct: More than ever, companies are looking to grow internationally (particularly in **Asia).**

When a full sentence is enclosed in parentheses, place ending punctuation <u>inside</u> the close parenthesis.

Incorrect: More than ever, companies are looking to grow internationally. (Asia, particularly China, is an increasingly popular **location).**

Correct: More than ever, companies are looking to grow internationally. (Asia, particularly China, is an increasingly popular **location.)**

Punctuation marks are placed immediately after a word. They are followed by a single space.*

Correct: With the development of many forms of technology and the improvement of **transportation, globalization** is occurring faster than ever.

Correct: More than ever, companies are looking to grow **internationally. Therefore**, foreign languages play a critical role in the ever-expanding global market.

DO NOT:

Leave a space between the word and the punctuation mark.

Incorrect: With the development of many forms of technology and the improvement of **transportation , globalization** is occurring faster than ever.

Omit the space after the punctuation mark.

Incorrect: With the development of many forms of technology and the improvement of **transportation,globalization** is occurring faster than ever.

Place the punctuation mark next to the following word, without a space.

Incorrect: With the development of many forms of technology and the improvement of **transportation ,globalization** is occurring faster than ever.

Numbers

Numbers 1-9 are typically written out; numbers 10 and above are written as numerals.

Correct: Throughout history there have been many senatorial bodies, **two** of which were the Spartan Gerousia and the Roman Senate.

The primary exception is when different numbers are used to refer to different categories of things. In such cases, one category can be written as words and the other in numerals.

Acceptable: Despite not publishing her first novel until she was **forty**, Edith Wharton wrote **15** novels as well as **85** short stories.

Ampersands

An ampersand ("&" sign) may be used in titles and names of organizations, but the word *and* should always be written out in the body of a text.

Incorrect: Despite not publishing her first novel until she was **forty**, Edith Wharton wrote 15 novels **&** 85 short stories.

Correct: Despite not publishing her first novel until she was **forty**, Edith Wharton wrote 15 novels **and** 85 short stories.

*During the typewriter era, two spaces were commonly used after a period. Today, however, one space is standard.

Citing Works

Use **quotation marks** to set off titles of **songs**, **poems**, **essays**, **chapters**, **articles**, and **short stories**.

Correct: One of Sylvia Plath's earliest works, **"Tulips"** is a study in poetic tension.

Correct: Jonathan Swift's essay **"A Modest Proposal"** is often held up as a model of satire.

Italicize or **underline** titles of **books**, **epic poems**, **plays**, **films**, **albums**, **aircraft**, **ships**, and **foreign terms**.*

Correct: One of the many theatrical devices in Tony Kushner's *Angels in America* is that each of the eight principal actors has other minor roles in the play.

Correct: The filming of **Gone with the Wind** was delayed for two years while 1,400 women were screened for the role of Scarlett O'Hara.

Correct: *Sfumato* is a painting technique for softening the transition between colors, mimicking an area beyond what the viewer is focusing on.

Miscellaneous Points

Always refer to an author by his or her **last name**.

Incorrect: The progress of Elizabeth and Darcy's relationship in Jane Austen's novel *Pride and Prejudice* reflects several key themes of the novel. Through the relationship of these two characters, **Jane** explores class expectations, social status, and marriage.

Correct: The progress of Elizabeth and Darcy's relationship in Jane Austen's novel *Pride and Prejudice* reflects several key themes of the novel. Through the relationship of these two characters, **Austen** explores class expectations, social status, and marriage.

A novel is a long work of narrative fiction—plays, memoirs, and short stories are not novels.

Incorrect: Shakespeare's *Julius Caesar* is a **novel** that centers on the assassination of an ancient Roman general by a group of conspirators.

Correct: Shakespeare's *Julius Caesar* is a **play** that centers on the assassination of an ancient Roman general by a group of conspirators.

In general, **the first person (I) is not used in academic papers**; it is understood that the ideas you are presenting are your own. **Unless your instructor explicitly permits this construction, you should err on the side of caution and avoid it.** Note that while very advanced writers sometimes break with this convention, most high school and beginning college writers do not yet have a compelling reason to do so.

Avoid: The two characters **that I think strive** for beauty most strongly in Toni Morrison's *The Bluest Eye* are Pauline and Pecola.

Better: The two characters **that strive** for beauty most strongly in Toni Morrison's *The Bluest Eye* are Pauline and Pecola.

*Note that political and legal documents, e.g., The Constitution, are an exception to this rule.

Exercise: Capitalization

In the following sentences, capitalize the first letter of any word incorrectly written in lower case. Some of the sentences may not contain an error. (Answers p. 269)

Example: At the end of w̶orld w̶ar I [W W], the music industry was already on its way to becoming big business in the u̶nited s̶tates [U S], exerting a strong influence on a̶merican [A] culture.

1. While competing at the olympics in beijing, the japanese sprinter Shingo Suetsugu set a record for the 200-meter dash on august 22, 2008.

2. In Charles Beard's analysis, the constitution is a Document that was created primarily to protect the rights of wealthy landowners.

3. Throughout the anglo-saxon epic poem *beowulf*, vengeance plays a central role in the actions of many of the characters.

4. Many early childhood experts have argued that watching too much tv is dangerous for young children because they have difficulty distinguishing between fantasy and Reality.

5. Civics was once a required class for students in many High Schools, but since the 1960s, the number of students required to study how the united states government works has declined dramatically.

6. As Odysseus and his crew journey home to the island of ithaka, they overcome many obstacles with the help of the mythological greek gods, yet they also lose a number of crew members along the way.

7. In september of 2015, *Harper's* magazine published William Deresiewicz's Essay "The Neoliberal Arts: How colleges have sold their soul to the market."

8. After burberry experienced a series of losses in the early 1980s, the ceo, Rose Marie Bravo, took steps to modernize the brand, and soon its popularity began to grow among celebrities.

9. According to Cowell, the court showdown between galileo and the catholic church is quite possibly the greatest standoff between faith and science that History has ever seen.

10. Modern Communication features such as caller id, call waiting, and voice mail help both companies and customers to save valuable time and calling charges.

Exercise: Punctuating Titles

In the following sentences, correct any missing or incorrect punctuation. Some of the sentences may not contain an error. (Answers p. 270)

Example: Based on the life of Gypsy Rose Lee, the musical **Gypsy** is set in Depression-era Seattle during the last days of the vaudeville era.

1. In his essay Why We Crave Horror Movies, Stephen King suggests that viewing paranormal acts on a screen can help people keep their own fears at bay.

2. Multiple readings of Oscar Wilde's novel The Picture of Dorian Gray reveal that the image of the painting referenced in the title can always be interpreted in new ways.

3. Rolled out on September 17, 1976, as the first orbiter in the space shuttle system, Endeavor was built to perform atmospheric test flights for NASA.

4. Chris Berg's article The Weight of the Word presents the argument that the United States government's attempts to close WikiLeaks were a fundamental breach of both free speech and freedom of the press.

5. Among Ike and Tina Turner's final joint hits were the cover version of Proud Mary (1971) and Nutbush City Limits (1973), with the former becoming one of Turner's most recognizable songs.

6. Set in sixteenth-century Venice, Shakespeare's play Othello was adapted from the Italian author Cinthio's short story "A Moorish Captain" (1565).

7. The narrator of Robert Browning's poem The Last Duchess recounts to a visitor that he keeps a painting of his former wife hidden behind a curtain that only he is allowed to draw back.

8. In the article Stuff Is Not Salvation, Anna Quindlen examines the American fixation with material possessions and offers a critique of consumer culture.

9. The director Nora Ephron, best known for her romantic comedy films, received an Academy Award nomination for Silkwood (1983), When Harry Met Sally... (1989), and Sleepless in Seattle (1993).

10. George Orwell's novel 1984 depicts a totalitarian society in which citizens are subject to constant surveillance from a leader known only as "Big Brother."

Chapter Two

Sentences and Fragments

We're going to begin this chapter with a short quiz.

Is It a Sentence?

For each statement below, circle "Sentence" if it can stand alone as an independent sentence and "Fragment" if it cannot. Try to complete the full exercise in less than two minutes. (Answers p. 270)

1. Louis Armstrong was one of the greatest jazz musicians of the twentieth century.

    Sentence   **Fragment**

2. He was one of the greatest jazz musicians of the twentieth century.

    Sentence   **Fragment**

3. Louis Armstrong, who was one of the greatest jazz musicians of the twentieth century.

    Sentence   **Fragment**

4. Who was one of the greatest jazz musicians of the twentieth century.

    Sentence   **Fragment**

5. Louis Armstrong, who was one of the greatest jazz musicians of the twentieth century, was a vocalist as well as a trumpet player.

    Sentence   **Fragment**

6. Today, he is considered one of the greatest jazz musicians of the twentieth century.

    Sentence   **Fragment**

7. He is, however, considered one of the greatest jazz musicians of the twentieth century.

    Sentence   **Fragment**

8. Armstrong now being considered one of the greatest jazz musicians of the twentieth century.

          Sentence   **Fragment**

9. Because of his virtuosic trumpet skills, Louis Armstrong is considered one of the greatest jazz musicians of the twentieth century.

          Sentence   **Fragment**

10. Although he was one of the most virtuosic trumpet players of his generation.

          Sentence   **Fragment**

11. Many people considering Louis Armstrong the greatest jazz musician of all time.

          Sentence   **Fragment**

12. Many of them consider him the greatest jazz musician of all time.

          Sentence   **Fragment**

13. Many consider him the greatest jazz musician of all time.

          Sentence   **Fragment**

14. Many of whom consider him the greatest jazz musician of all time.

          Sentence   **Fragment**

15. Having shown an unusual gift for music early in his childhood, Louis Armstrong, who was born in New Orleans on August 4, 1901.

          Sentence   **Fragment**

16. Having shown an unusual gift for music early in his childhood, Louis Armstrong, who was born in New Orleans on August 4, 1901, went on to become one of the greatest jazz musicians of the twentieth century.

          Sentence   **Fragment**

17. Moreover, Armstrong, who spent much of his early life in poverty, went on to become one of the greatest jazz musicians of the twentieth century.

          Sentence   **Fragment**

18. Nicknamed "Satchmo," Louis Armstrong, who was born in New Orleans on August 4, 1901, grew up to become one of the greatest jazz musicians of the twentieth century and, perhaps, one of the greatest musicians of all time.

          Sentence   **Fragment**

Every sentence must contain two elements:

1) A **subject** (noun, pronoun, or gerund)

2) A **verb** that corresponds to the subject

The verb and any additional information are known as the **predicate**.

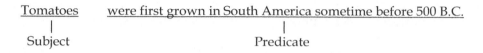

A sentence can contain only one word (*Go!* is a sentence because the subject, *you*, is implied) or consist of numerous clauses, but provided that it contains a subject and a verb (predicate), it can be considered grammatically complete.

Phrases and Clauses

A **phrase** is essentially any statement that does not contain a subject and a verb. It can contain nouns, *-ing* words (participles or gerunds), prepositions, adjectives, or adverbs.

- to the office
- having woken up early
- a beautiful sunrise

A **clause** is a statement that contains both a subject and a verb. **Independent clauses** can stand on their own as sentences; **dependent clauses** cannot. If you find it easier, you can also think of dependent clauses as **fragments**.

- The dog barks (Independent)
- It rang loudly (Independent)
- Although it rained yesterday (Dependent)

Now we're going to look at a variety of sentence types, as well as how they are constructed.

A. Simple Sentence

Sentence: The tomato grows.

This is known as a simple sentence because it contains only a subject (*the tomato*) and a verb (*grows*), which tells us what the subject does. Because it can stand on its own as an independent sentence, it can also be called an **independent clause**.

B. Prepositional Phrases

If we want to make our simple sentence a little longer, we can add a **prepositional phrase**. A prepositional phrase is a phrase that begins with a preposition—a **time** or **location** word that comes **before a noun**. Common prepositions include *in, to, with, from, for, at, by,* and *on.* (For a complete list, see p. 12.)

    Sentence: The tomato grows <u>**around**</u> **the world.**

Sentences can contain many prepositional phrases, sometimes one after the other.

    Sentence: The tomato grows <u>**in**</u> **many shapes and varieties** <u>**in**</u> **greenhouses** <u>**around**</u> **the world**.

A prepositional phrase can also be placed between the subject and the verb.

    Sentence: The tomatoes <u>**in the greenhouse**</u> grow in many varieties and colors.

A prepositional phrase can also be placed at the **beginning** of a sentence.

    Sentence: <u>**In the greenhouse,**</u> the tomatoes grow in many varieties and colors.

A prepositional phrase **cannot**, however, stand alone as a complete sentence.

    Fragment: In the greenhouse

    Fragment: In many shapes and varieties in greenhouses around the world

C. Pronoun as Subject

Nouns can also be replaced by **pronouns**—words such as *it, she,* and *they*. In the sentence *The tomato grows,* the singular noun *the tomato* (the subject) can be replaced with the singular pronoun *it.*

    Sentence: It grows.

This is still a sentence because it contains a subject (*it*) and a verb that corresponds to it (*grows*). **Grammatically, it is identical to the version with the noun.**

As is true for the original version, we can rewrite the longer versions of our sentence using pronouns.

    Sentence: **It** grows around the world.

    Sentence: **It** grows in many shapes and varieties in greenhouses around the world.

If we want to make the subject plural, we can replace it with the plural pronoun *they.*

    Sentence: **Tomatoes** grow.

    Sentence: **They** grow.

    Sentence: **They** grow in many shapes and varieties in greenhouses around the world.

It and *they* are the most common **subject pronouns**, but other pronouns can also be used.

People	Things	People or Things	
I	It	None	Several
You	Nothing	One	Many
S/he	Anything	Each	More
We	Everything	Every	Most
No one	Something	Any	Other(s)
Someone/somebody		Another	All
Anyone/anybody		Few	They
Everyone/everybody		Some	

"Group" Pronouns

One very common point of confusion often involves **"group" pronouns** such as *some, several, few, many,* and *others*. These pronouns can be used to begin clauses in two different ways, one of which creates an independent clause and the other of which creates a dependent clause. Let's start with these two sentences:

Sentence: Many tomatoes are grown in greenhouses around the world.

Sentence: Most people believe that the tomato is a vegetable.

People generally don't have too much trouble recognizing that these are sentences. They have clear subjects (*many tomatoes, most people*) and verbs (*are, believe*), and they make sense on their own. The problem arises when the nouns are removed.

Pronoun (of them) = Sentence

In this usage, the pronoun alone acts as a subject and is used to replace a noun. It is often followed by the phrase *of them*, but it can be used by itself as well.

Sentence: **Many (of them)** are grown in greenhouses around the world.

Sentence: **Most (of them)** believe that the tomato is a vegetable.

Pronoun + of which/whom = Fragment

When an indefinite pronoun is followed by *of which* or *of whom*, it creates a **dependent clause** which, by definition, cannot stand alone as a full sentence.

Fragment: **Many of which** are grown in greenhouses around the world

Fragment: **Most of whom** believe that the tomato is a vegetable

D. Adjectives and Adverbs

We can also add descriptive words, or modifiers, in the form of adjectives or adverbs.

Adjective: The **large red** <u>tomato</u> grows.

Adverb: Tomatoes <u>grow</u> **relatively quickly**.

Adverbs can also modify **clauses**. Note that a sentence to which an adverb is added is still a sentence.

Sentence: <u>Tomatoes are</u> **usually** <u>red</u>, but **sometimes** <u>they are also yellow, orange, or green</u>.

Sentence: **Furthermore**, <u>tomatoes are one of the most common ingredients in dishes worldwide</u>.

E. Participles and Gerunds

Every verb has two **participles**: present and past.

The **present participle** is formed by adding *–ing* to the verb.

talk	→	talking
paint	→	painting
grow	→	growing

The **past participle** is usually formed by adding *–ed* or *–n* to the verb.

talk	→	talked
paint	→	painted
grow	→	grown

Both present and past participles can act as adjectives and be used to describe (modify) nouns.

Present: The **growing** <u>tomatoes</u> are bright green, but they will soon turn red.

Past: The tomato's use as a **cultivated** <u>food</u> may have originated with the indigenous peoples of Mexico.

A **participial phrase begins with a participle** and can be formed in either the **present** or the **past**.

Present: **Originating in South America**, the tomato, one of the most popular salad ingredients, grows in many shapes and varieties in greenhouses around the world.

To form the past tense, use the present participle *having* + past participle of the main verb (*originated*).

Past: **Having originated in South America**, the tomato, one of the most popular salad ingredients, grows in many shapes and varieties in greenhouses around the world.

We can also use the past participle of the verb *grow*.

Past: **Grown originally in South America**, the tomato, one of the most popular salad ingredients, is now produced in many shapes and varieties in greenhouses around the world.

Participial phrases can appear in the beginning (as in the above examples), middle, or end of a sentence:

Middle: The tomato, **<u>cultivated</u> initially in South America during the first millennium B.C.,** is now grown in many shapes and varieties in greenhouses around the world.

End: The tomato is now grown in greenhouses around the world, **<u>having</u> first been cultivated in South America in the first millennium B.C.**

A participle cannot act as a main verb, and so a statement containing only a participle is a fragment.

Fragment: Originating/Grown in South America

Fragment: The tomato having initially been cultivated in the first millennium B.C.

Fragment: The tomato grown originally in South America

Gerunds are identical in appearance to present participles: they are created by adding *–ing* to the verb. (You do not need to worry about the difference between gerunds and participles right now.)

Although gerunds look like verbs, they act like nouns and can act as subjects.

Sentence: **Cultivating** tomatoes in greenhouses is common in regions where temperatures are low in the wintertime.

Because gerunds cannot act as verbs, a statement that contains only an *-ing* word is a **fragment**.

Fragment: Tomatoes **growing** in many shapes and varieties in greenhouses around the world

Sentence: Tomatoes **grow** in many shapes and varieties in greenhouses around the world.

Note that *to be*, the most common verb in the English language, is highly irregular: its gerund form, *being*, does not resemble its conjugated forms.

	Present	**Past**
Singular	is	was
Plural	are	were

Fragment:	Today, the tomato **being** grown in greenhouses around the world
Sentence:	Today, the tomato **is** grown in greenhouses around the world.
Fragment:	Originally, tomatoes **being** cultivated only in South America
Sentence:	Originally, tomatoes **were** cultivated only in South America.

F. Non-Essential and Essential Phrases and Clauses

Information can be inserted between a subject and a verb in the form of a **non-essential** or **essential clause**.

Non-essential clauses modify nouns. They often begin with **"w-words"** such as *who(se)*, *which*, and *where*, and they are most often **followed by verbs**.

Sentence:	The tomato, **which is one of the most popular salad ingredients,** grows in many shapes and varieties in greenhouses around the world.

These clauses are called "non-essential" because they are not central to the meaning or logic of a sentence. When they are removed, the sentence still makes sense.

Sentence:	The tomato, ~~which is one of the most popular salad ingredients,~~ grows in many shapes and varieties in greenhouses around the world.

A non-essential clause that begins with a noun or pronoun is called an **appositive**.

Sentence:	The tomato, **a popular salad ingredient,** grows in many shapes and varieties in greenhouses around the world.
Sentence:	The tomato, **one of the most popular salad ingredients,** grows in many shapes and varieties in greenhouses around the world.

Appositives can also appear as descriptions at the beginnings or ends of sentences.

Sentence:	**A popular salad ingredient,** the tomato grows in many shapes and varieties in greenhouses around the world.
Sentence:	In greenhouses around the world grow many shapes and varieties of the tomato, **a popular salad ingredient.**

In addition, participial phrases can be used non-essentially in the middle of a sentence.

Sentence:	The tomato, <u>having</u> **initially been cultivated only in South America,** is now grown around the world.
Sentence:	The tomato, <u>cultivated</u> **initially in South America during the first millennium B.C.,** is now grown in many shapes and varieties in greenhouses around the world.

Essential clauses are known as such because they are essential to meaning and logic. They begin with *that* and are **not set off by commas**. Like non-essential clauses, they are typically inserted between subjects and verbs (underlined below).

Sentence: <u>The small yellow fruits</u> **that were cultivated in South America during the first millennium B.C.** <u>bear</u> little resemblance to the large red tomatoes sold in supermarkets around the world today.

Non-essential and essential elements cannot stand alone as complete sentences.

Fragment: which grows in greenhouses around the world

Fragment: grown in greenhouses around the world

Fragment: a popular salad ingredient

Fragment: that were cultivated in South America during the first millennium B.C.

In addition, a sentence cannot **stop** right after a non-essential or essential clause. If it does, a fragment is created.

Fragment: The tomato, which is one of the most popular salad ingredients

Fragment: The tomato, used in a wide variety of dishes around the world

Fragment: The small yellow fruits that were originally cultivated in South America

G. Conjunctions

Conjunctions join phrases and clauses. Common examples include *and, but, so, yet, because, although, when,* and *while*.

Sentence: Tomatoes are cultivated in gardens **and** in greenhouses.

Sentence: **Although** tomatoes have been cultivated since the first millennium B.C., they did not become popular in the United States until the mid-nineteenth century.

Sentence: Tomatoes are brightly colored and full of flavor, **so** they are among the most popular salad ingredients.

A **single clause** that begins with a conjunction cannot stand alone as a sentence, however.

Fragment: **But** today, tomatoes are grown around the world

Fragment: **When** tomatoes were first brought to Europe from South America

Fragment: **Although** tomatoes have been cultivated since the first millennium B.C.

Every sentence must therefore have one main (independent) clause that does not begin with a conjunction.

Fragment: Often used in soups and stews, **and** <u>tomatoes are among the most popular ingredients worldwide</u>.

Sentence: Often used in soups and stews, <u>tomatoes are among the most popular ingredients worldwide</u>.

Note that when a clause begun by a conjunction contains a subject, it must contain a verb rather than an *-ing* word.

Fragment: Most tomatoes grown today have smooth surfaces, **although** <u>some older plants and most modern beefsteaks</u> **showing** pronounced ribbing.

Sentence: Most tomatoes grown today have smooth surfaces, **although** <u>some older plants and most modern beefsteaks</u> **show** pronounced ribbing.

When no subject is present, however, *-ing* can acceptably appear in the same phrase as some subordinating conjunctions, primarily ones indicating time (e.g., *while, when, before, after, since*).

Sentence: <u>Since</u> **becoming** a key ingredient in Italian cuisine in the nineteenth century, the tomato has grown in popularity worldwide.

Exercise: Sentences vs. Fragments

Now see how well you can identify sentences and fragments. (Answers p. 271)

1. Lan Samantha Chang, a critically acclaimed novelist who counts among her influences authors as varied as Charlotte Brontë and Edgar Allan Poe.

    Sentence   **Fragment**

2. The recipient of a MacArthur "genius" grant, Deborah Willis is a renowned photographer.

    Sentence   **Fragment**

3. The development of identity remaining one of psychologist Erik Erikson's greatest concerns throughout his career.

    Sentence   **Fragment**

4. A fungus that has been destroying bat populations throughout the United States in recent years.

    Sentence   **Fragment**

5. The plan to overhaul the country's higher education system being a model for moving other desperately needed projects forward.

    Sentence   **Fragment**

6. Physical differences among dog breeds are determined by variations occurring in only about seven genetic regions.

    Sentence   **Fragment**

7. Taking place in June of each year, and the Rochester Jazz Festival attracts more than 100,000 fans.

    Sentence   **Fragment**

8.   George Barr McCutcheon, a popular novelist and playwright who is best known for a series of novels set in the fictional eastern European country of Graustark.

Sentence   **Fragment**

9.   Between 1903 and 1913, the British suffragettes, a group devoted to helping women win the right to vote, resorted to increasingly extreme measures to make their voices heard.

Sentence   **Fragment**

10.   The sailing trip, which had begun in ideal weather conditions and rapidly turned perilous after storm clouds began to move in.

Sentence   **Fragment**

11.   Often thought of as a contemporary sport, but surfing was actually an important activity in Polynesian culture for many centuries before Europeans first observed it.

Sentence   **Fragment**

12.   Heralds, the predecessors of modern diplomats, traveled under the orders of kings or noblemen in order to convey messages or proclamations.

Sentence   **Fragment**

13.   The dam was declared a threat to the surrounding area because if it eroded, people could be put in danger.

Sentence   **Fragment**

14. High school students, who send a higher number of texts per day than members of any other age group and average more than 330 messages each month.

   Sentence   **Fragment**

15. Recent findings from research on moose, which have suggested that arthritis in human beings may be linked in part to nutritional deficits.

   Sentence   **Fragment**

Chapter Three

Joining and Separating Clauses

Two complete sentences can never be separated by only a comma (**comma splice**), nor can they be placed back-to-back without any punctuation whatsoever (**fused sentence**).

> Incorrect: Some animal species are able to make their own **vitamin C, people** lack the enzymes necessary to produce this compound and must obtain it through their diets.

> Incorrect: Some animal species are able to make their own **vitamin C people** lack the enzymes necessary to produce this compound and must obtain it through their diets.

There are three primary ways to **correctly** separate two independent clauses (complete sentences) from one another. **All of these options are grammatically identical;** they vary only in style and emphasis.

1) Period

2) Semicolon

3) Comma + Coordinating (FANBOYS) Conjunction

A. Period = Semicolon

Both periods and semicolons are used to separate two complete sentences from one another. Note that the first letter after a period is capitalized, whereas the first letter after a semicolon is not.

> Correct: Some animal species are able to make their own **vitamin C. People** lack the enzymes necessary to produce this compound and must obtain it through their diets.

> Correct: Some animal species are able to make their own **vitamin C; people** lack the enzymes necessary to produce this compound and must obtain it through their diets.

Although periods and semicolons have the same grammatical purpose, they also produce slightly different effects. A period provides a strong division between two statements, without implying any connection between them. The second statement simply adds information to the first. In contrast, a semicolon is used to imply a connection, without stating it outright.

"Strong" Transitions

Certain transition words (**conjunctive adverbs**) are strong enough to begin a sentence. Common examples include *however*, *therefore*, *thus*, *consequently*, *moreover*, *instead*, and *nevertheless*. Traditionally, these words followed a semicolon when used to begin a clause, but today a period is broadly accepted as well.

In this usage, conjunctive adverbs must not **follow** a comma, but they must be **followed by** a comma.

Incorrect:	Some animal species are able to make their own **vitamin C, however,** people lack the enzymes necessary to produce this compound and must obtain it through their diets.
Correct:	Some animal species are able to make their own **vitamin C; however, (or: vitamin C. However,)** people lack the enzymes necessary to produce this compound and must obtain it through their diets.

Note that these conjunctions can be used with two commas (non-essentially) in the **middle** of a clause.

Correct:	Some animal species are able to make their own **vitamin C;** people lack the enzymes necessary to produce this compound, **however,** and must obtain it through their diets.

B. Comma + Coordinating/FANBOYS Conjunction (Compound Sentence)

There are seven coordinating conjunctions, collectively known by the acronym FANBOYS.

For*, And, Nor, But, Or, Yet, So

FANBOYS conjunctions must always follow a comma when used to join independent clauses. **A sentence formed from two independent clauses + FANBOYS conjunction is called a compound sentence.**

Without a comma, a sentence that uses a FANBOYS conjunction to join two independent clauses is technically a run-on, regardless of its length.

Run-on:	Some animal species are able to make their own **vitamin C but people** lack the enzymes necessary to produce this compound and must obtain it through their diets.
Correct:	Some animal species are able to make their own **vitamin C, but people** lack the enzymes necessary to produce this compound and must obtain it through their diets.

In everyday writing, this rule is somewhat flexible: in short sentences, a comma may not be desirable for stylistic reasons. In general, however, the comma helps maintain a clear division between thoughts.

*The FANBOYS conjunction *for* means "because."

Note, however, that FANBOYS conjunctions are not normally followed by a comma.

Incorrect: Some animal species are able to make their own **vitamin C, but, people** lack the enzymes necessary to produce this compound and must obtain it through their diets.

When the subject is the same in both clauses and is **not** repeated in the second clause, no comma is needed.

Incorrect: People lack the enzymes necessary to produce **vitamin C, and must** obtain this compound through their diets.

Correct: People lack the enzymes necessary to produce **vitamin C and must** obtain this compound through their diets.

You can also think of the rule this way: *comma + FANBOYS = period*, so plug in a period.

Plug in: People lack the enzymes necessary to produce **vitamin C. Must** obtain this compound through their diets.

Because the second statement above clearly is not a sentence, no comma should be placed before *and*.

This rule is again somewhat flexible in everyday writing, however. When a sentence is very long and complex, a comma may be helpful—or even necessary—for the sake of clarity.

Acceptable: Unlike some animal species, human beings are born without the ability to produce the enzyme L-gulonolactone oxidase, **and must** obtain vitamin C through the consumption of foods such as oranges and grapefruit.

Note that *FANBOYS conjunction + verb* should never follow a period or semicolon.

Incorrect: Unlike some animal species, human beings cannot make **vitamin C. But must obtain (or: vitamin C; but must obtain)** this compound by consuming foods such as oranges and grapefruit.

When sentences are very long and complex, however, it is generally considered acceptable to place a FANBOYS conjunction after a semicolon in order to provide clear divisions between ideas and improve readability.

Acceptable: Some animal species, including bats and guinea pigs, are born with the ability to produce the enzyme L-gulonolactone **oxidase; but** human beings, who cannot manufacture it, must obtain it through foods such as oranges and grapefruit.

Likewise, a FANBOYS conjunction may sometimes be used to start a sentence for stylistic effect. This construction is more common in informal and journalistic writing, although it is usually fine to use it occasionally for emphasis in academic writing.

Acceptable: People are born with the ability to produce many of the compounds they need to survive. **But** that's not always the case.

C. Colon or Dash

When the second clause or sentence explains the first, a colon or dash can also be used to separate two clauses. In such cases, the first word after the punctuation mark should not be capitalized.

Correct: Because they are unable to produce vitamin C themselves, people must consume foods that contain **it: oranges**, grapefruit, and broccoli are all excellent sources of that compound.

Correct: Because they are unable to produce vitamin C themselves, people must consume foods that contain **it—oranges**, grapefruit, and broccoli are all excellent sources of that compound.

Note that a FANBOYS conjunction may be placed after a dash, for dramatic effect.

Correct: People are unable to produce vitamin C themselves—and that's why they must consume citrus fruits such as oranges and grapefruit.

Exercise: Joining and Separating Independent Clauses

In the following sentences, correct any missing or incorrect punctuation. Some of the sentences may not contain an error. (Answers p. 271)

Example: Anthropology is viewed as a branch of sociology in the United ~~States but~~ **States, but** it is considered an independent discipline in many other countries.

1. In large doses, many common substances found in household items have devastating effects, however, many toxicologists insist that they are thoroughly innocuous in minuscule amounts.

2. Organizers at the International Exhibition of 1862 debated whether photographs should be shown with the machines or with the paintings, for photography's status as an art form was then unclear.

3. The average family size in most countries has been steadily decreasing, so, there are fewer children overall than there used to be.

4. Over the past several years, the country's food prices have increased dramatically; and they are now at their highest rate in two decades.

5. Illegal logging was once rampant in Mexican forests but has recently declined as a result of pressure from environmental groups.

6. Naples has traditionally lacked the wealth and polish of some of its northern Italian counterparts — yet the city has played an important political and cultural role throughout Italian history.

7. Medieval fairs often attracted uncontrollable crowds and led to rioting, therefore the right to hold one could only be granted by royal charter.

8. Lyme disease causes muscle aches in its early stages and nervous system problems in its later ones: it is so named because the first cases occurred in the town of Lyme, Connecticut.

9. International sports competitions are symbolic showdowns that are more about winning than about universal friendship; they are, however, a far more civilized alternative to actual warfare.

10. During the nineteenth century, Detroit's roads and railways were improved; but, its manufacturing sector remained weak until after the Industrial Revolution.

Dependent Clauses (Complex Sentences)

Unlike independent clauses, dependent clauses (fragments) cannot stand on their own. Instead, they must be joined to an independent clause to form a **complex sentence**.

A. Subordinating Conjunction

Somewhere around third grade, you probably learned that you should never start a sentence with *because*. Although this "rule" is taught with the best of intentions, it's unfortunately only half right. In reality, it's perfectly acceptable to begin a sentence with *because*—sometimes, that is.

Here's the whole story: *Because* is a type of conjunction known as a **subordinating conjunction**. A clause that begins with a subordinating conjunction cannot stand on its own as a sentence and is thus dependent.

Common subordinating conjunctions include the following:

After	Before	Though	Whenever
(Al)though	Despite	Unless	Whereas
As	If	Until	Whether
Because	Since	When	While

Incorrect: **Although** some animal species are able to make their own vitamin C.

The dependent clause can be joined to an independent clause to create a complete sentence.

Correct: **Although** some animal species are able to make their own vitamin C, people lack the enzymes necessary to produce this compound and must obtain it through their diets.

When the dependent clause comes first, a comma must be placed after the dependent clause.

Incorrect: Although some animal species are able to make their own **vitamin C; people** lack the enzymes necessary to produce this compound and must obtain it through their diets.

Incorrect: Although some animal species are able to make their own **vitamin C people** lack the enzymes necessary to produce this compound and must obtain it through their diets.

Note that in the no-comma version, the two clauses blend into one another. The reader is forced to stop and think about where the division of ideas logically occurs. In contrast, the comma creates a clear break between the thoughts.

Correct: Although some animal species are able to make their own **vitamin C, people** lack the enzymes necessary to produce this compound and must obtain it through their diets.

When the independent clause comes first, things are less clear-cut.

Certain "strong" conjunctions, including *(al)though*, *while*, and *whereas*, should be set off by a comma.

Incorrect: Some animal species are able to make their own **vitamin C although people** lack the enzymes necessary to produce this compound naturally and must obtain it through their diets.

Correct: Some animal species are able to make their own **vitamin C, although people** lack the enzymes necessary to produce this compound naturally and must obtain it through their diets.

With "weaker" conjunctions, including *because*, *when*, and *until*, the comma typically creates an unnatural break and is therefore omitted.

Less good: People must obtain vitamin C through their **diets, because** they lack the enzymes necessary to produce this compound naturally.

Better: People must obtain vitamin C through their **diets because** they lack the enzymes necessary to produce this compound naturally.

When sentences are long and complex, however, a comma may be useful for improving clarity.

Acceptable: People must obtain ascorbic acid (vitamin C) by consuming citrus fruits such as oranges and green vegetables such as **broccoli, because** they lack the enzymes necessary to produce this compound naturally.

Note, however, that no comma should be placed **after** a subordinating conjunction.

Incorrect: People must obtain vitamin C through their **diets because,** they lack the enzymes necessary to produce this compound naturally.

Note also that a subordinating conjunction cannot serve as an introductory word at the beginning of a clause, after a period or semicolon. A conjunctive adverb such as *however* or *therefore* must be used instead.

Incorrect: Some animal species are able to make their own **vitamin C. Although, people** lack the enzymes necessary to produce this compound.

Correct: Some animal species are able to make their own **vitamin C. However, people** lack the enzymes necessary to produce this compound.

B. Relative Clause

A relative pronoun (e.g., *who* or *which*) **set off by a comma** can also be used to form a subordinate clause.

Incorrect: People can obtain vitamin C through citrus **fruits which** contain large amounts of that compound.

Correct: People can obtain vitamin C through citrus **fruits, which** contain large amounts of that compound.

C. Appositive or Participial Phrase

To review, appositives begin with nouns, and participial phrases begin with participles, either present or past. They can be placed anywhere in a sentence, but they **must always be set off by commas**.

Notice that when the appositive or participial phrase comes first, the noun that serves as the subject of the first clause is moved to the second clause.

Sentence 1:   <u>Vitamin C</u> is a compound not produced naturally in people.

Sentence 2:   It can be obtained through the consumption of citrus fruits such as oranges and grapefruit.

Combined: **A compound not produced naturally in people,** <u>vitamin C</u> can be obtained
(Appositive)   through the consumption of citrus fruits such as oranges and grapefruit.

Sentence 1:   People lack the enzymes necessary to produce vitamin C naturally.

Sentence 2:   They must obtain it by consuming foods such as oranges and grapefruit.

Combined: **Lacking the enzymes necessary to produce vitamin C naturally,** people must
(Part. Phrase)   obtain it by consuming foods such as oranges and grapefruit.

When a participial phrase is placed second, the subject of the second clause is removed, and the verb becomes a participle.

Sentence 1:   People must obtain vitamin C through their diets.

Sentence 2:   They must <u>consume</u> it through citrus fruits such as oranges and grapefruit.

Combined: People must obtain vitamin C through their diets, **consuming it through
citrus fruits such as oranges and grapefruit**.

In addition, the construction *with…-ing* (gerund) can be used as an alternative to *comma + and*.

Correct: People obtain vitamin C through their **diets, with many individuals
consuming** it through citrus fruits such as oranges and grapefruit.

D. Colon or Dash

Unlike periods and semicolons, colons and dashes can join two independent clauses OR an independent clause and a dependent phrase/clause. In case of the latter, the dependent item must be placed second.

Correct: People often obtain vitamin C from citrus fruits: **oranges and grapefruit, for
example**.

Correct: People often obtain vitamin C from citrus fruits—**oranges and grapefruit, for
example**.

Compound-Complex Sentences

To review:

Compound sentence – independent clause + FANBOYS + independent clause.

Independent	The production of ceramics in China began during the Neolithic period,
FANBOYS	**and**
Independent	it continues to this day.

Complex sentence – independent clause + dependent clause.

Note that either clause type can be placed first.

Independent	Jackie Robinson retired from baseball in 1957,
Dependent	**having** become one of the most famous athletes in the United States.

OR:

Dependent	**Having** become one of the most famous athletes in the United States,
Independent	Jackie Robinson retired from baseball in 1957.

A **compound-complex sentence** is created by joining a compound and a complex sentence:

independent clause + FANBOYS + independent clause + dependent clause

Again, the clauses can be presented in any order. Note that if a dependent clause appears first, a comma must be placed after it.

Dependent	**When** tomatoes were first brought to Europe from South America,
Independent	many people believed that the small yellow fruits were poisonous,
FANBOYS	**but**
Independent	the tomato plays a central role in many European cuisines today.

Exercise: Punctuating Sentences with Dependent Clauses

In the following sentences, make sure that all dependent clauses are correctly punctuated. Some of the sentences may not contain an error. (Answers p. 271)

                                                                          sculptures, his
Example: Although Rodin purposely omitted crucial elements from his ~~sculptures his~~ consistent use of the human figure demonstrated his respect for artistic tradition.

1. Because domesticated canines do not naturally live in pack structures some scientists scoff at dog-training approaches that require humans to act as pack leaders.

2. Freeways and transit systems have facilitated movement throughout the San Francisco metropolitan area; with millions of people taking up residence in the suburbs.

3. Since the city's government has curtailed spending on all non-essential services in an attempt to balance the budget the new theater company has been forced to suspend several of its productions.

4. While many design movements have political or philosophical beginnings or intentions the Art Deco style was invented for purely decorative purposes.

5. Whereas almost all general-interest books published in the United States are issued first in hardcover and then in paperback in Europe the paperback is commonly the only version.

6. The Rosetta Stone provided the key to the modern understanding of hieroglyphs because, it presented the same text in all three ancient Egyptian scripts.

7. Used as both food and medicine in many cultures for thousands of years garlic dates to at least the time of the Giza Pyramids.

8. Former space shuttle commander Pamela Melroy retired from NASA in 2007 having logged a total of nearly 40 days in orbit.

9. China was ruled by an emperor between the Qin Dynasty and the Qing Dynasty. Although, government bureaucracies were staffed by scholars selected by competitive examination and promoted according to merit.

10. The bowhead whale is thought to be the world's longest-living mammal; sometimes reaching up to 200 years in age.

Exercise: Appositives and Participial Phrases

For each question, combine the two statements by rewriting the indicated sentence as an appositive or participial phrase. (Answers p. 272)

Example:

Sentence 1:   The Hale-Bopp comet received an enormous amount of media coverage.

Sentence 2:   It became one of the most observed astronomical bodies in history. **(Participial phrase)**

The Hale-Bopp comet received an enormous amount of media coverage, becoming

one of the most observed astronomical bodies in history.

1.   Sentence 1:   Birds lack vocal cords. **(Participial phrase)**

      Sentence 2:   They are thought to sing with their throat muscles.

2.   Sentence 1:   Farmers in many parts of Brazil have successfully reduced the acidity of their soil.

      Sentence 2:   They have substantially increased food production. **(Participial phrase)**

3.   Sentence 1:   Copper was a metal widely used by the ancient Greeks. **(Appositive)**

      Sentence 2:   It had great significance because it was associated with the sacred island of Cyprus.

4. Sentence 1: During the 1970s, the demand for long-lasting foods caused manufacturers to add preservatives to simple dishes.

   Sentence 2: Thus, they reduced the quality of the flavors. **(Participial phrase)**

   _____

   _____

5. Sentence 1: Science fiction is shaping the language companies use to market virtual reality technologies.

   Sentence 2: This influences the types of experiences for which headsets are designed. **(Participial phrase)**

   _____

   _____

6. Sentence 1: The electric cargo bicycle is an efficient source of transportation. **(Appositive)**

   Sentence 2: It often outpaces its four-wheeled rivals for short-distance deliveries.

   _____

   _____

7. Sentence 1: The earliest type of armor to be invented was chainmail.

   Sentence 2: It was a protective covering made from thousands of interlocking metallic rings. **(Appositive)**

   _____

   _____

8. Sentence 1: Modern technology offers infinite possibilities for communication. **(Participial phrase)**

   Sentence 2: It also provides endless opportunities for distraction.

   _____

   _____

9.   Sentence 1:   Andy Warhol was a leading figure in the Pop Art movement. **(Appositive)**

           Sentence 2:   He was celebrated for his depictions of everyday objects.

_____

_____

10.   Sentence 1:   Lake Tahoe measures more than 250 square miles. **(Participial phrase)**

           Sentence 2:   It is larger than any other alpine lake in North America.

_____

_____

Comma Splices and How to Fix Them

A **comma splice** is created when a comma is used to separate two sentences. Although this construction may on <u>very</u> rare occasions be used for stylistic effect, it is incorrect in formal writing. **When people have difficulty identifying comma splices, it is typically not because they have trouble understanding the rule, but rather because they are not always sure when a statement is a sentence.**

Two factors in particular are typically responsible for this confusion:

   1) Adverbs

   2) Pronouns

A. Adverbs and Comma Splices

To review, adverbs modify verbs and are usually created by adding *–ly* onto the ends of adjectives: *slow* → *slowly; bright* → *brightly; clear* → *clearly*, etc.

Adverbs of time indicate when or how often events occurred. Sometimes they end in *–ly*, e.g., *currently, initially,* or *frequently,* but many common ones do not.

After(ward)	Before	Last	Often	Then
Already	First	Late(r)	Sometimes	Today
Also	Forever	Never	Soon	Tomorrow
Always	Just	Next	Still	Yesterday

The addition of an adverb to a sentence has no grammatical effect, regardless of where the adverb appears.

   Beginning: **Currently**, three versions of Edvard Munch's *The Scream* hang in Norwegian museums.

   Middle: Three versions of Edvard Munch's *The Scream* **now** hang in Norwegian museums.

   End: Three versions of Edvard Munch's *The Scream* hang in Norwegian museums **today**.

Because the above clauses are independent, they can only be joined to another complete sentence with a semicolon or *comma + FANBOYS*. Using a comma alone creates a comma splice.

   Incorrect: Edvard Munch created four versions of his painting *The Scream*, <u>currently</u>, **three versions** of the work hang in Norwegian museums.

   Correct: Edvard Munch created four versions of his painting *The Scream*; <u>currently</u>, **three versions** of the work hang in Norwegian museums.

Incorrect:	Edvard Munch created four versions of his painting *The Scream*, **three versions** of the work **now** hang in Norwegian museums.
Correct:	Edvard Munch created four versions of his painting *The Scream*; **three versions** of the work **now** hang in Norwegian museums.
Incorrect:	Edvard Munch created four versions of his painting *The Scream*, **three versions** of the work hang in Norwegian museums **today**.
Correct:	Edvard Munch created four versions of his painting *The Scream*; **three versions** of the work hang in Norwegian museums **today**.

B. Pronouns and Comma Splices

The second common point of confusion about independent clauses involves pronouns: words such as *it*, *they*, *s/he*, *this*, and *those* that are used to replace nouns.

The most important thing to understand about pronouns is that, like adverbs, they have no effect on whether a clause is independent or dependent. They are simply used to avoid making sentences wordy and repetitive.

Awkward:	The Mid-Autumn Festival dates back 3,000 years to China's Shang Dynasty, and **the Mid-Autumn Festival** is traditionally held on the fifteenth day of the eighth month.

In this version, the repetition of *the Mid-Autumn Festival* in the second clause is very awkward. The sentence would read much more smoothly if we replaced the noun in the second clause with the pronoun *it*.

Clear:	The Mid-Autumn Festival dates back 3,000 years to China's Shang Dynasty, and **it** is traditionally held on the fifteenth day of the eighth month.

That version sounds a lot better, right? The important thing to understand, however, is that there is no grammatical difference between this version and the first version.

If we were to separate the two clauses with only a comma, we would have a comma splice:

Incorrect:	The Mid-Autumn Festival dates back 3,000 years to China's Shang Dynasty, **it** is traditionally held on the fifteenth day of the eighth month.

One more example:

Clause #1:	The ramparts in Old Quebec are the only remaining fortified city walls in the Americas north of Mexico.
Clause #2:	The ramparts were constructed in Old Quebec by French settlers during the early seventeenth century.

Now we're going to replace some of the nouns in clause #2 with pronouns to avoid repetition:

Pronouns: **They** were constructed **there** by French settlers during the early seventeenth century.

Again, in context of the first sentence, the second sentence makes sense—we know that *they*, the subject, must refer to the ramparts, and that *there* must refer to Old Quebec. Out of context, however, it's unclear what those pronouns refer to. The clause does not tell us *what* was constructed by French settlers, or *where* it was constructed.

This is where a lot of people run into trouble: they incorrectly assume that because the clause's **meaning** is not entirely clear out of context, the clause cannot actually stand on its own **grammatically** as a complete sentence.

The clause does, however, have a subject (the pronoun *they*) and a main verb that corresponds to it (*were*), so it **can** actually stand on its own as a sentence—and it must follow a semicolon or *comma* + *FANBOYS*.

Incorrect: The ramparts in Old Quebec are the only remaining fortified city walls in the Americas north of Mexico, **they** were constructed **there** by French settlers during the early seventeenth century.

Correct: The ramparts in Old Quebec are the only remaining fortified city walls in the Americas north of Mexico**; they** were constructed **there** by French settlers during the early seventeenth century.

Alternately, it is sometimes possible to correct a comma splice by turning the second clause into a dependent clause beginning with *which* or *who*.

Incorrect: Ownership of the Arctic is governed by the United Nations Convention of the Law of the **Sea, it** gives Arctic nations an exclusive economic zone that extends 200 nautical miles from land.

Correct: Ownership of the Arctic is governed by the United Nations Convention of the Law of the **Sea, which** gives Arctic nations an exclusive economic zone that extends 200 nautical miles from land.

But remember, a sentence that is not a question cannot begin with *which* or *who*.

Incorrect: Ownership of the Arctic is governed by the United Nations Convention of the Law of the **Sea. Which** gives Arctic nations an exclusive economic zone that extends 200 nautical miles from land.

"Group" Pronouns

An additional point of confusion often involves **indefinite** or **"group" pronouns** such as *any, none, some, several, few, many, more, most, neither,* and *others.*

To review, these pronouns can be used to begin clauses in two different ways, one of which creates a comma splice and the other of which does not.

Pronoun (+ of them) = Comma splice

In this usage, the pronoun simply acts as a subject and is used to replace a noun. It is often followed by *of them*, but it can be used by itself as well.

Correct: Several of them have already been put into effect.

Correct: Several have already been put into effect.

Taken out of any context, the above examples don't make much sense, nor do they provide any real information. It is also likely that the second one sounds very strange to you. You might even be wondering whether it's really acceptable to use *several* that way, without a noun afterward (it's fine).

Regardless of how odd you find these examples, they are still sentences because they contain a subject (*several*) and a verb (*have been*) that corresponds to it.

Incorrect: The manufacturing company has created an advisory board to oversee the implementation of the new safety **regulations, several of them** have already been put into effect.

Incorrect: The manufacturing company has created an advisory board to oversee the implementation of the new safety **regulations, several** have already been put into effect.

The comma must be replaced by period, a semicolon, or *comma + FANBOYS.*

Correct: The manufacturing company has created an advisory board to oversee the implementation of the new safety **regulations. Several (of them)** have already been put into effect.

Correct: The manufacturing company has created an advisory board to oversee the implementation of the new safety **regulations; several (of them)** have already been put into effect.

Correct: The manufacturing company has created an advisory board to oversee the implementation of the new safety **regulations, and several (of them)** have already been put into effect.

Pronoun + of which/whom = No comma splice

When an indefinite pronoun is followed by *of which* or *of whom*, it becomes part of a dependent clause and can correctly be separated from an independent clause by only a comma.

Incorrect: The manufacturing company has created an advisory board to oversee the implementation of the new safety **regulations. Several of which** have already been put into effect.

Incorrect: The manufacturing company has created an advisory board to oversee the implementation of the new safety **regulations; several of which** have already been put into effect.

Correct: The manufacturing company has created an advisory board to oversee the implementation of the new safety **regulations, several of which** have already been put into effect.

Comma + FANBOYS should also not be used. This construction results in a jumbled sentence.

Incorrect: The manufacturing company has created an advisory board of outside **experts, and many of whom** are nationally recognized in their fields.

Correct: The manufacturing company has created an advisory board of outside **experts, many of whom** are nationally recognized in their fields.

Exercise: Independent vs. Dependent Clauses

In the following sentences, determine whether a comma or a period/semicolon should be used to separate the clauses. (Answers p. 272)

Example: The Philadelphia Zoo is the oldest zoo in the United States __;__ it opened less than a decade after the end of the Civil War.

1. *The Adventures of Huckleberry Finn* was originally intended for an adult audience ____ today, it is widely read as part of the high school curriculum in the United States.

2. The Euphrates river receives most of its water in the form of rainfall and melting snow ____ this results in peak volumes during the spring months and low volumes during the summer ones.

3. African-American life during the 1920s was documented in great detail by the writers and artists of the Harlem Renaissance ____ far less, however, is known about it during the 1930s.

4. Universities have historically offered a wide range of continuing education classes ____ some of them are now offered over the Internet as well as in traditional classrooms.

5. In 1930, John Maynard Keynes predicted that technology would give rise to a 15-hour workweek ____ instead, it gave rise to thousands of hours of pointless work.

6. Oils found in peanuts can provoke serious immune reactions in allergy sufferers ____ most of whom must be careful to avoid other types of nuts as well.

7. The First World War began in August of 1914 ____ it was directly caused by the assassination of Archduke Franz Ferdinand of Austria by the Bosnian revolutionary Gavrilo Princip.

8. Gwendolyn Knight painted throughout her life but did not start seriously exhibiting her work until relatively late ____ her first retrospective occurred when she was nearly 80 years old.

9. Black-backed woodpeckers live almost exclusively in severely burned forests ____ they thrive on insects that are adapted to fire and can detect heat up to 30 miles away.

10. Frederick Law Olmsted, who designed New York City's Central Park, also designed Montreal's Mount Royal Park ____ most of which is heavily wooded.

Chapter Four

Transitional Words and Phrases

There are three main types of transitions:

Continuers

Continuers are words such as *and, in addition, furthermore,* and *moreover,* which indicate that a sentence is continuing in the same direction it began.

> Correct: The sun streamed through the window into the living room, **and** its brightness was so great that it lit up the hall as well.

Contradictors

Contradictors are words such as *but, yet, although,* and *however* that indicate a sentence is shifting directions or introducing contradictory information.

> Correct: Antibiotics were not invented until the twentieth century, **but** many ancient cultures used specially selected plant extracts to treat infections.

> Correct: Antibiotics were not invented until the twentieth century; **however,** many ancient cultures used specially selected plant extracts to treat infections.

Cause-and-Effect Words

Common examples are *so, for, therefore, because,* and *since.* They indicate that an action or occurrence is causing a particular result, or that a result is occurring because of a particular action.

> Correct: The first astronauts were required to undergo mental evaluation before their flight **because** the psychological dangers inherent in space travel were judged to be as important as the physiological ones.

The chart on the following page lists many common transitional words and phrases.

Common Transitions

Continuers	Contradictors	Cause-and-Effect
Add Information Also* And Furthermore In addition Moreover **Give Example** For example For instance **Define, Clarify** Effectively Essentially In other words That is **Emphasize** In fact Indeed **Compare** Likewise Similarly **Sequence of Events** Finally Next Previously Subsequently Then While	Alternatively (Al)though But Conversely Despite Even so Even though However In any case In spite of Instead Meanwhile Nevertheless Nonetheless Otherwise Rather Regardless Still Whereas While Yet **Contrast** Alternately Alternatively In contrast On the contrary On the other hand	Accordingly As As a result As such Because Consequently For Hence Since So Thus Therefore To that end

Remember: coordinating, or FANBOYS, conjunctions (*for, and, nor, but, or, yet, so*) follow a comma when used to begin a clause; all other conjunctions follow a period or semicolon.

*In formal writing, *also* should not begin a clause. Use *in addition, furthermore,* or *moreover* instead.

Incorrect Conjunction Type

Conjunction errors can be tricky to catch because they are based on meaning rather than grammar. A transition that creates an illogical relationship may sound perfectly fine in the context of a sentence. It is only when you stop and consider the relationship between the statements that the problem becomes apparent.

Incorrect: Researchers are unable to drill into the Earth's core, but its chemical composition remains a mystery.

In the above sentence, the second statement indicates a result of the first: the Earth's chemical composition remains a mystery <u>because</u> its core is inaccessible.

Correct: Researchers are unable to drill into the Earth's core, **so** its chemical composition remains a mystery.

Correct: Researchers are unable to drill into the Earth's core; **therefore/thus**, its chemical composition remains a mystery.

To determine the relationship (compare/contrast/cause-and-effect) between a set of clauses, start by placing the statements next to one another.

For example, consider the following pair of sentences:

Sentence 1:   Many runners attempt to complete a marathon.

Sentence 2:   Most of them fail to do so because they lack the necessary stamina.

Then, determine whether the statements express similar or opposing ideas, or whether one statement is the result of the other.

In this case, the second statement contradicts the first: although many runners attempt to complete a marathon, they fail because they lack sufficient stamina. As a result, a contradictor must be used.

Correct: Many runners attempt to complete a marathon, **but/yet** most fail to do so because they lack the necessary stamina.

Correct: Many runners attempt to complete a marathon; **however,** most fail to do so because they lack the necessary stamina.

Note that conjunctive adverbs, e.g., *however, therefore, consequently, nevertheless, moreover,* can also be used non-essentially (between commas) in the middle of a sentence.

Remember that in terms of meaning, this construction is **identical** to the examples above: the transitional word or phrase connects the clause in which it appears to the **previous** statement—it does not connect two parts of the same clause. Only the placement of the transition changes.

Correct: Many runners attempt to complete a marathon; most fail to do so, **however,** because they lack the necessary stamina.

Ambiguous Transitions

Some transitions can be used to indicate more than one relationship.

- *While* and *as* both indicate that two actions are occurring at the same time; however, *while* is also commonly used as a synonym for *although*, and *as* is often used as a synonym for *because*.

- *Since* can indicate how long an action has been occurring, or it can act as a synonym for *because*.

In everyday writing, these uses are widely accepted; however, for maximum clarity and readability you should aim to use transitions that have just one, unambiguous meaning.

Ambiguous	Clear
As Since	Because
While	Although Whereas

Ambiguous: **As** rent-control laws have remained in place in New York City, rents for some apartments have remained relatively stable for decades.

Ambiguous: **Since** rent-control laws have remained in place in New York City, rents for some apartments have remained relatively stable for decades.

In the above sentences, the reader does not initially know whether the sentence will go on to describe something that happened during the time when rent-control laws remained in place, or whether it will indicate something that occurred because rent-control laws remained in place. Although the meaning becomes clear enough eventually, the reader is forced to stop and think just a little harder than necessary about what the sentence is trying to say.

Clear: **Because** rent-control laws have remained in place in New York City, rents for some apartments have remained relatively stable for decades.

In this version, the use of *because* immediately signals to the reader that the sentence will convey a cause-and-effect relationship.

When

Another potentially tricky conjunction is *when*.

Incorrect: Santiago's failure to complete the marathon surprised no one, least of all his training partners, **when** he had not spent enough time building the necessary stamina.

At first reading, the sentence may sound somewhat strange, but it is difficult to identify precisely why. At this point, the goal is to simplify the sentence into a more manageable form. If we consider the structure of the sentence, we notice that there are two commas in the interior of the sentence, indicating a non-essential clause. When we remove the non-essential clause, we are left with the following:

Incorrect: Santiago's failure to complete the marathon surprised no one, **when** he had not spent enough time building the necessary stamina.

Clearly, the fact that Santiago didn't complete the marathon was a <u>result</u> of his failure to build the necessary stamina.

Correct: Santiago's failure to complete the marathon surprised no one, least of all his training partners, **because** he had not spent enough time building the necessary stamina.

Note, however, that the phrase *when in fact* or *when in reality* can be used to signal that something is not as it seems.

Acceptable: Santiago believed that his training regimen was adequate **when in fact** it was nothing of the sort. It was no surprise when he did not finish the marathon.

That said, *but* is a stronger, clearer option that leaves no room for guessing where the sentence is going.

Better: Santiago believed that his training regimen was adequate, **but in fact** it was nothing of the sort. It was no surprise when he did not finish the marathon.

Double Conjunctions

It is both redundant and **grammatically unacceptable** to place conjunctions at the beginnings of two consecutive clauses. If one clause begins with a subordinating conjunction, the following clause should not begin with a coordinating conjunction. Either one or the other should be used.

Incorrect: **Although** Santiago had trained hard for the marathon, **but** he was unable to finish the entire course.

Correct: **Although** Santiago had trained hard for the marathon, **he** was unable to finish the entire course.

Correct: Santiago had trained hard for the marathon, **but** he was unable to finish the entire course.

Double conjunctions are relatively easy to spot when sentences are short; however, when they are longer and more complex, it is considerably easier to forget that you have already used a conjunction at the beginning of the sentence and accidentally place one at the beginning of a later clause.

Incorrect: **Although** 68 of the female delegates at the Seneca Falls convention signed *The Declaration of Sentiments*, a document that was based on the Declaration of Independence and that included demands for many basic rights for **women, but** only 32 of the male delegates did so.

Correct: **Although** 68 of the female delegates at the Seneca Falls convention signed *The Declaration of Sentiments*, a document that was based on the Declaration of Independence and that included demands for many basic rights for **women, only** 32 of the male delegates did so.

Correct: 68 of the female delegates at the Seneca Falls convention signed *The Declaration of Sentiments*, a document that was based on the Declaration of Independence and that included demands for many basic rights for **women, but only** 32 of the male delegates did so.

To avoid this error, try to keep your sentences to a reasonable length. Not only will this keep you on track grammatically, but it will also make it easier for readers to follow your ideas.

Glossary of Transitions

Accordingly
Consequently } **Therefore, as a result**

Correct: Dolphins are social animals. **Consequently**, they live in pods of up to a dozen animals.

Correct: Dolphins are social animals. **Accordingly**, they live in pods of up to a dozen animals.

Furthermore
Moreover } **In addition**

Correct: Dolphins are social animals. **Furthermore**, they are highly intelligent.

Correct: Dolphins are social animals. **Moreover**, they are highly intelligent.

In fact
Indeed } **Used to emphasize a preceding statement**

Correct: Dolphins are highly intelligent. **In fact**, they are one of the smartest mammals.

Correct: Dolphins are highly intelligent. **Indeed**, they are one of the smartest mammals.

Even so
Nevertheless
Still } **Despite this, however**

Correct: Dolphins are descended from land-dwelling animals. **Even so**, they can survive only in water.

Correct: Dolphins are descended from land-dwelling animals. **Nevertheless**, they can survive only in water.

Correct: Dolphins are descended from land-dwelling animals. **Still**, they can survive only in water.

Whereas – Although

> Correct: A salmon is a type of fish, **whereas** a dolphin is a type of mammal.

As such – *As a(n) + noun*

As such is one of the trickier transitions, and it's best explained with an example.

Let's start with this sentence:

> Correct: Dolphins are social animals. **Because** they are social animals, they live in pods of up to a dozen animals.

We can also write it this way:

> Correct: Dolphins are social animals. **As** social animals, they live in pods of up to a dozen animals.

These sentences are fine grammatically, but the repetition of the phrase *social animals* in the second sentence is awkward. To eliminate the repetition, we can replace the phrase *as social animals* with *as such*.

> Correct: Dolphins are social animals. **As such**, they live in pods of up to a dozen animals.

Likewise – Similarly, in the same way

> Correct: As mammals, dolphins are warm blooded. **Likewise,** they nourish their young with milk.

Meanwhile – At the same time; often used as a synonym for *however*, to indicate a contrast

> Correct: Many people think of dolphins as fish. **Meanwhile,** they ignore scientific research, which long ago established that dolphins are actually mammals.

Subsequently – Then, afterward

> Correct: In the 1980s, dolphin populations began to decline because too many animals were caught in fishing nets. **Subsequently,** fishing companies began taking steps to reassure customers that products were "dolphin safe."

That is – In other words; provides a definition or explanation, and often follows a dash.

> Correct: Dolphins are mammals – **that is,** they are warm blooded and nourish their young with milk.

Exercise: Transitions

For the following exercises, write a logical and grammatically appropriate transition in the blank provided. Some of the sentences may not require a transition. (Answers p. 273)

Example: The eyes of many predatory animals are designed to enhance depth perception; _____**however**_____, in other organisms, they are designed to maximize the field of vision.

1.   In the past, coffees were blended to suit a homogenous popular taste, _____ that has changed in response to a growing awareness of regional differences.

2.   People living in cities tend to eat more processed foods than those living in rural areas; _____, city-dwellers experience higher rates of health problems.

3.   The Taj Mahal is regarded as one of the eight wonders of the world; _____, some historians have noted that its architectural beauty has never been surpassed.

4.   Music serves no obvious evolutionary purpose; it has, _____ played a role in every known civilization on earth.

5.   There is no escaping the fact that most of the world's big cats are in serious trouble because of poaching, _____ tigers are no exception.

6.   Because small companies generally lack the financial resources to upgrade their software and set up protective barriers, _____ their security systems can be hacked more easily than those of large ones.

7.   No one truly knows where the pirate known as Blackbeard called home; _____, author Daniel Defoe, a self-appointed piracy expert, claimed that he came from the English city of Bristol.

8.   The correlation between bad moods and negative judgments is useful _____ it allows people to make informed guesses about how others are feeling from observing their actions and choices.

9.   _____ Frederic Chopin's charming and sociable personality drew loyal groups of friends and admirers, including the novelist George Sand, his private life was often painful and difficult.

10. Pyramids are most commonly associated with ancient Egypt, _____ it comes as a surprise to many people that Nubian civilization, located in modern-day Sudan, produced far more pyramids than Egyptian civilization ever did.

11. The two books recount the same series of events; _____, they do so from different perspectives and are not intended to be read in any particular order.

12. _____ eighteenth-century European sailors were convinced that citrus fruits could cure scurvy, a disease caused by a severe deficiency of vitamin C, but physicians dismissed that theory because it did not conform to prevailing beliefs.

13. _____ the lemur shares some traits with other primates, it is frequently mistaken for an ancestor of modern monkeys and apes.

14. Modern chemistry keeps insects from ravaging crops, lifts stains from carpets, and saves lives, _____ the constant exposure to chemicals is taking a toll on many people's health.

15. Thomas Jefferson believed that prisoners of war should be treated humanely; _____, during the American Revolution, he requested that British generals be held in private homes rather than behind bars.

Chapter Five

Relative and Non-Essential Clauses

Relative pronouns refer back to the noun that immediately precedes them; they are used to join clauses smoothly. Most of these words begin with *w*, so you can also think of them as "w-words." They include:

- Who
- Whose
- Whom
- Which
- That
- Where*
- When*

In the examples below, notice how the bolded pronoun in Sentence 2 becomes the relative pronoun in the combined version. Notice also how the relative clause is set off by a comma.

Which

Sentence 1:   J.R.R. Tolkien's *Lord of the Rings* novels are set in <u>Middle-earth</u>.

Sentence 2:   **It** is an imaginary continent inhabited by a variety of mystical creatures.

Combined: J.R.R. Tolkien's *Lord of the Rings* novels are set in <u>Middle-earth</u>, **which** is an imaginary continent inhabited by a variety of mystical creatures.

Who

Sentence 1:   W.E.B. Du Bois' intellectual gifts were recognized by many of his <u>high school teachers</u>.

Sentence 2:   **They** encouraged their pupil to further his education.

Combined: W.E.B. Du Bois' intellectual gifts were recognized by many of his <u>high school teachers</u>, **who** encouraged their pupil to further his education.

Where and *when* are sometimes considered relative adverbs, but in this context they function as relative pronouns.

That

Sentence 1:   ShapeShifter is a <u>computer program</u>.

Sentence 2:   **It** offers users the opportunity to design animations without purchasing expensive software or licenses.

Combined: ShapeShifter is a <u>computer program</u> **that** offers users the opportunity to design animations without purchasing expensive software or licenses.

Note that relative clauses beginning with *that* are never set off by commas.

Where

Sentence 1:   William Faulkner's novels are set mostly in <u>Mississippi</u>.

Sentence 2:   Faulkner was born in Mississippi and spent his entire life **there**.

Combined: William Faulkner's novels are set mostly in <u>Mississippi</u>, **where** Faulkner was born and spent his entire life.

When

Sentence 1:   Thomas Jefferson returned to the United States from Paris in <u>1820</u>.

Sentence 2:   **At that time**, he finished serving as the American ambassador to France.

Combined: Thomas Jefferson returned to the United States from Paris in <u>1820</u>, **when** he finished serving as the American ambassador to France.

Exercise: Using Relative Clauses to Join Sentences

For the following sentences, combine the two clauses by using a comma and a relative pronoun (*which, who, that, where, when*). The relative clause should be placed at the end. (Answers p. 274)

Example:

Sentence 1: Atlantic City was home to the United States' first boardwalk.

Sentence 2: It was the inspiration for the board game *Monopoly*™.

_____
Atlantic City was home to the United States' first boardwalk, which was the inspiration

_____
for the board game *Monopoly*™.

1. Sentence 1: *Clueless* is a movie.

   Sentence 2: It was based on Jane Austen's classic novel *Emma*.

_____

_____

2. Sentence 1: Ownership of the Arctic is governed by the 1958 Law of the Sea.

   Sentence 2: It gives Arctic nations an exclusive economic zone 200 nautical miles from land.

_____

_____

3. Sentence 1: The printing press was introduced in Europe by Johannes Gutenberg.

   Sentence 2: He devised a hand mold to create movable metal type.

_____

_____

4. Sentence 1:   SpaceX was founded in June 2002 by Elon Musk.

   Sentence 2:   His goal was to build a simple and relatively inexpensive reusable rocket.

   _____

   _____

5. Sentence 1:   Most volcanic activity occurs on the sea floor.

   Sentence 2:   There, tectonic plates are spreading the earth apart.

   _____

   _____

Embedded Clauses

Relative phrases and clauses can also appear in the middle of a sentence. Used this way, they allow you to "embed" one statement in another in order to make your writing smoother and more fluid.

Non-essential clauses often begin with *which* or *who(se)*, relative pronouns that refer back to the noun immediately preceding them. Typically inserted between the subject and the verb, they **are surrounded by commas** and can be crossed out of a sentence without affecting its basic meaning or structure.

These clauses allow you to indicate the relative importance of different ideas. By definition, non-essential information is less important than the main part of the sentence; it's more like an aside to the reader.

Which

Sentence 1:   Middle-earth is the setting for J.R.R. Tolkien's *Lord of the Rings* novels.

Sentence 2:   **It** is a land inhabited by a variety of mystical creatures.

To combine the two sentences, the subject pronoun *it* is replaced with the relative pronoun *which.* Then, the new clause is inserted between the subject and the verb in Sentence 1.

Combined: Middle-earth, **which is a land inhabited by a variety of mystical creatures,** is the setting for J.R.R. Tolkien's *Lord of the Rings* novels.

To reiterate, commas must be used to mark both the beginning and the end of the non-essential clause; it is incorrect to omit either or both of the commas. Without this punctuation, the reader will find it extremely difficult to follow the logic of the sentence.

Incorrect: **Middle-earth which** is a land inhabited by a variety of mystical creatures, is the setting for J.R.R. Tolkien's *Lord of the Rings* novels.

Incorrect: Middle-earth, which is a land inhabited by a variety of mystical **creatures is** the setting for J.R.R. Tolkien's *Lord of the Rings* novels.

Incorrect: **Middle-earth which is a land inhabited by a variety of mystical creatures is** the setting for J.R.R. Tolkien's *Lord of the Rings* novels.

Who

Sentence 1:   The works of the British writer J.R.R. Tolkien are still popular today.

Sentence 2:   **He** is generally considered the father of modern fantasy literature.

Embedded: The works of the British writer J.R.R. Tolkien, **who is generally considered the father of modern fantasy literature,** are still popular today.

Appositive

Non-essential clauses can also begin with nouns, in which case they are called **appositives**. Some appositives can be created by removing a relative pronoun. For example, let's revisit this sentence:

Sentence 1: <u>Middle-earth</u> is the setting for J.R.R. Tolkien's *Lord of the Rings* novels.

Sentence 2: It is **a land** inhabited by a variety of mystical creatures.

Embedded: Middle-earth, **a land inhabited by a variety of mystical creatures,** is the setting for J.R.R. Tolkien's *Lord of the Rings* novels.

Participles

Non-essential clauses can begin with either present (*-ing*) or past participles (*-ed, -own, -ung, -unk*).

Sentence 1: In 1937, J.R.R. Tolkien published the first volume of his *Lord of the Rings* trilogy.

Sentence 2: He **had** already published several important academic works.

Embedded: In 1937, **having** already published several important academic works, J.R.R. Tolkien published the first volume of his *Lord of the Rings* trilogy.

Now let's look at an example with a past participle:

Sentence 1: *The Hobbit* is the first volume in J.R.R. Tolkien's *Lord of the Rings* series.

Sentence 2: It was **published** in 1937.

Combined: *The Hobbit,* **published in 1937,** is the first volume in J.R.R. Tolkien's *Lord of the Rings* series.

Note that an adverb can acceptably be placed before the participle:

Correct: *The Hobbit,* <u>initially</u> **published in 1937,** is the first volume in J.R.R. Tolkien's *Lord of the Rings* series.

"Reporting" and "Arguing" Verbs

Verbs that involve "reporting" (e.g., *say, state, announce*) and "arguing" (e.g., *claim, insist, contend*) are sometimes used non-essentially in the middle of a clause in order to create a more interesting and sophisticated construction.

Beginning: **Critics agree** that buildings designed by Zaha Hadid are among the most important examples of contemporary architecture in the world.

Middle: Buildings designed by Zaha Hadid, **critics agree,** are among the most important examples of contemporary architecture in the world.

Transitions

Transitional words and phrases can also be used non-essentially rather than at the beginning of a clause. In such cases, the transition is commonly placed next to the verb (although other placements are certainly acceptable).

Middle: The great success of *The Lord of the Rings* directly led to a resurgence of the fantasy genre; Tolkien**, therefore,** is often viewed as the father of modern fantasy literature.

Note: while this construction is useful to make your sentence structure more varied, it is best used sparingly. If you employ it too frequently, it quickly becomes repetitive and clunky.

Emphasis

Non-essential clauses can be used to emphasize a previous statement. Such clauses often begin with adverbs such as *particularly* or *especially*; they may also begin with transitional words or phrases.

Correct: Writers of fantasy novels**, (and) particularly those who invent mystical creatures,** often cite J.R.R. Tolkien as one of their most important influences.

Prepositional Phrases

This is a less common usage, and one that can easily turn awkward, but it is useful for occasional effect.

Correct: One evening in 1977, forty or so intelligent, distinguished persons came together at the elegant St. Regis Hotel in New York City and**, with drinks in hand,** discussed the state of the English language.

Two Commas Do Not Always Signal a Non-Essential Clause

Important: Sentences that contain commas setting off embedded non-essential clauses may *also* contain commas that serve unrelated purposes. In such cases, you must consider the meaning of the sentence in order to determine whether and where non-essential clauses appear.

For example, the following sentence contains only one embedded non-essential clause that can be removed without creating a problem:

Correct: The sport of sumo wrestling**, whose competitors must attempt to force one another out of a circular ring,** originated in Japan, which remains the only country in the world where it is practiced.

Correct: The sport of sumo wrestling…originated in Japan, which remains the only country in the world where it is practiced.

If the information between a different set of commas is removed, however, we are left with nonsense:

Incorrect: The sport of sumo wrestling, whose competitors must attempt to force one another out of a circular ring, **originated in Japan,** which remains the only country in the world where it is practiced.

Incorrect: The sport of sumo wrestling, whose competitors must attempt to force one another out of a circular ring…which remains the only country in the world where it is practiced.

Logically, a circular ring cannot be *the only country in the world where it is practiced* because a circular ring is not a country. The two commas thus do not create a non-essential clause.

If you cannot instinctively determine where a non-essential clause belongs, take your pencil (not a pen!), draw a line through the section you want to test out, and read the sentence without it. If that doesn't work, erase the line, cross out a different section, and try again.

Essential Clauses

Essential clauses begin with *that* and are essential to the structure/meaning of a sentence.

Like non-essential clauses, these clauses can be embedded in the middle of a sentence in order to prevent sentences from becoming short and choppy.

When essential clauses are used to combine two sentences, the essential clause is typically placed between the subject and the verb of the first sentence.

Sentence 1: <u>Medications</u> are known as generic drugs.

Sentence 2: **They** are manufactured and sold without patent protection.

Combined: <u>Medications</u> **that are manufactured and sold without patent protection** <u>are</u> known as generic drugs.

Essential clauses are also known as **restrictive clauses** because they restrict the focus of a sentence to the description contained within the clause.

In the "combined" version above, for example, the clause is restrictive because the sentence is not referring to medications in general. Rather, it is restricting the focus to particular medications: ones manufactured and sold without patent protection.

Note that unlike non-essential clauses, **essential clauses should not be set off by commas**.

Incorrect: Medications**, that are manufactured and sold without patent protection,** are known as generic drugs.

It is also incorrect to place a comma before or after *that*.

| Incorrect: | **Medications, that** are manufactured and sold without patent protection are known as generic drugs. |

Incorrect: **Medications that,** are manufactured and sold without patent protection are known as generic drugs.

The only (rare) exception is when a non-essential clause is inserted after *that*.

Correct: Generic drugs are medications **that, for the most part,** cost significantly less than drugs still under patent protection.

Another semi-exception involves use of a comma at the **end** of an essential clause. Although not technically correct, this construction may sometimes be useful for the sake of clarity. It does, however, create somewhat of an awkward break and should therefore be used only when absolutely necessary.

Iffy: Medications that are manufactured and sold without patent **protection, are** known as generic drugs.

In addition, note that essential clauses can be acceptably written <u>without</u> *that + verb*. When this is the case, no commas should be used.

Incorrect: Medications, **manufactured and sold without patent protection,** are known as generic drugs.

Correct: Medications **manufactured and sold without patent protection** are known as generic drugs.

Exercise: Embedded Non-Essential and Essential Clauses

Combine the two sentences by embedding the second sentence in the middle of the first, before the underlined verb. (Answers p. 274)

Example:

Sentence 1:   The novel *A Tale of Two Cities* <u>revolves</u> around the themes of sacrifice and redemption.

Sentence 2:   It was written by Charles Dickens.

_____

The novel *A Tale of Two Cities*, which was written by Charles Dickens, revolves around
_____

the themes of sacrifice and redemption.
_____

1.   Sentence 1:   Frank Lloyd Wright <u>was</u> one of the most renowned architects of the twentieth century.

      Sentence 2:   He founded the Prairie School movement.

_____

_____

2.   Sentence 1:   Japan's bullet train <u>is</u> the world's fastest high-speed railway.

      Sentence 2:   It travels between the cities of Tokyo and Osaka.

_____

_____

3.   Sentence 1:   Sutter's Mill <u>was</u> located on the South Fork American River in Coloma, California.

      Sentence 2:   Gold was found there in 1849.

_____

_____

4. Sentence 1:   The design of Paris's Pompidou Center <u>marked</u> a radical break with tradition.

    Sentence 2:   Its exterior is covered with brightly colored tubes.

    _____

    _____

5. Sentence 1:   Genetic diseases <u>are</u> known as single-gene or Mendelian disorders.

    Sentence 2:   They result from a mutation on only one gene.

    _____

    _____

6. Sentence 1:   The Ottoman Empire <u>remained</u> at the center of interactions between Europe and Asia for 600 years.

    Sentence: 2:   Its capital was Constantinople.

    _____

    _____

7. Sentence 1:   Ray Dearlove <u>has</u> an ambitious plan to airlift 80 rhinos to Australia to save them from poachers.

    Sentence 2:   He is the founder of the Australian Rhino Project.

    _____

    _____

8. Sentence 1:   Researchers have found that regular aerobic exercise <u>may</u> boost verbal memory and learning.

    Sentence 2:   It is the kind that gets your heart pumping.

    _____

    _____

9. Sentence 1:   The last of the dense minerals <u>has</u> been found inside a meteorite.

    Sentence 2:   These minerals make up much of the Earth's crust and upper mantle.

    _____

    _____

10. Sentence 1:   Roald Dahl <u>was</u> a member of Britain's Royal Air Force in his youth.

    Sentence 2:   He earned fame as the author of children's books such as *Matilda* and *The BFG*.

    _____

    _____

Exercise: Punctuating Non-Essential and Essential Elements

In the sentences below, add and remove commas as necessary so that non-essential and essential elements are correctly punctuated. Some of the sentences may not contain an error. (Answers p. 275)

Example: When the *Mona* ~~*Lisa* already the most famous painting in the world~~ *Lisa*, already the most famous painting in the world, had its first American showing in 1962, thousands of viewers flocked to Washington, D.C., to see it.

1.   As a general rule, species living on land, particularly large species tend not to survive as long as those living in freshwater environments.

2.   The disruptions in sleep cycles, that almost inevitably accompany movement across time zones, can be reduced if travelers are exposed to light before setting out on a trip.

3.   Modern advertising which was introduced in the United States during the 1920s was created from techniques developed in the campaigns of Edward Bernays.

4.   Some traditional assumptions about how to treat jellyfish stings have recently been called into question: rinsing the injured areas with seawater, for example has been discovered to spread venom to other tissue.

5.   Testing animal cognition is tricky, and comparing and contrasting across species lines especially when distinct species-specific tests are used is particularly challenging.

6.   Proctor & Gamble, a multinational consumer goods company, headquartered in Cincinnati, Ohio, produces a variety of household products, including soap, oil, and toothpaste.

7.   Researchers have determined, that about 66 million years ago, an asteroid came streaking out of the sky and crashed into what is now Mexico's Yucatán Peninsula.

8.   Sweatshops were common in the early New York City garment industry; by the standards of the early 1900s however the Triangle Shirtwaist Company was not actually a sweatshop.

9.   The destruction of American swamps and marshes, long seen as wastelands that harbored deadly disease accelerated over the course of the twentieth century.

10.   A new software called DXplain some hospitals report, is helping doctors make diagnoses and avoid the types of errors that can sometimes cause harm to patients.

Non-Essential Clauses with Dashes and Parentheses

Although non-essential clauses are most frequently set off by commas, they can also be set off by dashes or parentheses. (In fact, non-essential clauses are also known as **parenthetical clauses**.)

Correct: The Tower of London — **which was begun by William the Conqueror in 1078** — is one of the largest and most imposing fortifications in England.

Correct: The Tower of London **(which was begun by William the Conqueror in 1078)** is one of the largest and most imposing fortifications in England.

Why use dashes or parentheses? For stylistic reasons.

- **Dashes** create a stronger break between the non-essential information and the rest of the sentence.

- **Parentheses** imply that the non-essential information is even less important than either commas or dashes do.

Despite these differences, **two commas, two dashes, and two parentheses are all grammatically interchangeable.**

The only **exception** involves transition words and phrases (e.g., *however, therefore, in fact*), which must be surrounded by commas when they are used non-essentially. Dashes and parentheses create too strong a break.

Incorrect: The Tower of London is nearly a thousand years old. It remains — **however** — one of the largest and most imposing fortifications in England.

Incorrect: The Tower of London is nearly a thousand years old. It remains **(however)** one of the largest and most imposing fortifications in England.

Correct: The Tower of London is nearly a thousand years old. It remains, **however,** one of the largest and most imposing fortifications in England.

The most important thing to know is that either two commas, two dashes, or two parentheses should be used — you cannot mix and match. For instance, a non-essential clause begun by a comma should not end with a dash or close parenthesis, and a non-essential clause begun by an open parenthesis should not end with a comma or dash.

Incorrect: The Tower of London **(which was begun by William the Conqueror in 1078,** is one of the largest and most imposing fortifications in England.

Correct: The Tower of London **(which was begun by William the Conqueror in 1078)** is one of the largest and most imposing fortifications in England.

Incorrect: The Tower of London, **which was begun by William the Conqueror in 1078** — is one of the largest and most imposing fortifications in England.

Correct: The Tower of London, **which was begun by William the Conqueror in 1078,** is one of the largest and most imposing fortifications in England.

Note that only **one form of punctuation should be used to set off a non-essential clause**. The primary **exception** is when a comma is required after a close parenthesis for other reasons, e.g., before a FANBOYS conjunction used to separate two independent clauses.

Incorrect: The tower of London was constructed as a prison in the eleventh **century, (1078 to be exact), but** it has been used as everything from a treasury to an armory.

Correct: The tower of London was constructed as a prison in the eleventh **century (1078 to be exact), but** it has been used as everything from a treasury to an armory.

Multiple Non-Essential Clauses

It is also possible for sentences to contain multiple non-essential clauses. Although this construction can require readers to make a significant effort to follow the various modifications, there is nothing inherently wrong with it from a grammatical standpoint.

Let's start with the following base sentence:

Correct: The country's human rights record is widely known to be poor, but leaders of the ruling party have nevertheless managed to avoid diplomatic consequences.

Now we're going to add the non-essential clauses one by one.

Correct: The country's human rights record, **which has recently come under close inspection,** is widely known to be poor, but leaders of the ruling party have nevertheless managed to avoid diplomatic consequences.

Correct: The country's human rights record, **which has recently come under close inspection,** is widely known to be poor, but leaders of the ruling party, **whose power has remained entrenched for decades,** have nevertheless managed to avoid diplomatic consequences.

A sentence may also include non-essential clauses with different types of punctuation.

Correct: The country's human rights record, **which has recently come under close inspection,** is widely known to be poor, but leaders of the ruling party— **whose power has remained entrenched for decades**—have nevertheless managed to avoid diplomatic consequences.

Correct: The country's human rights record, **which has recently come under close inspection,** is widely known to be poor, but leaders of the ruling party **(whose power has remained entrenched for decades)** have nevertheless managed to avoid diplomatic consequences.

Correct: The country's human rights record **(which has recently come under close inspection)** is widely known to be poor, but leaders of the ruling party, **whose power has remained entrenched for decades,** have nevertheless managed to avoid diplomatic consequences.

Avoiding Jumbled Sentences

As we've seen, a sentence that contains a non-essential or essential clause must also contain a main verb that corresponds to the main subject of the sentence.

Incorrect: George C. Williams, <u>who</u> **was** one of the most important thinkers in the field of evolutionary biology.

Here, the verb *was* belongs to the relative pronoun *who*, the subject of the new clause. It does not correspond to the main subject, *George C. Williams.*

In addition, the construction *comma + who* suggests that a non-essential clause is beginning, but there is never a second comma to end the clause. Instead, the sentence ends without a resolution.

The fastest and easiest way to turn this fragment into a sentence is to remove *comma + who*, eliminating the relative clause and making the entire sentence into a single main clause.

Correct: <u>George C. Williams</u> **was** one of the most important thinkers in the field of evolutionary biology.

Again, this type of error is relatively easy to catch in short sentences. When sentences are longer, it is much easier to get "lost" in them and to lose track of which verb belongs to which subject. This is a particular danger when you are writing quickly, or at the last minute (or both).

Incorrect: George C. Williams, who was one of the most important thinkers in evolutionary **biology, and who** made a number of lasting contributions to his field.

In the above sentence, we can identify what appears to be a non-essential clause (*who was…biology*) because it begins with *who* and is surrounded by commas. If we cross it out, however, we are left with nonsense.

Incorrect: George C. Williams […] **and who made** a number of lasting contributions to his field.

Clearly, this is not a sentence. Making it into one is relatively simple, though. Since the first word after the end of a non-essential clause is typically a verb, we can cross out all the excess words before the verb.

Correct: George C. Williams […] ~~**and who**~~ made a number of lasting contributions to his field.

With the elimination of those two words, the fragment suddenly becomes a sentence. And when we plug the non-essential clause back in, we get something much clearer.

Correct: <u>George C. Williams</u>, who was one of the most important thinkers in evolutionary biology, **made** a number of lasting contributions to his field.

Another possible solution is to remove the non-essential clause entirely.

Correct: <u>George C. Williams</u> **was** one of the most important thinkers in the field of evolutionary biology and **made** a number of lasting contributions to his field.

A different, less common problem occurs when a writer loses track of a sentence and creates the end of a non-essential clause when there is no beginning.

Incorrect: George C. Williams was one of the most important thinkers in the field of evolutionary **biology, made** a number of lasting contributions to his field.

Correct: George C. **Williams, who** was one of the most important thinkers in the field of evolutionary **biology, made** a number of lasting contributions to his field.

Let's look at one more example, this time with a dash.

Incorrect: Mobile robot technology—**a technology historically used by both the military and the police**—and it is now becoming widespread at businesses and hotels.

Reduce: Mobile robot technology—~~**a technology historically used by both the military and the police**~~— and it is now becoming widespread at businesses and hotels.

Cross out: Mobile robot technology [...] ~~**and it**~~ is now becoming widespread at businesses and hotels.

Correct: Mobile robot technology—**a technology historically used by both the military and the police**—is now becoming widespread at businesses and hotels.

Note: in very rare instances, a (coordinating) conjunction may follow a non-essential clause.

Correct: When Allen Ginsberg set out on a cross-country tour in 1965, he brought with him a portable **tape recorder <u>and</u> used** it to dictate what eventually became part of *The Fall of America: Poems of These States*.

Correct: When Allen Ginsberg set out on a cross-country tour in 1965, he brought with him a portable tape recorder, **then an expensive novelty, and** used it to dictate what eventually became part of *The Fall of America: Poems of These States*.

In the original sentence, *and* correctly follows *tape recorder*. The non-essential clause is simply used to modify that noun; the rest of the sentence can remain unchanged.

Jumbled sentences can also be created in sentences with essential ("that") clauses.

Incorrect:　　The mobile robot technology **that has historically been used by both the military and the police** and that is now becoming widespread at businesses and hotels.

When the essential clause is crossed out, the statement that remains is clearly ungrammatical.

Cross out:　　The mobile robot technology ~~that has historically been used by both the military and the police~~ and that is now becoming widespread at businesses and hotels.

Here, the verb *is* belongs to *that* — the subject of the essential clause.

Simplified:　　The mobile robot technology [...] and <u>that</u> **is** now becoming widespread at businesses and hotels.

To correct the sentence, we must restore the verb *is* to the sentence's main subject, *The mobile robot technology*.

Crossed out:　　The mobile robot technology ~~that has historically been used by both the military and the police and that~~ is now becoming widespread at businesses and hotels.

Correct:　　<u>The mobile robot technology</u> that has historically been used by both the military and the police **is** now becoming widespread at businesses and hotels.

Exercise: Correcting Non-Essential Clause Punctuation

In the sentences below, correct any problem in the construction or punctuation of non-essential items. Some of the sentences may not contain an error. (Answers p. 275)

Example: The Arts and Crafts movement—which was founded by the artist and writer William Morris in the ~~1860s, emphasized~~ natural materials and traditional craftsmanship.
> 1860s—emphasized

1. Ant colonies can live for up to 30 years, the lifetime of the single queen who produces all the ants but individual ants live at most a year.

2. Palm oil—currently the world's most popular edible oil—is used in hundreds of products, both edible and non-edible, and makes up a third of all the vegetable oil consumed across the planet.

3. The author Shirley Jackson, best known for her shocking short story "The Lottery," and who was born in San Francisco in 1916.

4. Patients who receive anesthesia during surgery are put into a semi-comatose state, not—as many people assume—a deep state of sleep.

5. Chosen as young girls, the priestesses of Vesta (goddess of the hearth), were granted rights, privileges, and power unavailable to other women in ancient Rome.

6. Grand Staircase-Escalante National Monument is home to more than 650 bee species, most likely because it mirrors the range of habitats—from sandstone canyons and sagebrush-peppered deserts to aspen and pine forests in which the insects live.

7. The scientific method—often presented as a fixed sequence of steps, actually represents a set of general principles.

8. In the early sixteenth century, colonization attempts by the world's newest major power, Spain were centered on the Caribbean islands and involved little contact with complex mainland civilizations.

9. The American Craftsman style, developed in Pasadena, California, in the 1890s by the architectural firm Greene & Greene, emphasized simplicity of form and the use of natural materials.

10. Telling the story of Odette, a princess turned into a swan by an evil sorcerer's curse, *Swan Lake*, one of the most popular ballets, was fashioned from Russian folk tales.

11. Richard Rodgers and Oscar Hammerstein, having achieved success independently began their collaboration with the musical *Oklahoma!* in 1943.

12. Human computers, who once performed basic numerical analysis for laboratories, and they were behind the calculations for everything from the first accurate prediction of the return of Halley's Comet to the success of the Manhattan Project.

13. Voyager 2—a space probe launched by NASA on August 20, 1977—, was actually launched 16 days before its twin, Voyager 1, on a trajectory that enabled encounters with Uranus and Neptune.

14. Batsford Arboretum, a 55-acre garden that contains Great Britain's largest collection of Japanese cherry trees and it is open daily to the public for most of the year.

15. Early European settlers first called the Boston area Trimountaine, (after its "three mountains," only traces of which remain today), but they later renamed it after Boston, England, the native city of several prominent colonists.

Chapter Six

Commas with Names and Titles

Names and titles can be **either essential (no commas) or non-essential (two commas)**. The most important thing to understand is that commas are not simply plunked in front of names and titles because "that's the rule." Rather, commas are used to indicate whether those elements are essential or non-essential.

When a name/title appears in the middle of a sentence (that is, not as the first or last words), there are generally only two correct options:

    1) Two commas: one before and one after the name or title

    2) No commas

It is always incorrect to place a comma at only the beginning of a non-essential phrase, so it is also incorrect to place one at only the beginning of a name or title.

    Incorrect: Best-selling **author, Amy Tan** combines fiction and family stories in her novels.

    Correct: Best-selling **author Amy Tan** combines fiction and family stories in her novels.

Note that this rule is unaffected by the length of the description before the name.

    Correct: **Best-selling Chinese-American author Amy Tan** combines fiction and family stories in her novels.

In this case, it is also incorrect to use two commas.

    Incorrect: **Best-selling author, Amy Tan,** combines fiction and family stories in her novels.

To test out the above version, cross out the name and see whether the sentence makes sense without it.

    Incorrect: **Best-selling author**…combines fiction and family stories in her novels.

No. The name is clearly required, so no commas should be used.

    Correct: **Best-selling author Amy Tan** combines fiction and family stories in her novels.

In many cases, crossing out a name will tell you whether commas are necessary. If the sentence does not make sense without the name, you can know for certain that commas are unnecessary. (Think: no sense = no commas.)

In some cases, however, just crossing out a name will not give you enough information to tell whether commas are necessary—the sentence will make sense both with and without the name.

In such cases, you can use the following guideline:

No commas = one of many

Commas = the only one

For example:

No commas: In Harper Lee's novel *To Kill a Mockingbird*, six-year-old "Scout" Finch lives with her <u>father</u> **Atticus** and <u>brother</u> **Jem** in a small Alabama town.

Commas: In Harper Lee's novel *To Kill a Mockingbird*, six-year-old "Scout" Finch lives with her <u>father</u>**, Atticus,** and <u>brother</u>**, Jem,** in a small Alabama town.

In the first version, the lack of commas implies that Scout has multiple fathers and multiple brothers. But in fact, that is not the case: Scout only has one of each. So although both versions are grammatically acceptable, only the second one is correct.

Now consider this pair of sentences:

Incorrect: Ada Lovelace and her <u>acquaintance</u>**, Charles Babbage,** were two of the most influential figures in the history of computer science: Babbage sketched out his ideas for an "analytical engine," while Lovelace demonstrated the machine's abilities.

Correct: Ada Lovelace and her <u>acquaintance</u> **Charles Babbage** were two of the most influential figures in the history of computer science: Babbage sketched out his ideas for an "analytical engine," while Lovelace demonstrated the machine's abilities.

Both versions of the sentence are grammatically correct, but here the no-comma option is more logical.

Commas around *Charles Babbage* imply that Babbage was Lovelace's **only** acquaintance. That's theoretically possible, but it's probably not what the writer meant to say. Without the commas, the implication is that Lovelace had multiple acquaintances, one of whom was Babbage. That just makes more sense.

Note that a single comma can be placed **after** a name if that punctuation is necessary for other reasons.

Correct: In Harper Lee's novel *To Kill a Mockingbird*, the protagonist is six-year-old **Scout,** <u>who</u> lives with her father and brother in a small town in Alabama.

In the above sentence, the construction *comma + who* is used to begin a dependent clause. The first clause just happens to end with a proper name.

Finally, when a person is addressed directly, the name is treated non-essentially and set off with commas.

Incorrect:	You **know Sophie your** essay on *To Kill a Mockingbird* is really impressive.
Incorrect:	You **know, Sophie (or: know Sophie,) your** essay on *To Kill a Mockingbird* is really impressive.
Correct:	You **know, Sophie, your** essay on *To Kill a Mockingbird* is really impressive.

Now let's look at some options with titles. They can be a bit trickier than names, but the same rule applies. When a title appears in the middle of a sentence, the two most common correct options are again **no commas (essential) or two commas (non-essential)**.

A single comma before or after the title should not be used.

| Incorrect: | Harper Lee's first novel**,** *To Kill a Mockingbird* was published in 1960. |
| Incorrect: | Harper Lee's first novel *To Kill a Mockingbird,* was published in 1960. |

In this case, omitting the commas entirely does not work either.

| Incorrect: | Harper Lee's <u>first novel</u> *To Kill a Mockingbird* was published in 1960. |

By definition, Lee could have published only one *first* novel. Only one = commas.

| Correct: | Harper Lee's <u>first novel</u>**,** *To Kill a Mockingbird,* was published in 1960. |

When a title refers to a work that *is* one of many, however, no commas should be used.

| Correct: | Harper Lee's novel *Go Set a Watchman* was published in 2016. |

The lack of commas in this version implies that Harper Lee published multiple novels, one of which was *Go Set a Watchman*. And in fact, that is the case: Lee did publish more than one novel.

Note that if the title is placed at the **end** of the sentence, it should be set off with a comma as well. Again, it is acceptable to use only one comma here—there is nowhere to place a second comma afterward.

| Correct: | In 1960, Harper Lee published her <u>first novel</u>**,** *To Kill a Mockingbird*. |

"Who" Clauses

Like many names and titles, clauses beginning with *who* are often grammatically acceptable either with or without commas, but they convey different meanings depending on whether the commas are present.

For example, consider the following.

Version 1:   <u>People</u>, **who** attend large open-air events such as sporting matches and music festivals, often turn to camping as a cheap form of accommodation.

The commas above indicate that the sentence is focusing on people in general. The fact that they attend large open-air events such as sporting matches and music festivals is secondary.

Version 2:   <u>People</u> **who** attend large open-air events such as sporting matches and music festivals often turn to camping as a cheap form of accommodation.

The lack of commas in the second version indicates that the sentence is **not discussing people in general** but rather a **specific group** of people: those who attend large open-air events such as sporting matches and music festivals. In the absence of any context, this version simply makes more sense: not all people use camping as a cheap form of accommodation.

Grammatically, these sentences are acceptable both ways; the focus of the sentence merely shifts depending on whether the commas are used. When a sentence that can be written either with or without commas appears in a paragraph, however, only one version will normally create a logical meaning.

To decide whether commas are necessary, you can also approach things this way: look at the noun immediately before the word *who*.

- If **two commas** are used, the clause describes the preceding noun **in general**.

- If **no commas** are used, the clause restricts the description to that **specific noun**.

Note that you may need to read the surrounding paragraph for context in order to determine whether the focus is general or specific. If you're not sure, try crossing out the clause and reading the paragraph without it. If it no longer makes sense, the clause is essential, and no commas should be used. (There are exceptions, but they must be considered on a case-by-case basis.)

Let's look at an example.

> The store where I work has a return policy I have always found amusing. Normally, customers have one year from the purchase date to return unwanted or defective goods; however, <u>customers</u>, **who make purchases on February 29th,** have *four* years to return their items. Because February 29th occurs only once every four years, customers have nearly 1,500 days to decide whether they truly want a toaster or pair of shoes.

The commas around *who make purchases on February 29th* imply that the passage is discussing customers in general; however, the clause clearly is focusing on a specific group of customers: those who make purchases on February 29th.

In addition, consider what happens to the meaning of the passage if the clause is removed:

> The store where I work has a return policy I have always found amusing. Normally, customers have one year from the purchase date to return unwanted or defective goods; however, **customers**...have *four* years to return their items. Because February 29th occurs only once every four years, customers are allowed nearly 1,500 days to decide whether they truly want a toaster or pair of shoes.

Without the clause specifying that *customers* refers only to people who purchase items on February 29th, the reference to that date in the following sentence does not make sense.

The passage also contradicts itself because it initially states that customers normally have only one year to return unwanted items. It is illogical to then say that *customers have four years to return their items.*

The clause is thus **essential** and does not require commas:

> The store where I work has a return policy I have always found amusing. Normally, customers have one year from the purchase date to return unwanted or defective goods; however, **customers who make purchases on February 29th** have *four* years to return their items. Because February 29th occurs only once every four years, customers are allowed nearly 1,500 days to decide whether they truly want a toaster or pair of shoes.

Proper Names

"Who" clauses that <u>follow</u> proper names are **virtually always non-essential** because they are used to provide descriptive information about a person and are not crucial to the basic meaning of a sentence.

Incorrect: Henri Becquerel **who shared in the 1903 Nobel Prize in Nuclear Physics** is credited with the discovery that the radiation emitted by uranium salts emanates spontaneously from the uranium itself.

Correct: Henri Becquerel**, who shared in the 1903 Nobel Prize in Nuclear Physics,** is credited with the discovery that the radiation emitted by uranium salts emanates spontaneously from the uranium itself.

Exercise: Essential vs. Non-Essential Elements

In the following sentences, add or eliminate commas as necessary. Some of the sentences may not contain an error. (Answers p. 276)

Example: Mildly shocking when it was first produced in 1984, the ~~play, Equus,~~ play Equus has attracted far less controversy during recent performances.

1. Karl Marx, in collaboration with Frederich Engels, provides a detailed critique of capitalism in the book, *The Communist Manifesto*.

2. Although the medieval philosopher, Peter Abelard was expected to pursue a military career, he rejected that option, choosing to become a scholar instead.

3. The explorer James Cook, who demonstrated a talent for cartography, was responsible for mapping the entrance to the Saint Lawrence River during the siege of Quebec.

4. Nearly a fifth of researchers, who work with mice, are estimated to become allergic to those animals; however, the real number may be higher because some people may not report their symptoms.

5. While working as an instructor for the U.S. Navy, George Lucas produced his first film *Electronic Labyrinth: THX 1138 4EB*, which won first prize at the 1967–68 National Student Film Festival.

6. The original Olympics were banned in A.D. 393 by Roman emperor, Theodosius I, but despite that prohibition, Europeans persisted in holding the Games during the Dark and Middle Ages.

7. Because the director harshly criticized actors, who dared to question his instructions, he earned a reputation for being an exceptionally poor colleague.

8. Some scholars, including the historian, Niall Ferguson, have suggested that populist governments are usually so incompetent that they prove short-lived.

9. Groundbreaking when it was released in 1990, the documentary, *The Civil War*, possessed a collage-like quality, presenting an incredible number of stories in rapid succession.

10. The novelist Willa Cather is often seen reverently as a symbol of the American Midwest, but this view conflicts with the reality that Cather was a writer who belongs to the modern world.

Chapter Seven
People vs. Things

Some relative pronouns refer to people only; some refer to things only; and some refer to people and things.

People	Things	People & Things
Who Whom	Which That	Whose (That)

Which can refer only to things, never to people. Note that legal entities such as companies count as things.

Incorrect: King Henry VIII was a British <u>monarch</u> **which** ruled England during the Tudor period and was known for his many wives.

Correct: Fines for pollution were levied against the manufacturing <u>company</u>, **which** has pledged to dispose of waste in a more environmentally friendly manner.

Conversely, *who(m)* can only be used to refer to people, never things.

Incorrect: Fines for pollution were levied against the manufacturing <u>company</u>, **who** has pledged to dispose of waste in a more environmentally friendly manner.

Correct: King Henry VIII was a British <u>monarch</u> **who** ruled England during the Tudor period and was known for his many wives.

Note, however, that *whose* can refer to either people or things.

Correct: Conductor Marin Alsop is a consummate <u>musician</u> **whose** every gesture reveals her commitment to and passion for her art.

Correct: Although it is a smaller city than either London or New York, Dublin has a thriving <u>theater scene</u> **whose** productions often achieve international renown.

Although *that* is commonly used to refer to both things and people, the second use is somewhat inelegant and controversial because it implies that you are viewing people as objects. To be truly correct, reserve *which* and *that* for things and *who* for people.

Iffy: Although certain genetic mutations always result in the development of a disease, <u>patients</u> **that** have identical mutations can display widely varying symptoms.

Better: Although certain genetic mutations always result in the development of a disease, <u>patients</u> **who** have identical mutations can display widely varying symptoms.

Note that *which* is always preceded by a comma and is used to set off a non-essential clause.

Incorrect: The mutation **<u>which</u> was recently identified** has been linked to several diseases.

Correct: The mutation**, <u>which</u> was recently identified,** has been linked to several diseases.

In contrast, *that* is never preceded by a comma and is used to set off an essential clause.

Incorrect: The mutation**, <u>that</u> was recently identified,** has been linked to several diseases.

Correct: The mutation **<u>that</u> was recently identified** has been linked to several diseases.

Who vs. Whom

At the simplest level, there are two main things you need to know about *who* and *whom*.

1) **Who comes before a verb.**
2) **Whom comes after a preposition (e.g., *of*, *to*, *with*, *by*, *for*, *from*).**

Before a Verb

Incorrect: Emily Dickinson was not only a poet but also a distinguished letter-writer **whom** <u>exchanged</u> thousands of pieces of correspondence with friends and family.

Correct: Emily Dickinson was not only a poet but also a distinguished letter-writer **who** <u>exchanged</u> thousands of pieces of correspondence with friends and family.

After a Preposition

Incorrect: Among Emily Dickinson's favorite writing partners was her sister-in-law, Susan Huntington, **with who** Dickinson exchanged hundreds of letters.

Correct: Among Emily Dickinson's favorite writing partners was her sister-in-law, Susan Huntington, **with whom** Dickinson exchanged hundreds of letters.

Although formal English has traditionally prohibited the use of prepositions at the ends of sentences (more about that in a little bit), writers do of course end their sentences with prepositions all the time.

When *whom* would normally follow a preposition, it should be used even if the preposition appears at the end of the sentence.

Correct: Among Emily Dickinson's favorite writing partners was her sister-in-law, Susan Huntington, **whom** Dickinson exchanged hundreds of letters **with**.

Important: When the construction *pronoun + of whom* appears, it is acceptable for a verb to be placed after *whom*. The use of *whom* is determined by the preposition *of*, not by the verb.

Incorrect: The members of the youth orchestra, <u>many of who</u> **have** been studying music since a young age, are frequently praised for their exceptional playing.

Correct: The members of the youth orchestra, <u>many of whom</u> **have** been studying music since a young age, are frequently praised for their exceptional playing.

You can also think of it this way: when *pronoun + of whom* is used, the entire phrase is one unit that acts as the subject. As a result, a verb can be placed immediately afterward.

Subjects and Objects

The *who* vs. *whom* rules we've just looked at are fairly straightforward to master in the sense that it isn't really necessary to know anything about subjects or objects to apply them.

To fully understand how *who* and *whom* are used, however, you must understand how subject and object pronouns work.

Each subject pronoun has an object counterpart.

Subject	Object
I	Me
You	You
S/he	Her, Him
We	Us
They	Them

In terms of relative pronouns:

- **Who** corresponds to subject pronouns.
- **Whom** corresponds to object pronouns.

Let's start with something very simple.

Correct: I <u>saw</u> **James** yesterday.

James is the direct object of the verb *saw*, so *James* can thus be replaced with the object pronoun *him*.

Correct: I <u>saw</u> **him** yesterday.

Now, if we want to rewrite the sentence using a relative pronoun, the object form *whom* must be used.

Correct: James is the person **whom** I saw yesterday.

If you're not sure whether *whom* is correct, check whether an object pronoun (*him*, *her*, *them*) can be placed after the verb. If it can, *whom* should be used.

Correct: In sincerely trying to find the truth about factual claims, people must often decide **whom** to believe.

Substitute: People must often decide to believe **them.**

Because an object pronoun follows the verb *believe*, *whom* is the correct form.

Let's look at another example:

Correct: John Brown, who led the raid on Harpers Ferry in 1859, was a man **whom** Lincoln disowned until the beginning of the Civil War.

Substitute: Lincoln disowned John Brown.

→   Lincoln disowned **him**.

Because *John Brown* can be replaced with the object pronoun *him*, it is again correct to use *whom*.

Now let's look at something really tricky:

Incorrect: John Brown was a man **whom** Lincoln believed was responsible for stoking tensions between the states.

The above sentence can be rewritten as follows:

Substitute: Lincoln believed that **John Brown** was responsible for stoking tensions between the states.

→   Lincoln believed that **he** was responsible for stoking tensions between the states.

Correct: John Brown was a man **who** Lincoln believed was responsible for stoking tensions between the states.

Where & When

Where is for places (physical locations) only. To refer to works of art or literature, use *in which*.

Incorrect:	The novel *Life of Pi*, written by Yann Martel, is a story **where** the protagonist survives on a raft in the ocean for nearly a year, accompanied only by a tiger.
Correct:	The novel *Life of Pi*, written by Yann Martel, is a story **in which** the protagonist survives on a raft in the ocean for nearly a year, accompanied only by a tiger.

When a place is being referred to, *where* and *in which* are both acceptable. *In which* is just a bit more formal.

Correct:	Although Einstein predicted black holes, regions of space **where** gravity is so intense that not even light can escape, he had difficulty believing they could exist.
Correct:	Although Einstein predicted black holes, regions of space **in which** gravity is so intense that not even light can escape, he had difficulty believing they could exist.

When is for **times** and **time periods**.

Incorrect:	The Middle Ages was a period **where** many farmers were bound to the lands they worked.
Correct:	The Middle Ages was a period **when** many farmers were bound to the lands they worked.

Preposition + which is also an acceptable alternative to *when*.

Correct:	The Middle Ages was a period **in/during which** many farmers were bound to the lands they worked.

Whereby & Wherein

In some cases, *whereby* and *wherein* can be used in place of *by which* or *according to which*. These constructions typically appear in the context of systems/processes or phenomena.

Correct:	Scientific inquiry is <u>a process</u> **whereby** researchers traverse the abyss between the known and the unknown, suspended by intuition, adventurousness, a healthy dose of stubbornness, and a measure of luck.
Correct:	"Follow Friday" is a Twitter <u>phenomenon</u> **wherein** users of the social media service list, in a tweet or two every Friday, the handful of users they recommend following.

Although these pronouns may strike you as odd or antiquated, they are in fact acceptable. That said, they should be used sparingly. Excessive use of them can easily make writing seem clunky and pretentious.

Ending Clauses and Sentences with Prepositions

Consider the following sentence. Notice that the last word, *on*, is a preposition.

Informal: In the early days of mass automobile production, the Ford Model-T was the car most Americans **relied on**.

The sentence can also be rearranged so that the preposition is placed in the middle and followed by *which*.

Formal: In the early days of mass automobile production, the Ford Model-T was the car **on which** most Americans **relied**.

For many traditional grammarians, the first construction would be considered downright incorrect. In fact, the prohibition against ending sentences (and clauses) with prepositions was for a long time handed down as an ironclad rule. In reality, however, it is one of the odder quirks of the English language. Unlike grammatical rules that evolved to make writing clearer and easier to follow, this one is quite arbitrary.

To make a long story short, in the seventeenth century, when English was still jockeying for equal status with Latin as a language of the educated classes, a well-known writer (reportedly John Dryden) decided that because Latin sentences could not be ended with prepositions, then the same should be true of "proper" English.

Unfortunately, this proclamation ignored a key difference between Latin and English. In Latin, it is effectively impossible to end a sentence with a preposition. English, however, is also a Germanic language. In German, it is not only possible but often necessary to end sentences and clauses with prepositions—and when it comes to phrasal verbs (verbs followed by prepositions, e.g., *rely on*, *relate to*, *wonder about*), English is much closer to German than it is to Latin. Thus, from a strictly linguistic standpoint, the statement "you can't end a sentence with a preposition" is, to put it bluntly, nonsense.

That said, tradition exerts a strong pull, and there are undoubtedly still grammar purists who are inclined to view the placement of a preposition at the end of a clause or sentence as a type of sacrilege in formal writing.

As a result, you should use both your ear and common sense: consider both your audience and the impression you want to create. For example, compare the two versions of the following sentence.

Acceptable: Although *Mansfield Park* ends with the heroine's marriage to **the man she has set her heart on**, the novel expresses a strong degree of ambivalence toward the pursuit and achievement of marriage, especially for women.

More formal: Although *Mansfield Park* ends with the heroine's marriage to **the man on whom she has set her heart**, the novel expresses a strong degree of ambivalence toward the pursuit and achievement of marriage, especially for women.

Because this sentence is already quite complex, the use of *preposition + whom* in the second version comes off as slightly stilted and overly correct. In contrast, placing the preposition at the end of the clause causes the sentence to flow more naturally and makes the writing seem a bit less stuffy.

In other cases, *preposition + which/whom* may simply add a degree of formality.

Less formal: Among Emily Dickinson's favorite writing partners was her sister-in-law, Susan Huntington, **whom** Dickinson exchanged hundreds of letters **with**.

More formal: Among Emily Dickinson's favorite writing partners was her sister-in-law, Susan Huntington, **with whom** Dickinson exchanged hundreds of letters.

One preposition that should not be placed unnecessarily at the end of a clause or sentence is *at*. Although constructions such as *I didn't know where he was at* are common in spoken English, they are unacceptable in formal writing because they are overly casual and draw the reader's attention away from the main action.

Awkward: Seeking to obtain a better understanding of where citrus trees **originated at**, researchers studied the genomes of more than 50 types of citrus fruit.

Better: Seeking to obtain a better understanding of where citrus trees **originated**, researchers studied the genomes of more than 50 types of citrus fruit.

In addition, note that when *preposition + which* is used, a separate preposition should not <u>also</u> be used at the end of the sentence.

Incorrect: Not only have amateur astronomers contributed to many important discoveries, but astronomy also remains one of the few sciences **in which** non-professionals can still play an active **role for**.

Because you would say <u>*in* astronomy</u>, *in* is the only preposition that can be used.

Correct: Not only have amateur astronomers contributed to many important discoveries, but astronomy also remains one of the few sciences **in which** non-professionals can still play an active **role**.

Exercise: People vs. Things

For the following sentences, correct any pronoun error involving references to people and things.
(Answers p. 277)

who
Example: Folk singers, jazz musicians, and painters were among the artists ~~which~~ were profiled by photographer and filmmaker George Picker over the course of his career.

1.   For delicate patients which cannot handle the rigors of certain treatments, some doctors are now rejecting the assembly line of modern medical care for gentler, more traditional options.

2.   In its later years, the Bauhaus architectural movement became a kind of religion in which heretics had to be excommunicated by those who held the true light.

3.   In 1623, Galileo published a work where he championed the controversial theory of heliocentrism, thus provoking one of the greatest scientific controversies of his day.

4.   Keyless entry systems often make uses of hidden cameras, which allow residents to screen visitors discreetly and determine whom to allow inside.

5.   It has taken many decades for scientists to piece together the riddle of just where modern cats first became domesticated at.

6.   When readers whom obtain their news from electronic rather than printed sources send articles to their friends, they tend to choose ones that confirm their pre-existing biases.

7.   In his utopian novel *Walden Two*, B.F. Skinner invents a world in which emotions such as envy have become obsolete because people are conditioned as children to reject them.

8.   Most evidence points toward the deep past, approximately four billion years ago, as the era during which Mars could have held marine environments in.

9.   One of the least popular Romance languages, Romansch is traditionally spoken by people who inhabit the southern regions of Switzerland.

10.   Ada Lovelace, for who the programming language Ada is named, was a pioneer in computer science, foreseeing how an "analytical engine" could be built more than a century before the first such machine was constructed.

Chapter Eight

Colons, Hyphens, and Dashes

Colons

Colons have three major uses:

1) Introduce a list

2) Introduce an explanation

3) Introduce a block quotation

Important: A colon must **follow** a full sentence that can stand on its own as a complete thought. However, a colon does not need to be **followed by** a complete sentence.

A. Colon Before a List

Incorrect:	The Great Bear Rainforest contains: Western Red Cedar, Sitka Spruce, and Douglas Fir trees.
Correct:	The Great Bear Rainforest contains three principal tree species: the Western Red Cedar, the Sitka Spruce, and the Douglas Fir.

Note that *including* and *such as* should <u>not</u> be followed by a colon. Even though they are typically used to introduce lists, there essentially is no way to create a standalone sentence that ends with them.

Incorrect:	The Great Bear Rainforest contains a variety of tree species, **including:** the Western Red Cedar, the Sitka Spruce, and the Douglas Fir.
Correct:	The Great Bear Rainforest contains a variety of tree species, **including** the Western Red Cedar, the Sitka Spruce, and the Douglas Fir.
Incorrect:	The Great Bear Rainforest contains a variety of tree species **such as:** the Western Red Cedar, the Sitka Spruce, and the Douglas Fir.
Correct:	The Great Bear Rainforest contains a variety of tree species **such** as the Western Red Cedar, the Sitka Spruce, and the Douglas Fir.

B. Colon Before an Explanation

When a colon comes before an explanation, a complete sentence typically follows the colon.

Correct: The Amazon parrot does not make an ideal pet for most people **for one major reason: it** requires much more attention and affection than many other animals do.

When a colon is used this way, it is typically an alternative to a period or semicolon. The colon merely signals to the reader that an explanation is coming, in a way that the period and semicolon do not.

Correct: The Amazon parrot does not make an ideal pet for most **people: it** requires much more attention and affection than many other animals do.

Correct: The Amazon parrot does not make an ideal pet for most **people; it** requires much more attention and affection than many other animals do.

Correct: The Amazon parrot does not make an ideal pet for most **people. It** requires much more attention and affection than many other animals do.

When the second clause does <u>not</u> serve to explain the first, a semicolon or period must be used instead.

Incorrect: Hersheypark was created as a leisure park for the employees of the Hershey Chocolate **Company: the** decision was later made to open it to the public.

Correct: Hersheypark was created as a leisure park for the employees of the Hershey Chocolate **Company; the decision** was later made to open it to the public.

C. Colon Before a Block Quotation

Multi-line citations should be set off as block quotations and introduced by a colon. For example, consider the following excerpt from a paper on Jane Austen's novel *Mansfield Park*:

[Maria's] only desire now is to be free of her father's control, and to take refuge from her disappointed feelings in the splendor of being Mrs. Rushworth, living a life of "fortune and consequence" (188). In case we have any doubt about Maria's motives for marriage, **the narrator, with breathtaking irony, tells us the following:**

> In all the important preparations of the mind she was complete; being prepared for matrimony by a hatred of home, restraint, and tranquility; by the misery of disappointed affection and contempt of the man she was to marry. The rest might wait. The preparation of new carriages and furniture might wait for London and spring, when her own taste could have fairer play. (188)[1]

Note: If the statement following a colon is restricted to a single sentence, then the first word after the colon does not need to be capitalized. If, however, a colon is used to set off a multi-sentence explanation (as is the case above), then the first word after the colon should be capitalized.

[1]https://www.alyve.org/english/docs/writingLab/sampleMLA-Austen.pdf

Hyphens and Dashes

Although hyphens and dashes look similar, they have two separate functions and are not interchangeable.

Hyphens

Hyphens (-) are shorter than dashes and are used to join compound words that form a single idea.

They are used with certain prefixes, including *ex-* (former), *pro-* (in favor of), *anti-* (against), and *self-*.

Correct:	**Anti-globalization** protestors have been assembling in anticipation of the rally, with thousands more expected to arrive over the next few days.
Correct:	A remarkable **self-publicist**, Margaret Cavendish was a composer of poetry, a writer of philosophy, and an inventor of romances.

They can also be used with verbs and adjectives.

Correct:	Many students have a tendency to **second-guess** themselves during exams, changing their correct answers to incorrect ones.

When a compound adjective comes **before** a noun, a hyphen should be used.

Correct:	Amusement parks grew out of **industrial-era leisure** gardens, offering spaces where workers could go to escape from grim urban environments.

No hyphen should be used when the adjective comes **after** the noun, however.

Correct:	Amusement parks grew out of leisure <u>gardens</u> of the **industrial era**, offering spaces where workers could go to escape from grim urban environments.

In addition, hyphens should be used between two-word numbers that are written out.

Correct:	Even after reading for several hours, I still had **fifty-seven** pages to go before I finished the assignment.

Hyphens are also used with ages. When an age precedes a noun, the construction is *x-year-old noun*.

Correct:	As a **six-year-old** <u>prodigy</u>, Mozart was brought to exhibit his musical talents at the courts of Vienna and Prague.

If the age itself is a noun, the full phrase should be hyphenated as well.

Correct:	As a **six-year-old**, Mozart was brought to exhibit his musical talents at the courts of Vienna and Prague.

When the age follows a form of the verb *to be*, however, no hyphens should be used.

Correct:	Mozart was brought to exhibit his prodigious musical talents at the courts of Vienna and Prague when he <u>was</u> just **six years old**.

Dashes

There are two types of **dashes**: the en dash (–), and the slightly longer em dash (—).

En dashes denote ranges, e.g., page numbers and dates. Do not place a space between the numbers and the dashes.

Correct:	The professor assigned us pages 107–152 for tomorrow.
Correct:	Although the match lasted for nearly three hours, the final score was only 2–1.
Correct:	Readers are eagerly anticipating the release of the magazine's January–February issue.

Em dashes have three major uses:

A. Set off a non-essential clause (two dashes = two commas)

Dashes can be used to set off non-essential information. Stylistically, they create a stronger break than commas do.

Correct:	London—**which is a very old city**—has buildings from many different eras.

When a sentence contains multiple non-essential clauses, a dash can also help clarify where ideas begin and end.

Confusing:	London, **which is a very old city, having been settled as early as the second century A.D.,** has buildings from many different eras.
Clearer:	London—**which is a very old city, having been settled as early as the second century A.D.**—has buildings from many different eras.

B. Introduce a list or explanation (dash = colon)

When a dash is used to introduce a list or explanation, it is grammatically identical to a colon: it must follow a complete, standalone sentence but can be followed by either a sentence or a fragment. The dash vs. colon distinction is purely stylistic; the dash merely creates a stronger break.

List

Incorrect:	The Great Bear Rainforest **contains**—**Western Red Cedar**, Sitka Spruce, and Douglas Fir trees.
Correct:	The Great Bear Rainforest contains three main tree **species**—**Western Red Cedar**, Sitka Spruce, and Douglas Fir.

Explanation

Incorrect: The Amazon parrot does not make an ideal pet for most people **because—it** requires much more attention and affection than many other animals do.

Correct: The Amazon parrot does not make an ideal pet for most **people—it** requires much more attention and affection than many other animals do.

Note that when dashes are used to introduce explanations or clarifications, they are often used with the transitional phrase *that is*.

Correct: Regret may be an unpleasant emotion, but it serves an important **purpose— that is,** it causes people to correct their future behavior in order to avoid harmful consequences.

C. Create a dramatic pause

A single dash can also be used to create a dramatic pause or sense of suspense. Again, a dash used this way must follow a complete sentence but can be followed by a sentence (as in the first example below) or a fragment (as in the second example).

Correct: Mushrooms are **everywhere—they** are found on forest floors, in gardens, and in networks connecting below our feet.

Correct: J.R.R. Tolkien's *Lord of the Rings* novels are set in Middle-earth—**a land inhabited by a variety of mystical creatures**.

In the sentence above, the dash creates a sense of suspense by breaking the sentence into two parts, requiring the reader to wait for a second to learn what Middle-earth is.

In addition, a noun from earlier in the sentence may be repeated, for stylistic effect.

Combined: J.R.R. Tolkien's *Lord of the Rings* novels are set in **a land** called Middle-earth— **a land** inhabited by a variety of mystical creatures.

Em vs. En Dashes

In British and Canadian English, and increasingly in American English, en dashes along with a space are used instead of em dashes because they provide a cleaner, more streamlined look.

Particularly when sentences are long, the extra space around the dash can help readers to process text more easily. For that reason, magazines and newspapers generally prefer this construction.

Compare:

Em dashes: In 1688, John Dryden was removed from the post of British poet **laureate—a**
(no space)   **post that was normally held for life—because** of his staunch refusal to swear
                 an oath of allegiance to the king.

En dashes: In 1688, John Dryden was removed from the post of British poet **laureate – a**
                 post that was normally held for life – because of his staunch refusal to swear
                 an oath of allegiance to the king.

From a visual perspective, the en dashes set off the non-essential information more clearly.

Alternately, em dashes may be used with a space, a construction that tends be easier than the no-space version to read on a screen.

Em dashes: In 1688, John Dryden was removed from the post of British poet **laureate — a**
(space)   **post that was normally held for life — because** of his staunch refusal to
                 swear an oath of allegiance to the king.

Although some readers might express a preference for the classic construction of em dashes without a space, you can generally use any of these options. Just make sure to be consistent.

Avoid using en dashes without a space; this construction is simply too cramped to be read comfortably on either paper or a screen.

Avoid: In 1688, John Dryden was removed from the post of British poet **laureate-a**
                 post that was normally held for life–because of his staunch refusal to swear
                 an oath of allegiance to the king.

Exercise: Colons and Dashes

For the following exercises, determine whether the colon or dash is used correctly, and remove or change the punctuation as necessary to fix any error. (Answers p. 277)

Example: Originally constructed as a Hindu temple, Angkor Wat is admired ~~for: the~~ **for the** immense scale of its architecture, its extensive bas-relief collection, and the many guardian spirits that decorate its walls.

1.   In experiments on monkeys, mice, and dogs, as well as in multiple test-tube trials, a small number of Lyme Disease bacteria have been found to survive—a wide array of antibiotics.

2.   In creating psychoanalysis, Freud developed therapeutic techniques such as: free association and transference, establishing their central role in the analytic process.

3.   There are many theories about why flying might leave passengers more vulnerable to crying— sadness, excitement, or homesickness are all possible explanations.

4.   As inhabitants of the digital world, most people are exposed daily to: dozens of photographs of friends, loved ones, celebrities, and strangers.

5.   Tipping as a phenomenon has long fascinated economists—paying extra, even though we are not legally required to do so, seems to go against our own best interest.

6.   The artificial sweetener Sucralose is increasingly being used as what experts call a "tracer"—that is, a substance used to help identify the origins of environmental contamination.

7.   Vanilla has become one of the most beloved and lucrative spices in the world: an estimated 18,000 products contain the flavor, and prices hover at around $300 per pound.

8.   Crux is a constellation located in the southern part of the Milky Way: it is among the most easily identified star clusters because of its high visual magnitude.

9.   As gaping holes of logic appear in Marc Antony's oration, we begin to see what sorts of artifices made his speech so cunning; its use of circumstantial evidence, its largely emotional pleas, and its desperate engagement of the citizens.

10.   After 1765, growing political differences between Great Britain and its colonies led to protests against taxation without representation—protests that culminated with the Boston Tea Party.

Chapter Nine

Questions and Question Marks

Question marks are used at the ends of questions, in place of periods.

Questions can be formed two ways:

1) Interrogative pronouns (*who, what, when, where, why, how*)

Incorrect: <u>What</u> explains Agatha Christie's continuing appeal to **readers.**

Correct: <u>What</u> explains Agatha Christie's continuing appeal to **readers?**

2) Verb before subject (with *be, have, do, will, can/could, should, would*)

Incorrect: **Can** selfies become artistic statements, as self-portraits once **were.**

Correct: **Can** selfies become artistic statements, as self-portraits once **were?**

Note that in British English, inverted questions are commonly formed with *have + subject + got*, e.g., *Have they got enough money to pay their rent?* In American English, however, *do + subject + have* is used instead, e.g., *Do they have enough money to pay their rent?*

Direct vs. Indirect Speech

Direct speech does exactly what its name implies: it asks questions directly. In this construction, the verb comes before the subject, and **a question mark is used**.

Correct: When Orson Welles' *War of the Worlds* was broadcast as a radio play in 1938, some listeners asked themselves, "<u>**Is this** a piece of theater or a live broadcast?</u>"

Although the question here is clearly linked to the first part of the sentence in terms of meaning, it is a separate statement that makes sense grammatically on its own. In addition, the verb, *is*, precedes the subject, *this*. A question mark is therefore necessary.

In **indirect speech**, a question is embedded in a longer sentence, and the subject comes before the verb. **No question mark is used.**

Often, this construction involves clauses begun by *whether* or *if*, although other "w-words" or *how* can be used as well.

Correct: When Orson Welles' *War of the Worlds* was broadcast as a radio play in 1938, some listeners could not tell **whether/if it was a piece of theater or a live broadcast.**

Notice that in this version, the subject (*it*) comes before the verb (*was*).

Let's look at another example.

Incorrect: If you spend time in a room with people who are yawning, it is almost certain that you will eventually join them. The only question is **whether you will begin to yawn immediately or manage to resist for a minute or two?**

Because the clause in question begins with *whether*, and the subject (*you*) and verb (*will*) are in the normal order, a period should be used.

Correct: If you spend time in a room with people who are yawning, it is almost certain that you will eventually join them. The only question is **whether you will begin to yawn immediately or manage to resist for a minute or two.**

If we make the question into a separate clause, a question mark can be used.

Correct: If you spend time in a room with people who are yawning, it is almost certain that you will eventually join them. The only question **is, will you begin to yawn immediately or manage to resist for a minute or two?**

Even cleaner: If you spend time in a room with people who are yawning, it is almost certain that you will eventually join them. The only question is **this: will you begin to yawn immediately or manage to resist for a minute or two?**

When a "w-word" or a phrase indicating uncertainty is used, a flipped verb and noun should not follow; the result is extremely awkward and ungrammatical, regardless of punctuation.

Incorrect: It is still not fully clear **why did Bach begin** recycling old material instead of composing new works from scratch. (**or:** scratch?**)**

Correct: It is still not fully clear **why Bach began** recycling old material instead of composing new works from **scratch.**

Incorrect: The purpose of an experiment is to determine **do observations** of the real world agree with or conflict with the predictions derived from a **hypothesis.**

Correct: The purpose of an experiment is to determine **whether observations** of the real world agree with or conflict with the predictions derived from a hypothesis.

Exercise: Forming Indirect Questions with "Whether"

Rewrite the underlined portion of each sentence indirectly, using a "whether" clause. (Answers p. 278)

Example: Because human behavior is driven by emotion as well as logic, it is exceedingly difficult for economists to predict <u>will markets rise or fall</u> in the short term.

    whether markets will rise or fall

1. When I am asked to write a blurb for the back cover of a novel, I don't spend a lot of time <u>wondering, "Is the book really worth readers' money?"</u>

2. Many people have argued that the medium in which journalists publish should have no bearing on <u>can they receive</u> the protection of a state's law shielding them from lawsuits.

3. The philosopher Alex Rosenberg of Duke University has <u>asked, "Is neuroscience</u> actually a bigger threat to humanity than artificial intelligence?"

4. A recent GPS system failure has raised the <u>question, could complex digital systems on earth continue</u> to function if satellite clocks were wiped out?

5. Americans remain heavily split on the issue of <u>should they consume</u> genetically modified foods (GMOs) and organic products.

Exercise: Question Mark or Period?

In the following sentences, add or remove question marks as necessary, and rewrite ungrammatical constructions. Some of the sentences may not contain an error. (Answers p. 278)

Example: For astrophysicists studying the birth of the universe, a key question is whether scientists can test an entire theoretical model rather than just specific ~~parts of it?~~
parts of it.

1.   Although oil prices have begun to rebound, market analysts question whether a significant price recovery is truly about to occur?

2.   Ponderous, pretentious, even ridiculous, Hemingway's fiction goes more out of fashion every year — why, then, is it still so widely read?

3.   Although the concept of debt dates to the ancient world, scholars still debate whether the Venetians were truly the inventors of corporate stock?

4.   While most editors are concerned with how accurate a biography is, others are more interested in how fast it can be published?

5.   While Yiddish words and phrases pepper modern American English, linguists are uncertain whether the language itself will survive.

6.   The vast majority of American parents who pay an allowance tie the money to have their children done chores around the house?

7.   Although people generally believe that they are directly and immediately aware of their own thoughts, some philosophers have asked whether conscious thought and judgment are illusions.

8.   The majority of experiments performed by cognitive psychologist Elizabeth Spelke have been designed to test how much babies and young children understand about the world around them?

9.   When selecting shoes and equipment, mountain climbers must ask themselves the following question: will their chosen route take them over rock, snow, or ice.

10.   Following his release from captivity, King Louis IX of France used his influence to show crusaders how could they rebuild their defenses and conduct diplomacy?

Chapter Ten

Punctuating Quotations

Quotation marks serve a variety of purposes:

1) Signal direct citations, in speech and in texts

Correct: According to Sophie Hannah, the author of *How to Hold a Grudge*, grudges are an **"important and fascinating part of human experience."**

2) Call attention to unusual or specialized terminology

Correct: Taking actions without fully considering their risks is a phenomenon that is known as **"reaching for yield."**

3) Set off definitions

Correct: The dictionary of gestures will help you understand what it means when someone pulls on their earlobe with their thumb and index finger **("watch out"** in Greece and Turkey) or wiggles it around **("delicious"** in Portugal and Brazil).

4) Convey non-literal or ironic meanings

Correct: We may say that an electric **"eye"** that opens a door when someone approaches **"sees"** that person, but we don't think there's any literal seeing going on.

Periods and Commas

In American English, periods and commas go **inside** quotation marks; in British English, they go outside.

American: The term "graphic **novel,"** **which** is applied more broadly than the term **"novel,"** includes fiction, non-fiction, and anthologized work.

British: The term "graphic **novel",** **which** is applied more broadly than the term **"novel",** includes fiction, non-fiction, and anthologized work.

American:	As the playwright Sacha Guitry once observed, "You can pretend to be serious, but you can't pretend to be **witty."**
British:	As the playwright Sacha Guitry once observed, "You can pretend to be serious, but you can't pretend to be **witty".**

When a textual citation (page, chapter, volume, etc.) is included after a quotation, the quotation marks should be placed right after the quotation, <u>before</u> the page reference and the period.

Incorrect:	As Fitzgerald states, Gatsby "had never really accepted…**his parents (99)."** At a young age, he began his journey to make something out of himself.

Think about the error in the above sentence from a logical standpoint: the page number is not actually part of the quoted material, and so it makes no sense to include it in the quotation marks. Likewise, it is incorrect to place the page reference after the period because doing so creates an unnecessary stop between the sentences. Readers are forced to stop and reorient themselves before moving on.

Incorrect:	As Fitzgerald states, Gatsby "had never really accepted…**his parents". (99)** At a young age, he began his journey to make something out of himself.
Correct:	As Fitzgerald states, Gatsby "had never really accepted…**his parents" (99).** At a young age, he began his journey to make something out of himself.

Semicolons, Colons, and Dashes

Semicolons, colons, and dashes are placed **outside** quotation marks.

Correct:	The French writer Charles de Brosses was the first person to use the geographical designation **"Polynesia";** originally, it referred to all the islands of the Pacific.
Correct:	International Morse code is based on a system of "dots" and **"dashes":** sequences of short and long signals that correspond to letters of the alphabet.
Correct:	International Morse code is based on a system of "dots" and **"dashes" —** sequences of short and long signals that correspond to letters of the alphabet.

Question Marks and Exclamation Points

Question marks and exclamation points can be placed **either inside or outside** quotation marks.

If the question or exclamation is **restricted to a word or phrase** within the sentence, place the punctuation **inside** the quotation marks. Note that this construction often involves a direct quotation set off by a comma.

Correct:	The policeman asks Tom Buchanan, **"What color car are you driving?"**

If the **entire statement** is a question or exclamation, place the punctuation **outside** the quotation marks. Note that the quoted portion of the sentence does not need to be a question.

Correct:	<u>What</u> do we mean when we talk about **"quality of life"**?

The same is true for exclamation points.

If the exclamation is restricted to a word or phrase, place the exclamation point inside the quotation marks.

> Correct: The sign read, **"Keep Off the Lawn!"**

If the exclamation lasts the entire sentence, place the exclamation point outside the quotation marks. Note that the information in quotation marks does not need to be an exclamation.

> Correct: Please stop yelling at me to **"chill out"**!

Important: while exclamation points are often used in everyday writing, especially on social media, they can make academic writing seem overly casual and immature, and so they should be used sparingly.

Direct and Indirect Speech

When you are referencing a person or a text, the use of quotation marks depends on whether you are citing the material directly or indirectly.

- In **direct speech**, a person's words are cited directly. Quotation marks are required, and a comma may be used to set off the quotation.
- In **indirect speech ("that")**, the writer restates a person's words. No quotation marks are used, and no comma is used to set off the quotation.

In the "direct" version below, the quote is set off by a reporting verb (*responds*), and the first word is capitalized.

> Correct: When the police ask Tom Buchanan what color car he was driving at the time of the accident, **he responds, "It's a blue car, a coupe."**

In the "indirect" version, no quotation marks are used, and the first word is not capitalized.

> Incorrect: When the police ask Tom Buchanan what color car he was driving at the time of the accident, **he responds <u>that</u> "he was driving a blue coupe."**

> Correct: When the police ask Tom Buchanan what color car he was driving at the time of the accident, **he responds <u>that</u> he was driving a blue coupe.**

As is generally true for "that" clauses, no comma should be placed either before or after the word *that*.

> Incorrect: When the police ask Tom Buchanan what color car he was driving at the time of the accident, he **responds, that (or: responds that,)** he was driving a blue coupe.

The indirect version can also be written without *that*. If this word is removed, no comma should replace it.

Incorrect: When the police ask Tom Buchanan what color car he was driving at the time of the accident, he **responds, he** was driving a blue coupe.

Correct: When the police ask Tom Buchanan what color car he was driving at the time of the accident, he **responds he** was driving a blue coupe.

When a direct quotation is integrated into a sentence rather than being <u>immediately</u> preceded by a reporting verb (e.g., *say, respond, tell*), **no comma** should be used. Unless the first word of the quotation falls at the beginning of a sentence in the original text, it should not be capitalized.

Incorrect: Tom Buchanan <u>told</u> the police officer that he was **driving, "a blue car, a coupe."**

Note how the comma interrupts the flow of the sentence and creates an illogical break. You wouldn't write *He was **driving, a** blue car*, so you wouldn't use the comma in context of a quotation either.

Correct: Tom Buchanan <u>told</u> the police officer that he was **driving "a blue car, a coupe."**

Interrupted Quotations

Quotations can be interrupted internally by reporting phrases, e.g., *he said, she asked, they announced*. **These phrases should be set off by commas, and separate quotation marks must be used for each section.**

Incorrect: "The internet hasn't so much changed people's relationship to **news" says James Meek "as** altered their self-awareness in the act of reading it."

Incorrect: "The internet hasn't so much changed people's relationship to news," says **James Meek "as** altered their self-awareness in the act of reading it."

Incorrect: "The internet hasn't so much changed people's relationship to **news" says** James Meek, "as altered their self-awareness in the act of reading it."

Incorrect: "The internet hasn't so much changed people's relationship to **news, says James Meek, as** altered their self-awareness in the act of reading it."

Correct: "The internet hasn't so much changed people's relationship to **news," says James Meek, "as** altered their self-awareness in the act of reading it."

If the quotation is interrupted at the end of a sentence, however, a period should be used.

Incorrect: "The internet hasn't so much changed people's relationship to **news," says James Meek, "It has, however,** altered their self-awareness in the act of reading it."

Correct: "The internet hasn't so much changed people's relationship to **news," says James Meek. "It has, however,** altered their self-awareness in the act of reading it."

Quotations Within Quotations

Quotations within quotations should be set off by single quotation marks.

Incorrect: At the beginning of *The Great Gatsby*, Nick Carraway states that Gatsby had none of that **"flabby** impressionability which is dignified under the name of the **"creative temperament"**—it was an extraordinary gift for hope, a romantic readiness such as I have never found in any other person and which it is not likely I shall ever find **again."**

Correct: At the beginning of *The Great Gatsby*, Nick Carraway states that Gatsby had none of that **"flabby** impressionability which is dignified under the name of the **'creative temperament'**—it was an extraordinary gift for hope, a romantic readiness such as I have never found in any other person and which it is not likely I shall ever find **again."**

When internal quotations fall at the end of a sentence, a single close quotation mark should be placed after the period, before the double close quotation marks.

Incorrect: Nick Carraway describes Gatsby as having none of that "flabby impressionability which is dignified under the name of the **'creative temperament."**

Correct: Nick Carraway describes Gatsby as having none of that "flabby impressionability which is dignified under the name of the **'creative temperament.'"**

Ellipses

When quotations are too long to be included in full, the omitted material must be replaced by three dots known as **ellipses**.

Original: At the beginning of *The Great Gatsby*, Nick Carraway states that Gatsby had none of that "flabby impressionability which is dignified under the name of the 'creative temperament'—it was an extraordinary gift for hope, **a romantic readiness such as I have never found in any other person and** which it is not likely I shall ever find again."

Correct: At the beginning of *The Great Gatsby*, Nick Carraway states that Gatsby had none of that "flabby impressionability which is dignified under the name of the 'creative temperament'—it was an extraordinary gift for **hope…which** it is not likely I shall ever find again."

Note that when you remove words from a quotation, you are expected to make a good-faith attempt to adhere as closely as possible to the original meaning. You may not, for example, alter quotations in a way that changes their significance or implications, or remove key material that might weaken or contradict your analysis.

Brackets

Sometimes, you may also need to add clarifying information to a quotation, in order to provide necessary context for your reader or integrate the citation more smoothly into your analysis. Added material should be placed in brackets to signal that it was not part of the original quotation.

Original: At the beginning of the novel, Nick Carraway states that "there was something gorgeous about **him**, some heightened sensitivity to the promises of life."

Incorrect: At the beginning of the novel, Nick Carraway states that "there was something gorgeous about **Gatsby**, some heightened sensitivity to the promises of life."

Incorrect: At the beginning of the novel, Nick Carraway states that "there was something gorgeous about **[Gatsby]**, some heightened sensitivity to the promises of life."

Setting Up Quotations

In *They Say/I Say*, their masterful introduction to college-level writing, professors Gerald Graff and Cathy Birkenstein describe what a colleague of theirs has termed "hit and run quotations"—quotations that are unceremoniously plopped into the middle of a paragraph, without any introduction. For example, consider the following paragraph from an essay on whether colleges should implement honor codes:

> One reason that honor codes are so difficult to enforce is that cheating is so much easier than it used to be. **"The Internet provides an inexhaustible source of information, and it's tempting to simply insert phrases directly into reports" (Altbach, 12).** There are also numerous websites that offer term papers to prospective cheaters. You can even get a customized paper written for you by a team of so-called experts.

The point of the quotation is clear enough, but the statement itself is simply dropped into the paragraph—the writer does nothing to announce it. Compare it to this version:

> One reason that honor codes are so difficult to enforce is that cheating is so much easier than it used to be. <u>**As Boston College scholar Philip Altbach points out**</u>**, "the Internet provides an inexhaustible source of information, and it's tempting to simply insert phrases directly into reports" (12).** There are also numerous websites that offer term papers to prospective cheaters. You can even get a customized paper written for you by a team of so-called experts.

Here, the quote is integrated seamlessly into the surrounding text. It is no longer necessary to stop and re-orient oneself within the argument. Subtly but importantly, the inclusion of Philip Altbach's name also gives the impression that you are engaged in a conversation, not just sticking quotations in because you are required to do so.

Exercise: Punctuating Quotations

In the following sentences, add or remove punctuation involving quotations as necessary. Some of the sentences may not contain an error. (Answers p. 278)

Example: The existentialist philosopher Jean-Paul Sartre asserted ~~that, "existence must come before essence"~~ — in other words, people do not choose to be born but are free to determine how to live their lives.

> *that existence must come before essence*

1. In *The Library: A Catalogue of Wonders*, Stuart Kells asserts that, libraries represent people's attempt to impose order in a world of chaos.

2. With its generous margins and legible type, the first edition of the *American Heritage Dictionary* was designed to be "an agreeable companion," as editor William Morris put it.

3. As Fauvelle points out in *The Golden Rhinoceros: Histories of the African Middle Ages*, a ruler of Mali set out with 2,000 ships to discover, "the furthest limit of the Atlantic Ocean" nearly 200 years before Columbus.

4. In his book *Toward a New Architecture*, the modernist architect Le Corbusier states "The motor car is an object with a simple function (to travel) and complicated aims (comfort, resistance, appearance)."

5. Thomas Hobbes believed that a strong centralized government is necessary to keep us in line because our nature would otherwise lead us to have lives that are "solitary, poor, nasty, brutish, and short."

6. When Mr. Darcy's feelings have grown too strong to repress, he approaches Elizabeth Bennet and proclaims, "You must allow me to tell you how ardently I love and admire you (Chapter 34)."

7. The author and illustrator Edward Gorey created his modern Gothic aesthetic with the self-described aim of making his readers "as uneasy as possible."

8. As one mother who successfully paid her children to complete their chores commented, "In behavioral psychology, this phenomenon is called "positive reinforcement."

9. "Social media stars are good at whatever made them famous, says branding consultant Jeremiah Boehner, but they're not always good businesspeople."

10. According to Joseph Campbell, the hero's journey features a descent into the "belly of the beast;" during this phase, the hero is brought low, and his ego is diminished.

11. In the words of the writer and child psychologist Bruno Bettelheim, "Fairy tales can help children confront and resolve conflicts in their own lives." (*The Uses of Enchantment*, 72).

12. Nutritional specialist Anne Collins states, "Parental behavioral patterns concerning shopping, cooking, eating and exercise have an important influence on a child's energy, balance and ultimately their weight."

13. The American Petroleum Institute has worked with many oil industry protection companies to stymie the renewable energy movement, in some cases even, "posing as environmentalist groups in order to attract the support of environmentalists while simultaneously pushing their anti-renewable agenda."

14. While talking about the luncheon, Woolf admits that "it is part of the novelist's convention not to mention soup and salmon and ducklings," but "[she] shall take the liberty to defy that convention." (723-724)

15. "Our intention is to affirm this life," the composer John Cage wrote in the introductory remarks to a 1956 dance performance that he created with his partner Merce Cunningham, not to bring order out of chaos."

Chapter Eleven

Additional Comma Uses and Misuses

Commas Should Be Used:

A. After introductory words and phrases

Correct: **At first,** it looked as if the storm was going to miss us by a few hundred miles.

Correct: **In medicine,** a prodrome is an early symptom that might indicate the start of a disease before specific symptoms occur.

Note that such words and phrases do not always appear at the beginning of a sentence.

Correct: Ignorance can often be propagated under the guise of balanced debate: **for example,** the synthesis of two opposing views does not always result in a rational conclusion.

B. Between items in a list

In any list of three or more items, serial commas are used to separate the items. Note that the use of a comma before *and* (i.e., the "Oxford comma") is typically optional.

Correct: The museum's open-storage display brings over 900 vintage World's Fair souvenirs out of attics, desk drawers, **shoeboxes, and museum** archives for visitors to view.

Correct: The museum's open-storage display brings over 900 vintage World's Fair souvenirs out of attics, desk drawers, **shoeboxes and museum** archives for visitors to view.

When the meaning would be ambiguous without a comma between the last two items, however, then one should be used for clarity.

Incorrect: The dairy company's overtime rules do not apply to the processing, preserving, freezing, **packing for shipment or distribution** of perishable foods.

In the above sentence, the lack of a comma in the phrase *packing for shipment or distribution* makes it unclear whether overtime rules do not apply to two acts (1. the packing of perishable foods for shipment, and 2. the distribution of perishable foods), or a single act (packing perishable foods so that they can be shipped and distributed).

If the overtime rules in fact refer to two separate acts, then a comma must be used for clarity.

Correct: The dairy company's overtime rules do not apply to the processing, preserving, freezing, **packing for shipment, or distribution** of perishable foods.

The example above is a modified version of a sentence that was the subject of a $10 million lawsuit. Based on the ambiguous wording of their contract, truck drivers argued that their employer had unfairly withheld overtime pay. They won.

Note: when list items are very long or are punctuated internally by commas, semicolons may also be used.

Correct: Among Marie Curie's achievements were the development of the theory of **radioactivity;** the invention of techniques for isolating radioactive **isotopes;** and the discovery of the elements polonium and radium.

Correct: Conference organizers have narrowed the venue for next year's event to three possible locations: **Boulder, Colorado; Austin, Texas; or Sacramento, California**.

C. Between two adjectives whose order could be reversed, OR that could be separated by the word *and*

When two adjectives can be written in either order, then a comma should be placed between them.

Correct: One of the Queens Museum's recent exhibits featured works by contemporary artists from Japan, Taiwan, and Ireland, offering patrons the chance to see a kind of **innovative, passionate (or: passionate, innovative)** art that larger museums often ignore.

Alternately, if the word *and* can be placed between the adjectives, a comma can be used in its place.

Correct: One of the Queens Museum's recent exhibits featured works by contemporary artists from Japan, Taiwan, and Ireland, offering patrons the chance to see a kind of **innovative and passionate** art that larger museums often ignore.

D. With geographic locations

Place a comma between streets and cities, and between cities and states/provinces.

Incorrect: The Massachusetts Institute of Technology is located at **77 Massachusetts Avenue Cambridge MA**.

Correct: The Massachusetts Institute of Technology is located at **77 Massachusetts Avenue, Cambridge, MA**.

A comma should be placed **after** a city name and **around** state/province/country names.

Incorrect: The conference will be held in **Albuquerque New Mexico** in July.

Correct: The conference will be held in **Albuquerque, New Mexico,** in July.

Incorrect: Next year, we are planning to visit **Seoul, South Korea** for two weeks.

Correct: Next year, we are planning to visit **Seoul, South Korea,** for two weeks.

However, no comma should be placed between states and zip codes.

Incorrect: The Massachusetts Institute of Technology is located at 77 Massachusetts Avenue, Cambridge, **MA,** 02139.

Correct: The Massachusetts Institute of Technology is located at 77 Massachusetts Avenue, Cambridge, **MA** 02139.

E. With dates

Place a comma between a month/day and a year when the day follows the month.

Incorrect: The Allied invasion of Normandy occurred on **June 6 1944**.

Correct: The Allied invasion of Normandy occurred on **June 6, 1944**.

When the day comes before the month (European-style), no commas should be used.

Incorrect: The Allied invasion of Normandy occurred on **6 June, 1944**.

Correct: The Allied invasion of Normandy occurred on **6 June 1944**.

When a date appears in the middle of a sentence, the year must be surrounded by commas.

Incorrect: John Adams believed that **July 2, 1776** would be celebrated as Independence Day in the United States.

Correct: John Adams believed that **July 2, 1776,** would be celebrated as Independence Day in the United States.

F. With titles

Titles such as Jr., M.D., or Esq. should be set off by commas.

Incorrect:	Martin Luther King, **Jr.** was actually born Michael Luther King, **Jr.** but later had his first name changed to Martin.
Correct:	Martin Luther King, **Jr.,** was actually born Michael Luther King, **Jr.,** but later had his first name changed to Martin.
Incorrect:	Beginning in 1989, Neil Patrick Harris played the title role of a child prodigy doctor on *Doogie Howser,* **M.D.** for which he was nominated for a Golden Globe.
Correct:	Beginning in 1989, Neil Patrick Harris played the title role of a child prodigy doctor on *Doogie Howser,* **M.D.,** for which he was nominated for a Golden Globe.

G. After i.e. and e.g.

The abbreviations i.e. (*id est,* Latin for *that is*) and e.g. (*exempli gratia,* Latin for *for example*) are commonly used to introduce definitions and examples. In American English, they are traditionally set off by commas.

Iffy:	People often obtain vitamin C through the consumption of citrus fruits, **e.g.** oranges and grapefruit.
Standard:	People often obtain vitamin C through the consumption of citrus fruits, **e.g.,** oranges and grapefruit.

Exercise: Adding Commas

Punctuate the following sentences by adding commas as necessary. (Answers p. 279)

Example: The poet Langston Hughes claimed ~~Paul Lawrence Dunbar Carl Sandburg and Walt Whitman~~ **Paul Lawrence Dunbar, Carl Sandburg, and Walt Whitman** as his primary influences and is known for his ~~colorful insightful~~ **colorful, insightful** portrayals of African-American life.

1. Emmy-winning actor André Braugher, the youngest of four children, was born July 1 1962 in Chicago Illinois the son of a postal worker and a heavy-equipment operator.

2. Large-scale social strife economic stagnation and an exploding population all conspired to weaken the Qing Dynasty in nineteenth-century China.

3. A staff writer at *The New Yorker* and the Dina and Raphael Recanati Chair of Medicine at Harvard Medical School in Boston Massachusetts Jerome E. Groopman M.D. grew up in Queens New York.

4. The Battle of Antietam was fought on September 17 1862 between Confederate General Robert E. Lee's Army of Northern Virginia and Union General George B. McClellan's Army of the Potomac near Sharpsburg Maryland and Antietam Creek.

5. As a result of farming deforestation and other developments giant pandas have been driven out of the lowland areas where they once lived and now dwell in a few mountain ranges in Sichuan China.

6. Long after ancient warriors had ceased to use chariots in warfare, ordinary citizens continued to rely on them for traveling long distances celebrating during festivals and racing them in sporting events.

7. Most modern brachiopods, also known as lamp shells, prefer quiet calm water; they often attach to the undersides of stones or other hard objects.

8. British Prime Minister Winston Churchill was born at Blenheim Palace, his family's home in Oxfordshire England on 30 November 1874, a time when Britain was the dominant world power.

9. Among cities in the United States, Philadelphia Pennsylvania is unique in that it holds the title of UNESCO World Heritage City—an honor that was bestowed on it on November 6 2015.

10. Based on the letters of Robert Gould Shaw, the film *Glory* premiered in limited release in the United States on December 14 1989 and in wide release on February 16 1990.

Commas Should <u>NOT</u> Be Used:

A. Between compound items

Compound items consist of two of the same part of speech (e.g., nouns, verbs, adjectives) joined by the word *and*. When two elements are linked this way, no comma is necessary.

The easiest way to apply this rule is as follows: because *comma* + *and* = period, replace the period with *comma* + *and*. If two complete sentences are not present, no comma should be used.

Compound Noun

Incorrect:	**Ada Lovelace, and Charles Babbage** were two of the most influential figures in the history of computer science and mathematics.
Plug in:	**Ada Lovelace. Charles Babbage** were two of the most influential figures in the history of computer science and mathematics.
Correct:	**Ada Lovelace and Charles Babbage** were two of the most influential figures in the history of computer science and mathematics.

Compound Adjective

Incorrect:	Ada Lovelace and Charles Babbage were two of the most **important, and influential** figures in the history of computer science and mathematics.
Plug in:	Ada Lovelace and Charles Babbage were two of the most **important. Influential** figures in the history of computer science and mathematics.
Correct:	Ada Lovelace and Charles Babbage were two of the most **important and influential** figures in the history of computer science and mathematics.

B. Between subjects and verbs

Incorrect:	<u>Ada Lovelace and Charles Babbage</u>, **were** two of the most influential figures in the history of computer science, and mathematics.
Correct:	<u>Ada Lovelace and Charles Babbage</u> **were** two of the most influential figures in the history of computer science and mathematics.

This rule holds true even when subjects are extremely long and complex.

Incorrect:	<u>What is remarkable about Ada Lovelace's work on Babbage's "analytical engine,"</u> **is** that Lovelace foresaw many of the ways in which computers are used today.
Correct:	<u>What is remarkable about Ada Lovelace's work on Babbage's "analytical engine"</u> **is** that Lovelace foresaw many of the ways in which computers are used today.

C. Before or after a preposition

Prepositions are **location** and **time** words such as *of, for, from, to, in, with, by, about, between, before,* and *after*.

Of all the errors involving commas, this one is usually easiest to hear; commas incorrectly placed before or after prepositions tend to create unnatural and illogical breaks.

Incorrect:	Ada Lovelace and Charles Babbage were two of the most influential **figures, in** the history of computer science and mathematics.
Incorrect:	Ada Lovelace and Charles Babbage were two of the most influential figures **in, the** history of computer science and mathematics.
Correct:	Ada Lovelace and Charles Babbage were two of the most influential **figures in** the history of computer science and mathematics.

The only **exception** is when a preposition is used immediately before or after a non-essential clause. This construction can easily become very awkward, though, and should generally be avoided.

Correct:	Although Ada Lovelace lived nearly a century before the first computer was built, she, **in a way that was unique among nineteenth-century mathematicians,** predicted many of the modern computer's capabilities.
Correct:	As a young woman, Ada Lovelace began work on Charles Babbage's "analytical engine," generally considered the precursor to the modern computer, **at a time** when most people could hardly imagine such a machine.

D. Between adjectives, when one modifies the other

Incorrect:	Created in Jamaica during the late 1960s, reggae music emerged from a number of sources ranging from **traditional, African** songs and chants to contemporary jazz.
Correct:	Created in Jamaica during the late 1960s, reggae music emerged from a number of sources ranging from **traditional African** songs and chants to contemporary jazz.

E. Between adjectives and nouns

Incorrect:	Headquartered in New York, the National Academy of Television Arts and Sciences (NATAS) is a **national, organization** that has local chapters around the country.
Correct:	Headquartered in New York, the National Academy of Television Arts and Sciences (NATAS) is a **national organization** that has local chapters around the country.

F. Between two adjectives separated by *but* or *yet*

Although common, a single comma creates an awkward and unnecessary break.

    Incorrect: Parrots are **challenging, yet loyal** pets that can live for decades.

    Correct: Parrots are **challenging yet loyal** pets that can live for decades.

If you want to create a strong break between the adjectives, however, two commas can be used.

    Acceptable: Parrots are **challenging, yet loyal,** pets that can live for decades.

G. Before or around "self" words

"Self" words (**emphatic pronouns**) are used to **emphasize** that a particular person or people is being referred to. Each pronoun has an emphatic counterpart.

I = Myself	We = Ourselves
You (sing.) = Yourself	You (pl.) = Yourselves
S/he = Himself, Herself	They = Themselves

It is always **incorrect** to place commas before, after, or around these words.

    Incorrect: The Tower of London, which lies within the Borough of Tower Hamlets, is separated from the **city, itself** by a stretch of open space.

    Incorrect: The Tower of London, which lies within the Borough of Tower Hamlets, is separated from the city **itself, by** a stretch of open space.

    Incorrect: The Tower of London, which lies within the Borough of Tower Hamlets, is separated from the **city, itself, by** a stretch of open space.

    Correct: The Tower of London, which lies within the Borough of Tower Hamlets, is separated from the city **itself** by a stretch of open space.

However, when a comma would normally be necessary (e.g., before a FANBOYS conjunction or to set off a non-essential clause), it is acceptable to place one after an emphatic pronoun.

    Correct: The Tower of London is separated from the city **itself, but** it is nevertheless one of London's most popular tourist attractions.

    Correct: The Tower of London, which is separated from the city **itself,** is nevertheless one of London's most popular tourist attractions.

Exercise: Eliminating Unnecessary Commas

In the following sentences, remove any unnecessary comma. Some sentences may not contain an error. (Answers p. 280)

Example: The grasslands of northeast Montana are a priority for conservation because of their extraordinary ~~biodiversity, and~~ high percentage of ~~remaining, native~~ prairie.
         biodiversity and   **remaining native**

1. Although it lacks traditional circus elements such as animals, and clowns, Cirque du Soleil continues to draw thousands of spectators around the world each year.

2. Some of the most powerful telescopes in the world are now peering across vast distances of space, watching for the faintest dip of light or wobble, that could suggest the presence of another world.

3. Although Tchaikovsky's music is popular with audiences around the world, early listeners often dismissed it as vulgar, and uninspired.

4. The Black Sea coast is characterized by the presence of steep yet beautiful mountains that extend along the entire length of the coast, separating it from the inland Anatolian plateau.

5. Sherlock Holmes' creator, Arthur Conan Doyle, was a physician, himself, and there is evidence that Holmes is modeled on Joseph Bell of the Royal Edinburgh Infirmary, one of the leading doctors of the day.

6. Because of the dearth of written records from the twelfth century, little factual information exists, about the early life of Genghis Khan.

7. It is unclear whether caffeine actually helps people retain information, but early research suggests that it can increase the sensitivity of neurons involved in learning, and memory.

8. The chariot, together with the horse itself, was introduced to the Egyptians by the Hyksos invaders in the sixteenth century B.C. and undoubtedly contributed to the Egyptians' military success.

9. New Zealand, one of the last lands to be settled by humans, developed fascinating, distinctive, forms of wildlife during its long isolation.

10. Among the reforms introduced during Napoleon's reign were the abolition of all feudal privileges and historic taxes and the reorganization of local, administrative systems.

Chapter Twelve

Apostrophes: Possessive vs. Plural

Singular	Plural (-s, -es)	Singular Possessive (-'s)	Plural Possessive (-s')
Bird	Birds	Bird's	Birds'
Business	Businesses	Business's	Businesses'
Party	Parties	Party's	Parties'

To form the **plural** of a regular noun (including decades), add *–s*. When a noun ends in *–s*, add *–es*; when it ends in *–y*, drop that letter and add *–ies*.

Correct: The **birds** are flying.

Correct: The **businesses** are open today.

Correct: The **parties** oppose the new law.

Correct: The **1960s** were a very exciting decade.

To form the **possessive** of a singular (regular) noun, add *apostrophe* + *–s*, including ones ending in *–s* and *–y*.

Correct: The **bird's** wings are red.

Correct: The **business's** policy is new.

Correct: The **party's** candidate is popular.

This rule also applies to proper names, including ones that end in *–s*.

Correct: **Douglas's** coat

Correct: **Pamela Erens's** novel

However, for names of **famous historical/literary figures** ending in *–s*, an apostrophe alone can be used.

Acceptable: **Dickens'** novels = The novels written by Dickens

Acceptable: **Moses'** staff = The staff belonging to Moses

To form the **possessive** of a plural (regular) noun, add *–s* or *–es* + *apostrophe.*

Note that while the apostrophe is placed **before** the *–s* to make singular nouns possessive, it is placed **after** the *–s* to make plural nouns possessive.

Correct: The **birds'** wings are red. = The wings of the birds are red.

Correct: The **businesses'** policies are new = The policies of the businesses are new.

Correct: The **Wangs'** house is blue. = The house belonging to the Wangs is blue.

The plural forms of **irregular nouns** are <u>not</u> created by adding *–s* to their singular forms. Instead, these nouns change in a variety of ways in the plural forms. Some common examples are listed below.

Singular	Plural
Child	Children
Fish	Fish
Foot	Feet
Mouse	Mice
Person	People
(Wo)man	(Wo)men

To form the possessive of a plural irregular noun, add *apostrophe* + *–s.*

Correct: The **mice's** whiskers = The whiskers of the mice

Correct: The **children's** books = The books belonging to the children

Because these plural forms are <u>already</u> different from their singular forms, the fact that both singular and plural possessive are formed by adding *apostrophe* + *–s* does not cause confusion.

As a general rule, you can determine whether a noun should be possessive by checking the following word. If that word is a noun, the noun is possessive and should take an apostrophe. If you think about it, this is entirely logical: the only thing a noun can possess is another noun.

Incorrect: The dogs <u>fur</u> is gray.

Because *fur* is a noun—that is, you can put *the* in front of it—an apostrophe is needed.

Correct: The dog's <u>fur</u> is gray.

Contraction with Verb

Apostrophe + *–s* is also used to form a **contraction** between a noun and the verb *is* or *has.*

Correct: The **artist's** known for her abstract works. = The **artist is** known for her abstract works.

Correct: The **reporter's** worked all over the world. = The **reporter has** worked all over the world.

Pronouns

A pronoun is a word such as *it(s)*, *s/he*, *they/their*, or *which* that can replace a noun in a sentence. For example, the sentence <u>I.M. Pei</u> *is a well-known architect* can be re-written as <u>He</u> *is a well-known architect*.

The most important thing to understand is that **apostrophes and –s are used differently for pronouns than for nouns**. The addition of –s alone only affects whether a pronoun is possessive, not whether it is plural.

- Possessive = –s only.* **Do not add an apostrophe.**

- Contraction with a verb = *apostrophe* + –s *(is)*, –re *(are)*, –d *(would)*, –m *(am)*, or –ve *(have)*.

Again, you can determine whether a pronoun is possessive by checking the word after it. If that word is a noun, the pronoun is possessive (no apostrophe).

A. It's vs. Its

It's = it is, it has

Its = possessive of *it*. Used before a noun.

Its' & **Its's** = do not exist

The easiest way to choose between *its* and *it's* is simply to plug in *it is*. If *it is* makes sense in context, an apostrophe is needed. If *it is* does not make sense, the apostrophe is incorrect. Alternately, you can check whether the word after the pronoun is a noun.

Incorrect:	Some critics of the Internet have argued that it is a danger because **it's (it is)** <u>vastness</u> threatens people's intellectual health.
Incorrect:	Some critics of the Internet have argued that it is a danger because **its'** vastness <u>threatens</u> people's intellectual health.
Correct:	Some critics of the Internet have argued that it is a danger because **its** <u>vastness</u> threatens people's intellectual health.

Because you would not say, *it is a danger because <u>it is</u> vastness threatens people's intellectual health*, no apostrophe should be used. In addition, the word after *its* is a noun, as indicated by the ending *–ness*.

B. They're, Their, and There

Although the same rules apply to *they're* vs. *their* as apply to other pronouns, an extra degree of confusion is often present because of a third identical-sounding pronoun: *there*.

They're = they are

Their = possessive of *they*. Used before a noun.

There = a place

---

*When the possessive form of a pronoun is placed before a noun (e.g., *its cover*, *their books*), it technically becomes a **possessive adjective**. In practice, however, these forms are effectively pronouns, and they are treated here as such.

In general, it's easiest to think of *there* as separate from *they're* and *their*, which both involve *they*. To check *their* vs. *they're*, plug in *they are*. If it makes sense, the apostrophe is needed; if it doesn't, no apostrophe should be used.

To check *there*, simply ask yourself whether the pronoun is referring to a place. The context provided by a sentence or paragraph will make it clear whether this is the case.

They're

Incorrect: Although **their** usually powered by rowers, canoes may also have sails or motors.

Incorrect: Although **there** usually powered by rowers, canoes may also have sails or motors.

Correct: Although **they're (they are)** usually powered by rowers, canoes may also have sails or motors.

Their

Incorrect: Deactivated viruses form the basis of many vaccines known for **they're (they are)** <u>effectiveness</u> in preventing disease.

Incorrect: Deactivated viruses form the basis of many vaccines known for **there** <u>effectiveness</u> in preventing disease.

Correct: Deactivated viruses form the basis of many vaccines known for **their** <u>effectiveness</u> in preventing disease.

Because *effectiveness* is a noun, *their* should be used.

There

Incorrect: Because Denver is located close to the Rocky Mountains, snow often falls **they're**.

Incorrect: Because Denver is located close to the Rocky Mountains, snow often falls **their**.

Correct: Because Denver is located close to the Rocky Mountains, snow often falls **there**.

Because the sentence is clearly talking about a place, *there* is required.

C. You're vs. Your

You're = you are

Your = possessive form of *you*. Used before a noun.

To determine which version is correct, plug in *you are*.

Incorrect: The first few hours of the workday can have a significant effect on **you're** level of productivity over the following eight hours.

Correct: The first few hours of the workday can have a significant effect on **your** level of productivity over the following eight hours.

D. Who's vs. Whose

Who's = who is, who has

Whose = possessive form of *who*. Note that unlike *who*, *whose* can refer to both people and things.

Incorrect:	Jessye Norman is an American opera singer **whose** <u>known</u> for her moving performances.
Correct:	Jessye Norman is an American opera singer **who's (who is)** <u>known</u> for her moving performances.

On the other hand:

Incorrect:	Jessye Norman is an American opera singer **who's** <u>performances</u> many people find moving.
Correct:	Jessye Norman is an American opera singer **whose** <u>performances</u> many people find moving.

Because the pronoun is followed by a noun (*performances*), the possessive form is required.

The same rule applies to the pronouns below as applies to the ones discussed in the previous pages.

- *Apostrophe + –s, –re, –d,* or *–ve* = contraction with verb

- No apostrophe = possessive

	Pronoun + verb	Possessive	Incorrect
I	I'm	--	Im
You	You're, You've, You'd	Your(s)	Your's, Yours'
He, She	S/he's, S/he'd	His, Her(s)	His', Her's, Hers'
We	We're, We've, We'd	Our(s)	Our's, Ours'
That	That's	--	Thats, Thats'

Exercise: Possessive vs. Plural

For the following sentences, write the correct form of the underlined noun or pronoun in the space provided. Some of the underlined words may already be in the correct form. (Answers p. 280)

Example:

In an attempt to boost school spirit, the university is increasing <u>it's</u> support for student organizations and giving away tickets to athletic <u>event's</u>.

its _____

events _____

1. Like <u>today's</u> astronauts, future space colonists are likely to be selected on the basis of <u>they're</u> suitability for long-duration spaceflight.

_____

_____

2. Fiction allows readers to understand other <u>peoples'</u> <u>action's</u> by entering into <u>characters'</u> minds and seeing situations from their interior points of view.

_____

_____

_____

3. During the <u>1920's</u>, most of the works written by Langston Hughes focused on <u>African American's</u> struggle for equality.

_____

_____

4. Digital technology has become so embedded in our culture that we find it almost impossible to recognize that forms of computation without <u>algorithm's</u> effectively control much of the world.

_____

5. Recognized today as one of the <u>worlds'</u> leading authorities on the Sphinx, archaeologist Mark Lehner has conducted field research on the pyramids at Giza for nearly four decades.

_____

6. Recent studies have suggested that if you consume a small amount of dark chocolate daily, <u>your</u> more likely to be healthy overall.

_____

7. Circadian rhythms dictate many of the <u>bodies</u> most fundamental <u>process'</u>, including eating, sleeping, and producing hormones.

_____

_____

8. <u>Its</u> not yet clear how much plastic is consumed by corals in the wild, or what harm it might do to these important marine organisms, <u>whose</u> lives are already threatened by environmental dangers like warming seas and pollution.

_____

_____

9. In Sandra <u>Cisneros's</u> novel *The House on Mango Street*, the protagonist discovers that liberation can be found through creativity and literature.

_____

10. News <u>stories</u> sometimes distort events in ways that create a negative perception of certain groups, leading to stereotypes, <u>bias'</u>, and false assumptions.

_____

_____

Chapter Thirteen

Pronoun Agreement

A **pronoun** is a word such as *he*, *she*, *it*, *them*, *their*, or *us* that is used to replace a noun.

- **The ball** is on the floor.   →   **It** is on the floor.
- **Katie** threw the ball.   →   **She** threw the ball.

An **antecedent** is the noun to which a pronoun refers. Although *ante-* means "before," an antecedent can appear either before or after the noun. (If you find *antecedent* confusing, you can use *referent* instead.)

All pronouns must **agree** with their antecedents in number: singular pronouns must agree with singular nouns, and plural pronouns must agree with plural nouns. For example:

- Katie dribbled the <u>ball</u>, and then she shot **it** at the basket.

The pronoun and the antecedent agree because the singular noun *ball* is the antecedent of the singular pronoun *it*. Now, consider this:

- Katie dribbled the <u>ball</u>, and then she shot **them** at the basket.

Here, the antecedent and the pronoun disagree because the antecedent *ball* is singular and the pronoun *them* is plural.

Speaking in General: One, You & We

English has three pronouns that can be used to create impersonal or general constructions: *one*, *you*, and *we*.

Although there are situations in which one of these options may be preferable—*one*, for example, is more formal than either *you* or *we*—**the only rule is that pronouns should not be mixed and matched within a sentence or paragraph.**

Incorrect:	If **one** wants to avoid insect invasions, **you** should refrain from leaving crumbs lying on the floor.
Incorrect:	If **you** want to avoid insect invasions, **we** should refrain from leaving crumbs lying on the floor.
Correct:	If **you** want to avoid insect invasions, **you** should refrain from leaving crumbs lying on the floor.

Singular vs. Plural

Sometimes different pronouns are used to refer to people and to things.

People (e.g., actors, judges, athletes):

With Singular Nouns	With Plural Nouns
He or she	They
His or her	Their

Note: Because many writers find *he or she/his or her* wordy and awkward, a common alternative is to use *they* or *their*. While this option technically creates a disagreement, it is also a simple, relatively mainstream solution. That said, it is still looked down on by some grammar purists, so consider your audience when using this option.

Debatable:	<u>A person</u> who wishes to become an Olympic-caliber athlete must devote virtually all of **their** time to training.
Correct:	<u>A person</u> who wishes to become an Olympic-caliber athlete must devote virtually all of **his or her** time to training.
Incorrect:	<u>People</u> who wish to become Olympic-caliber athletes must devote virtually all of **his or her** time to training.
Correct:	<u>People</u> who wish to become Olympic-caliber athletes must devote virtually all of **their** time to training.

Things (e.g., cities, books, ideas):

With Singular Nouns	With Plural Nouns
It	They
Its	Their
This	These
That	Those

Incorrect: When <u>the economy</u> does poorly, **their** performance is of great public interest.

Correct: When <u>the economy</u> does poorly, **its** performance is of great public interest.

Incorrect: <u>The lights</u> began to flicker wildly, and moments later **it** went out altogether.

Correct: <u>The lights</u> began to flicker wildly, and moments later **they** went out altogether.

Collective nouns refer to groups, e.g., *committee, board, council, jury, university, agency, institute, government, city, country*). In American English—unlike British English—these nouns are considered **singular**.

Incorrect: <u>The university</u> recently released **their** updated financial aid policies.

Correct: <u>The university</u> recently released **its** updated financial aid policies.

Indefinite Pronouns

Indefinite pronouns, which are used to indicate unspecified amounts, can also serve as antecedents. The pronouns that refer back to them must agree in number.

Singular	Plural	Singular or Plural
(N)either	Few	Any
No one	Both	None
Anybody	Several	Some
Anyone	Many	Most
One	Others	All
Each		
Everybody		
Everyone		

Again, *they/their* is often used as a more concise alternative to *he or she/his or her* for singular indefinite pronouns.

Debatable: **Each** of the committee members is expected to submit **their** vote by anonymous ballot at the meeting.

Correct: **Each** of the committee members is expected to submit **his or her** vote by anonymous ballot at the meeting.

Also note that certain pronouns can be either singular or plural, depending on the noun that follows.

Correct: <u>Most of the **water**</u> from the Euphrates River comes from rainfall and melting snow: <u>it</u> achieves peak volumes in the spring and is lower in the summer.

Correct: According to some scholars, <u>most of the ancient **Kushites**</u> survived by working <u>their</u> land and did not receive goods from the state.

The Former and the Latter

When two nouns are used in a sentence, *the former* can be used to refer back to the noun mentioned first, and *the latter* can be used to refer to the noun mentioned second.

Correct: Space travel poses inherent physical and psychological dangers, but **the former** (= physical dangers) are easier to assess than **the latter** (= psychological dangers).

Emphatic Pronouns

Emphatic pronouns are used for emphasis, or to indicate that a person/thing is both the subject and the object of an action. Like other pronouns, emphatic pronouns must agree with their antecedents in number.

I = Myself	We = Ourselves
You (sing.) = Yourself	You (pl.) = Yourselves
S/he = Himself, Herself	They = Themselves

Incorrect: Researchers in Texas have discovered that <u>the damaged heart</u> of a newborn mouse is capable of fully regenerating **themselves** without surgical intervention.

Correct: Researchers in Texas have discovered that <u>the damaged heart</u> of a newborn mouse is capable of fully regenerating **itself** without surgical intervention.

In addition, make sure that emphatic pronouns refer back to their logical antecedents.

Incorrect: What has been criticized is the author's refusal to discuss her work publicly, not the quality of the <u>writing</u> **herself**.

Correct: What has been criticized is the author's refusal to discuss her work publicly, not the quality of the <u>writing</u> **itself**.

Ambiguous Antecedent

Incorrect: **Cranston and Nathaniel Paschall** began working for Boeing, their family's airplane manufacturing company, after he decided to train as an aviation engineer.

Because there are two male names, the antecedent is ambiguous—we do not know whether *he* refers to Cranston or Nathaniel.

Correct: **Cranston and Nathaniel Paschall** began working for Boeing, their family's airplane manufacturing company after **Nathaniel** decided to train as an aviation engineer.

Correct: **Cranston and Nathaniel Paschall** began working for Boeing, their family's airplane manufacturing company, after **the latter** decided to train as an aviation engineer.

Let's look at another example:

Incorrect: In the report released by the treasury committee, **it** stated that significant budget cuts would be necessary for the following year.

In the above sentence, we do not know for sure who or what the word *it* refers to. The treasury committee? The report itself? The sentence gets the basic point across, but the meaning isn't precise.

There are a couple of ways to fix this problem and make the antecedent clear.

We can either eliminate the pronoun completely:

Correct: The report released by the treasury committee **stated** that significant budget cuts would be necessary for the following year.

Or, we can make it clear what *it* refers to:

Correct: The treasury committee stated in **its** report that significant budget cuts would be necessary for the following year.

Missing Antecedent

Any pronoun that appears in a sentence must have a clear antecedent that is a noun, pronoun, or gerund. If a sentence includes a pronoun without an antecedent, that sentence is not correct, no matter how obvious its intended meaning may be.

Incorrect: In some countries, extreme weather conditions have led to shortages of food; as a result, **they** must struggle to receive adequate nutrients.

Correct: In some countries, extreme weather conditions have led to shortages of food; as a result, **citizens** must struggle to receive adequate nutrients.

In the incorrect version, it is understood that the word *they* refers to the citizens of countries with extreme weather conditions—it would not make sense for this word to refer to *some countries* (countries themselves cannot receive nutrients). The problem is that no noun anywhere in the sentence explicitly says who *they* are. The second version of the sentence correctly supplies the noun.

"Trick" Antecedent

One of the trickiest antecedent problems involves modifiers "posing" as antecedents. This error requires some illustration to make clear, so let's start by looking at an example.

Incorrect: The ancient Egyptian temple complex at Karnak, situated on the eastern bank of the Nile, was **their** sacred place of worship.

Given the context, *their* must logically refer to the ancient Egyptians. The problem is that the noun *Egyptians* is not present. *Egyptian* is acting as an adjective that modifies *temple complex*, so it cannot be an antecedent.

To fix the sentence, we must supply the noun *Egyptians*.

Correct: The temple complex at Karnak, situated on the eastern bank of the Nile, was **the ancient Egyptians'** sacred place of worship.

Another very common version of this problem involves authors' names.

Incorrect: In the novel *Beloved*, **she** tells the story of Sethe, a woman who escapes slavery and makes her way to Cincinnati, Ohio.

In the above sentence, the reader can reasonably infer that *she* refers to the author; however, the author's name does not actually appear in the sentence. A slightly better, but still problematic, version is this:

Incorrect: In Toni Morrison's novel *Beloved*, **she** tells the story of Sethe, a woman who escapes slavery and makes her way to Cincinnati, Ohio.

At first glance the above sentence might appear acceptable. The problem is that the name *Toni Morrison* is possessive—the true subject is *Beloved*. As a result, *she* does not have a real antecedent.

One solution is to retain the introductory phrase and simply begin the following clause with *the author*.

Better: In Toni Morrison's novel *Beloved*, **the author** tells the story of Sethe, a woman who escapes slavery and makes her way to Cincinnati, Ohio.

An even better option is to provide only the book title in the introductory phrase and place the author's name after.

Even better: In her novel *Beloved*, **Toni Morrison** tells the story of Sethe, a woman who escapes slavery and makes her way to Cincinnati, Ohio.

Or, you can eliminate the introductory phrase altogether:

Also good: Toni Morrison's novel *Beloved* tells the story of Sethe, a woman who escapes slavery and makes her way to Cincinnati, Ohio.

Do So vs. Do It

Another common problem involving "fake" antecedents involves the phrases *do it* and *do so*.

Incorrect: Activists who defend endangered species from poaching **do it** on the grounds that such animals, once gone, are irreplaceable.

What does *it* refer to in this sentence? *Defending* endangered species. The problem is that the gerund *defending* doesn't actually appear in the sentence, only the verb *defend*. As a result, there is no real antecedent, and the correct phrase is *do so*.

Correct: Activists who defend endangered species from poaching **do so** on the grounds that such animals, once gone, are irreplaceable.

"Vague" Pronouns

When used alone, the pronouns *this*, *that*, *which*, and *what* have a tendency to be somewhat vague and ambiguous. Although these constructions are very common, you should be careful not to overuse them. Otherwise, you risk composing paragraphs like the following (real) example:

> The problem with just stating complex points like **that**, unfortunately, is that people cannot just read **that** and understand the entire meaning of **that**. There is a lot more behind that message, and with **that** in mind Steinbeck knew he needed to make his readers see a full picture of **what was happening**.

Let's look at some specific strategies for eliminating these types of constructions.

Vague: Today, London is one of the most important financial centers in the world, but **this** has been hard-won.

Clear: Today, London is one of the most important financial centers in the world, but **this** <u>status</u> has been hard-won.

Although the reader can reasonably assume that *this* refers to London's becoming one of the most important financial centers in the world, the use of the pronoun alone makes the meaning somewhat imprecise. The addition of the noun *status* makes the meaning clearer and easier for the reader to absorb.*

In other instances, you may be best served by finding an alternative construction. For example, consider the following:

> Conflict and human experience are necessary ingredients in a great novel. *The Great Gatsby* contains both of these elements. **This** causes the reader to stay intrigued and curious to know what will happen next.

It is reasonable to assume that *this* refers to the fact that *The Great Gatsby* is filled with conflict and human experience. Because that meaning is not made explicit, however, the reader must pause and piece it together.

One option for improving the paragraph is to use an *–ing* word (participle) to join the last two sentences.

> Conflict and human experience are necessary ingredients in a great novel. *The Great Gatsby* contains both of these elements, **causing** the reader to stay intrigued and curious to know what will happen next.

Notice how much smoother this version is. In addition, the verb *causing* makes the relationship between the two statements immediately clear.

---

*When *this*, *that*, *these*, and *those* are followed by a noun, they technically act as **demonstrative adjectives** rather than pronouns. This grammatical distinction is not important in practice, however, and so they are treated as pronouns here.

Transitional words and phrases (*however, therefore, in addition*) also clearly indicate relationships between ideas.

> Conflict and human experience are necessary ingredients in a great novel. *The Great Gatsby* contains both of these elements. **As a result**, the reader stays intrigued and curious to know what will happen next.

The transition spells out the relationship between the last two sentences, instantly making the meaning clearer and easier for the reader to follow.

Which can create similar problems. Technically, *which* should be used to refer only to the noun that immediately precedes it, but it is commonly used to refer to entire actions. Although this usage is extremely common and is generally accepted, it also forces readers to work a bit harder than necessary to absorb the writer's meaning.

Vague: In March of 2010, Australian Jessica Watson became the youngest person ever to sail around the world, **which** she accomplished at the age of just 16.

Based on the information in the sentence, *which* logically refers to the fact that Watson sailed around the world, or to her accomplishment of sailing around the world.

From a technical standpoint, though, *which* lacks a proper antecedent—the noun *accomplishment* or the gerund *sailing* never actually appears in the sentence. For maximum clarity, a noun should be used.

Clear: In March of 2010, Australian Jessica Watson became the youngest person ever to sail around the world, **a <u>feat</u> (that)** she accomplished at the age of just 16.

Clear: In March of 2010, Australian Jessica Watson became the youngest person ever to sail around the world, **accomplishing that <u>feat</u>** at the age of just 16.

Another very common problem involves clauses beginning with the pronouns *what* and *how*. (These are formally known as noun clauses). Rather than tell the reader specifically what people did or in what way, the writer will simply refer to *what they did/how they did it*.

This type of construction invariably makes writing much weaker. Not only is it vague, but it can also seriously hinder a reader's ability to follow the writer's argument.

Vague: In Harper Lee's novel *To Kill a Mockingbird*, the character Atticus must face a mob that wants to lynch him because of **what he did**.

Specific: In Harper Lee's novel *To Kill a Mockingbird*, the character Atticus must face a mob that wants to lynch him **because he dared to defend Tom Robinson, an African-American man, in court**.

Vague: In *Hamlet*, members of the court begin to believe that the protagonist has gone mad because of **how he behaves**.

Specific: In *Hamlet*, members of the court begin to believe that the protagonist has gone mad because of **his erratic and seemingly irrational behavior**.

Exercise: Pronoun Agreement

In the following sentences, correct any errors involving pronouns. Some sentences may not contain an error. (Answers p. 281)

Example: As an animal develops from a fertilized egg into an embryo, ~~their~~ *its* cells may diversify into a seemingly limitless range of types and tissues.

1. Not until the early twentieth century did the city become capable of maintaining their population and cease to be dependent on rural areas for a constant stream of new inhabitants.

2. Cleota Davis, the mother of jazz legend Miles Davis, was an accomplished pianist in her own right, but she hid that fact from her son until he was an adult.

3. In 1294 Boniface VIII began his papacy, replacing St. Celestine V, who had declared that it was permissible for a pope to resign and then promptly did that.

4. The nitrogen cycle describes its movement from the air into organic compounds and then back into the atmosphere.

5. If you exercise to prevent diabetes, one may also want to avoid vitamins C and E since these antioxidants have been shown to correlate with it.

6. Autobiographies are often structured differently from memoirs, which follow the development of an author's personality rather than the writing of his or her works.

7. Once common across southwest Asia, the Indian cheetah was driven nearly to extinction during the late twentieth century and now resides in the fragmented pieces of their remaining habitat.

8. In Marjane Satrapi's graphic novel *Persepolis*, a combination of comic-strip form and political commentary, she depicts her childhood and adolescence in Tehran and Vienna.

9. Always a site of contemplation, the art museum has lately seized on the wellness trend, marketing themselves as places of refuge from our frenzied lives.

10. Each of the chapters in Annie Dillard's *Pilgrim at Tinker Creek* has their own title, and so many readers mistakenly believe that the book is a compilation of essays.

11. In George Orwell's novel *1984*, he depicts a totalitarian society in which people use a simplified form of English known as "newspeak."

12. The city's economy has weakened significantly in the past decade, and this has led to an overwhelming loss of manufacturing jobs.

13. Google's dominance as an Internet search function has allowed the company to expand its ambitions to include virtually all aspects of the online world.

14. As the son of an electrical worker, Einstein learned about physics not only by reading about it but also by observing the technology their applications could produce.

15. Japan's status as an island country means that they must rely heavily on other countries for the supply of natural resources that are indispensable to national existence.

Chapter Fourteen

Objects and Complements

Verbs are typically referred to as "action words," but this description can be somewhat misleading. In fact, there are two main types of verbs:

1) **Action verbs** indicate specific activities.
   Examples: *talk, write, travel, speak, jump, go, read, think*

2) **Being verbs**, also known as **linking verbs**, indicate states of being, seeming, and feeling.
   Examples: *be, become, seem, appear, feel, stay, remain, taste*

Action verbs can be either **transitive** or **intransitive**.

Transitive verbs are followed by **direct objects: nouns** or **pronouns**. These objects are called "direct" because they immediately follow verbs.

- He **reads** <u>the newspaper</u> online every morning.

- They always **watch** <u>television</u> after dinner.

- She **takes** <u>the subway</u> home from school.

Intransitive verbs are followed by **prepositions** (e.g., *to, of, on, by, with*).

The noun that follows the preposition is the **indirect object** of the verb. It is called "indirect" because it does not immediately follow the verb. In the sentences below, the indirect objects are underlined.

- My sister **stays** IN <u>the shower</u> forever.

- Because I overslept, I **arrived** AT <u>school</u> fifteen minutes late.

- We **went** to <u>the movie</u> WITH <u>friends</u>.

Linking verbs (e.g., *to be*, *to become*, *to seem*) are followed by **complements**, either **adjectives** or **nouns**.

- The members of the class **remained** <u>calm</u> throughout the fire drill. (The adjective *calm* is the complement of *remained*.)

- My younger brother wants to **become** <u>a superhero</u> when he grows up. (The noun *superhero* is the complement of the verb *become*.)

When a plural noun is used as the complement, it must agree in number with the noun to which it refers (i.e., its antecedent).

Incorrect: My younger <u>brothers</u> want to **become** <u>a superhero</u> when they grow up.

Correct: My younger <u>brothers</u> want to **become** <u>superheroes</u> when they grow up.

A common point of confusion about this construction involves non-essential clauses. When they are present, singular antecedents can falsely appear plural.

Incorrect: <u>Mozart</u>, along with Haydn and Beethoven, **were members** of the First Viennese School of classical music.

In this case, it does in fact seem as if the subject is plural. Notice, though, that the sentence contains two commas, which set off a non-essential clause. Because the true subject (*Mozart*) is singular, the complement must be singular as well.

Cross out: <u>Mozart</u>~~, along with Haydn and Beethoven,~~ **were** <u>members</u> of the First Viennese School of classical music.

Correct: <u>Mozart</u>, along with Haydn and Beethoven, **was** <u>a member</u> of the First Viennese School of classical music.

You should, however, be careful not to take this rule so literally that it cuts into the logic or clarity of a sentence.

Awkward: <u>Cell phones</u> can be **distractions** in a school environment, cutting into class time and reducing students' academic success.

Although *cell phones* is plural, the singular *distraction* makes more sense here. Cell phones can be understood to cause a general state of distraction, not a series of individual distractions.

Better: <u>Cell phones</u> can be **a distraction** in a school environment, cutting into class time and reducing students' academic success.

Exercise: Direct Object, Indirect Object, or Complement?

In the following sentences, determine whether the underlined word is a direct object, an indirect object, or a complement. (Answers p. 282)

Example: Augustus Caesar commissioned <u>the Pantheon</u>, a monument to all the deities of Rome, as part of a construction program undertaken in the aftermath of the Battle of Actium.

_____ Direct object _____

1. Large fires, far from destroying forests, can act as catalysts that stimulate <u>biodiversity</u> and promote ecological health throughout an ecosystem.

   _____

2. Although it is estimated that around 10 meteorites crash to <u>Earth</u> from outer space every day, researchers discover only a few of these objects each year.

   _____

3. Ineligible for the draft because of a heart murmur, Milton Mezzrow spent the World War I years becoming <u>a part</u> of the Chicago jazz scene.

   _____

4. Although they are under substantial threat, coral reefs remain <u>incubators</u> of the ocean's ecosystem, providing food and shelter to a quarter of all marine life.

   _____

5. While the fugitive initially managed to elude capture, he was finally caught after a popular true-crime show displayed <u>his picture</u> for several consecutive episodes.

   _____

6. Not until the 1600s did European society begin to tolerate the pursuit of idle interests, a shift that led to the rise of modern science.

    _____

7. The body's circadian rhythms, which control sleep cycles, are more sensitive to light at night—even when a person's eyes are closed.

    _____

8. As the assistant director for building operations at New York City's Museum of Modern Art, Nelson Nieves oversees the huge team of workers who maintain the building and keep it running.

    _____

9. Because the philosopher Ludwig Wittgenstein was a deeply charismatic figure, his philosophy could not be clearly separated from his life.

    _____

10. In contrast to motor vehicles, which run on a flat surface but can move in many directions, rail vehicles are guided by the track on which they run.

    _____

Exercise: Noun Agreement

In the following sentences, make sure that complements and antecedents agree. (Answers p. 282)

Example: The Mississippi and the Nile are ~~an example~~ ^{examples} of rivers that form large deltas because of the large amount of sediment deposited at their mouths.

1. Both Wilfred Daniels and Leonard Chuene, who became powerful figures in South African sports, grew up as a promising athlete who could never compete internationally because of apartheid.

2. Because they evolved in the warm climate of Africa before spreading into Europe, modern humans had a body adapted to tracking prey over great distances.

3. Many of the great classical composers, including Mozart, Bach, and Mendelssohn, were born into musical families and began studying an instrument seriously when they were a child.

4. Thomas Abercrombie, along with his older brother, became a photographer after building a camera out of mirrors, discarded lenses, and scraps of plastic.

5. Known for creating a unique sound through the use of non-traditional instruments, Miles Davis joined Louis Armstrong and Ella Fitzgerald as the greatest jazz musicians of the twentieth century.

6. Inscribed ostrich eggs and pieces of shell jewelry are an example of early human attempts to record thoughts symbolically rather than literally.

7. Joseph Charles Jones and George Bundy Smith, who fought for African Americans as a civil rights activist during the early 1960s, were separated for nearly forty years after being arrested in Alabama in 1961.

8. The Opium Wars, which introduced the power of western armies and technologies to China, marked the end of Shanghai and Ningpo as an independent port city.

9. Although neither came from a literary family, novelists Amy Tan and Maxine Hong Kingston became an avid reader while growing up near San Francisco.

10. The military and the orchestra are examples of distinct entities that must interact with their own subsystems or units in order to survive.

Chapter Fifteen

Pronoun Case

Case refers to whether a pronoun is used as a **subject** or an **object**.

A subject is:

1) The person/thing that is the main focus of the sentence, OR

2) The person/thing performing the action described in the sentence.

In the following sentences, the subject is in bold:

1. **Jonah** read the book.
   (Who read the book? Jonah)

2. **The coat** is more attractive than warm.
   (What is more attractive than it is warm? The coat)

3. Having caught the flu, **Sarah and Ansel** had to stay home from school.
   (Who caught the flu? Sarah and Ansel)

All subjects can be replaced by **subject pronouns**:

I	We
You (s.)	You (pl.)
S/he, It, One	They

If we replace our subjects in the above sentences with pronouns, they become:

1. **Jonah** read the book.
   → **He** read the book.

2. **The coat** is more attractive than warm.
   → **It** is more attractive than warm.

3. Having caught the flu, **Sarah and Ansel** had to stay home from school.
   → Having caught the flu, **they** had to stay home from school.

An **object** is the person or thing that receives an action. To review from the previous chapter, objects can be either direct (after a verb) or indirect (after a preposition).

In the sentences below, the object is in bold.

1. Jonah read **the book**.
    (What was read? The book)

2. Akil threw **the basketballs** across the court.
    (What did Akil throw? The basketballs)

3. Serena waved to **Sam and me** from the parking lot.
    (To whom did Serena wave? Sam and me)

All objects can be replaced by **object pronouns**:

Me	Us
You (s.)	You (pl.)
Her/Him, It, One	Them

If we replace the objects in the above sentences with object pronouns, they become:

1. Jonah read **the book**.
    → Jonah read **it.**

2. Akil threw the basketballs across the court.
    → Akil threw **them** across the basketball court.

3. Serena waved to **Sam and me** from the parking lot.
    → Serena waved to **us** from the parking lot.

Notice that proper names (*Jonah, Serena, Sam, Akil, Sarah*) can be either subjects or objects, but pronouns can generally be only one or the other. The only exception is *you*, which has the same subject and object forms.

For example, in the sentence *Katie threw the ball to James*, *Katie* is the subject and *James* is the object. Both are proper names. We can rewrite the sentence several ways to include pronouns:

*   **She** threw the ball to James. (*Katie* replaced with subject pronoun)

*   Katie threw the ball to **him**. (*James* replaced with object pronoun)

*   **She** threw the ball to **him**. (*Katie* replaced with subject pronoun and *James* with object pronoun)

What we cannot do, however, is the following:

*   **Her** threw the ball to James.

*   Katie threw the ball to **he**.

*   **Her** threw the ball to **he**.

When pronouns are used incorrectly with singular subjects or objects, as in the above sentences, the error is usually pretty easy to spot. Most people would not say, *My little brother always wants to play with I*, or *Him went to the store for some milk*. When the subject or object is plural, however, people tend not to be so sure.

For example, statements like the following sentence are notorious for causing confusion:

Incorrect: Roosevelt High School's annual prize for citizenship was presented to **Annabel and he** by the vice-principal at the spring awards banquet.

The only thing to remember is that what goes for singular goes for plural. When you see a subject or object pronoun paired with another noun, cross out *and + noun*, and check whether the pronoun can stand on its own.

Incorrect: Roosevelt High School's annual prize for citizenship was presented to ~~Annabel and~~ **he** by the vice-principal at the spring awards banquet.

Since you would say, *The prize was presented to <u>him</u>* rather than *The prize was presented to <u>he</u>*, the sentence must be rewritten as follows:

Correct: Roosevelt High School's annual prize for citizenship was presented to **Annabel and him** by the vice-principal at the spring awards banquet.

To reiterate:

Incorrect: After giving a stern lecture on the necessity of checking the validity of our sources, the teacher gave **Jonah and I** back the report we had turned in at the beginning of the week.

In the above sentence, we can notice that there is a pronoun (*I*) paired with a proper name (*Jonah*). When we cross out *proper name + and,* we are left with:

Incorrect: After giving a stern lecture on the necessity of checking the validity of our sources, the teacher gave ~~Jonah and~~ **I** back the report we had turned in at the beginning of the week.

Would you say, *The teacher gave I back the report*? Obviously not. So you wouldn't say, *The teacher gave my friend and I back our report* either. Rather, you would say, *The teacher gave **me** back the report.*

Correct: After giving a stern lecture on the necessity of checking the validity of our sources, the teacher gave **Jonah and me** back the report we had turned in at the beginning of the week.

Sometimes, however, the word *and* will not appear.

Incorrect: It seems terribly unfair <u>to</u> **we** students that school should start at 7:30 a.m.

Correct: It seems terribly unfair <u>to</u> **us** students that school should start 7:30 a.m.

When this is the case, there are a couple of ways to check the pronoun.

1) Cross out the noun after the pronoun

Would you say, *It seems terribly unfair to ~~we~~ students*? Probably not. Instead, you'd say, *It seems terribly unfair to us*. So you would also say, *It seems terribly unfair to us students that school should start at 7:30 a.m.*

2) Know *preposition + object pronoun*

A pronoun that follows a preposition is the object of that preposition. As a result, an object pronoun must be used.

To is a preposition, so it must be followed by an object pronoun; however, *we* is a subject pronoun. The object pronoun *us* must therefore be used instead.

Between You and Me... Or Should That Be *I*?

As is true for all other prepositions, *between* must always be followed by an object pronoun.

That said, phrases involving *between* are a very common source of confusion (*between you and me* or *between you and I?*) because they always involve two singular objects. Something can only exist between two people or things, so there is no way to cross out *and + pronoun* without creating nonsense.

Note that **the order in which the pronouns are presented does not matter**; both must be in object form, regardless of which comes first. For example:

Incorrect	Correct
Between you and I	Between you and me
Between s/he and I Between I and him/her	Between him/her and me Between me and him/her
Between I and they Between they and I	Between me and them Between them and me
Between them and I	Between them and me

Incorrect: Although the start of the class was delayed, I still missed the first few minutes because the meeting between **my boss and I** ran much later than expected.

Correct: Although the start of the class was delayed, I still missed the first few minutes because the meeting between **my boss and me** ran much later than expected.

Exercise: Pronoun Case

In the following sentences, correct any errors involving pronoun case. Some sentences may not contain an error. (Answers p. 282)

Example: Because other patrons in the gallery had begun to complain, the guide asked Corey and ~~I~~ **me** to lower our voices as we walked through the museum.

1. Although our parents have little difficulty distinguishing between my twin sister and I, our teachers are much more easily fooled by our seemingly identical appearance.

2. It is exceedingly difficult for we voters to choose between the two candidates because their positions on so many issues are so similar that they are effectively indistinguishable.

3. After listening patiently to their admittedly flimsy excuses, the principal decided to sentence she and Akiko to a week of detention.

4. Along with our project, the professor handed Sabrina and I a note requesting that we remain after class in order to discuss our research methods.

5. Though extremely long, the meeting between they and their advisor was unusually productive because it provided many new ways of thinking about a familiar subject.

6. Evidently moved by the strength of their testimony, the jury awarded him and Thomas a two million dollar settlement for the injuries they had sustained in the accident.

7. When the gubernatorial candidate arrived at the auditorium to give a speech, we found it nearly impossible to distinguish between she and her assistant, so similar were they in height and appearance.

8. My lab partner and myself were awarded first prize in the science fair for our work on the breakdown of insulin production in people who suffer from diabetes.

9. The conference between my professor and me went surprisingly well, despite the anxiety I had felt about the meeting earlier in the week.

10. An unfamiliar subject when the class began, Roman history became increasingly fascinating to he and Alexis over the course of the semester.

Chapter Sixteen

Subject-Verb Agreement

Number answers the question "how many?" It indicates whether a verb is **singular** or **plural**.

All verbs must agree with their subject in number:

- Singular subjects take singular verbs.

- Plural subjects take plural verbs.

In English, the endings of most singular and plural verb forms are identical, e.g., *I go, we go, you go*.

The only variation occurs in the third-person **singular** form (*s/he, it, one*), which always ends in *–s*. (When a verb ends in *–sh* or *–ch*, the third-person singular form ends in *–es*, e.g., *she wishes, he watches*).

Note that this is the **opposite of nouns**, which take an *–s* in the plural.

To reiterate: third-person <u>singular</u> verbs end in *–s*; third-person <u>plural</u> verbs do not.

Subject Number	Correct	Incorrect
Singular	The student speaks.	The student speak.
Plural, Simple	The students speak.	The students speaks.
Plural, Compound	The student **and** the teacher speak.	The student **and** the teacher speaks.

The verb *to be*, the most common verb, is unique in that it has different third-person singular and plural conjugations in both the present and the past. *To have, to do,* and *to go* also have slightly irregular third-person singular forms.

	Present	Past
Singular	is	was
Plural	are	were

	3rd Person Singular
To have	S/he, it has
To do	S/he, it does
To go	S/he, it goes

What Can Be a Subject?

I. Noun

Correct: **Bats** are able to hang upside down without discomfort because they possess specialized tendons in their feet.

II. Pronoun

Pronouns are words that replace nouns, e.g., *she, he, it, one, you, this, that, there, each, some,* and *many*.

Correct: **They** are able to hang upside down without discomfort because they possess specialized tendons in their feet.

Correct: **Some (of them)** are able to hang upside down without discomfort because they possess specialized tendons in their feet.

Less commonly, the pronouns *how, that, what,* and *whether* can also be used as subjects, sometimes as part of a much longer complete subject (underlined). While the constructions below may sound odd to you, they are acceptable.

Correct: **That (= The fact that)** Aldous Huxley exhibited many shortcomings in his ability to develop believable characters and create compelling storylines was overshadowed by his capacity to navigate a staggering panorama of ideas in his fiction.

Correct: **Whether (= The question whether)** markets will continue to rise or will begin to demonstrate signs of sluggishness over the next several months remains to be seen.

Correct: **How** bats hang upside down was a mystery until it was discovered that they possess specialized tendons in their feet.

Correct: Although the technologies necessary for space travel were developed only recently, **what** drives humans' fascination with exploring the stars has remained unchanged for hundreds of years.

III. Gerund

Gerund = *Verb + -ING*

Correct: **Hanging** upside down for long periods is a skill that both bats and sloths possess, but bats race quickly away when startled whereas sloths make no attempt to move.

IV. Infinitive

Infinitive = *To + Verb*

Infinitives are most commonly used to create the parallel construction *to do x is to do y*.

Correct: **To hang** upside down from a branch for a long period of time is to experience the world much as a bat or sloth does.

Separating Subjects and Verbs

When simple subjects are placed next to their verbs, disagreements are typically easy to identify. When sentences become longer and more complex, however, verbs can be separated from their subjects in a variety of ways. In some instances, a very significant amount of information may be placed between the subject and the verb, making it easy to lose track of the subject and create or overlook a disagreement.

A. Compound Subject (noun + and + noun)

On their face, compound subjects are very straightforward: they simply consist of two nouns, singular or plural, joined by the word *and*. These subjects are **always plural** and thus take plural verbs.

When sentences are short and simple, as in the examples on the previous page, disagreements involving compound subjects are usually fairly obvious.

When they appear in the context of long sentences, however, disagreements can be quite subtle and are remarkably easy to overlook. (In fact, this error is so easy to miss, regardless of how well someone knows the rules, that it is not uncommon to find it in the pages of major newspapers!)

Incorrect: Louise Glück's straightforward language **and** unadorned style **gives** her poems an air of accessibility that masks the intensity of their content.

Correct: Louise Glück's straightforward language **and** unadorned style **give** her poems an air of accessibility that masks the intensity of their content.

Notice that in the above set of sentences, the disagreement error is very difficult to hear. In addition, people naturally tend to focus on the part of the subject that appears right before the verb (*unadorned style*) and not notice the first half (*straightforward language*).

B. Subject – Non-Essential Clause – Verb

To review, **non-essential clauses** describe nouns, often subjects. They can begin with "w-words" (relative pronouns), nouns, or participles. Because they are not crucial to either the meaning or the structure of a sentence, they can be crossed out without causing any grammatical problems.

Consider the following sentence:

Correct: Moroccan green tea, **(which is) prepared with a healthy dose of sugar and mint leaves,** is one of the most popular drinks across North Africa.

Crossed out: Moroccan green tea […] is one of the most popular drinks across North Africa.

The sentence that remains makes complete sense on its own.

Even when a subject and a verb are separated by a non-essential clause, they must still agree. Don't get distracted by a noun at the end of a non-essential clause!

In the example below, for instance, *leaves* (plural) appears before the verb; however, that noun is part of the non-essential clause. The verb must agree with *Moroccan green tea* (singular).

Incorrect: Moroccan green tea, which is prepared with a healthy amount of sugar and mint leaves, are one of the most popular drinks across North Africa.

Correct: Moroccan green tea, which is prepared with a healthy amount of sugar and mint leaves, is one of the most popular drinks across North Africa.

Also watch out for constructions like the following:

Incorrect: Moroccan green tea, along with spiced ginger coffee, **are** one of the most popular drinks across North Africa.

Correct: Moroccan green tea, along with spiced ginger coffee, **is** one of the most popular drinks across North Africa.

While the subject appears plural (compound), the commas indicate a non-essential clause. The subject is in fact singular.

You must also make sure that the verb(s) within a non-essential clause agree with the subject.

Incorrect: Moroccan green tea, which **are** prepared with a healthy amount of sugar and mint leaves, is one of the most popular drinks across North Africa.

Correct: Moroccan green tea, which **is** prepared with a healthy amount of sugar and mint leaves, is one of the most popular drinks across North Africa.

Essential Clauses with "That"

Essential clauses beginning with *that* can also be placed between subjects and verbs. Because these clauses are not set off by commas and do not provide a visual cue that the subject and the verb have been separated, they can be trickier to work with than non-essential clauses.

Incorrect: <u>A beverage</u> *that has long been used as a form of medicine in many countries* **are** green tea.

Correct: <u>A beverage</u> *that has long been used as a form of medicine in many countries* **is** green tea.

Although the verb comes after *countries* (plural), that noun is part of the essential clause *that has long been used as a form of medicine* and does not affect the number of the verb. The verb must agree with the singular subject, *beverage*.

C. Subject – Prepositional Phrase – Verb

A prepositional phrase is simply a phrase that begins with a preposition (e.g., <u>*in*</u> *the box*, <u>*under*</u> *the table*, <u>*over*</u> *the hill*). Prepositional phrases are commonly inserted between subjects and verbs. Even if you haven't studied this structure formally, you most likely use it in your own writing already.

In the sentences below, the subject is underlined, the prepositional phrase is italicized, and the verb is in bold. **Note that the last word of a prepositional phrase is always the last word right before the verb.** If you ever need to cross out prepositional phrases in order to simplify a sentence, make sure you do not cross out verbs!

Incorrect: <u>Changes</u> *in the balance of trade* **seems** remote from everyday concerns, but they can drastically affect how we spend our money.

Correct: <u>Changes</u> *in the balance of trade* **seem** remote from everyday concerns, but they can drastically affect how we spend our money.

In the above sentences, the subject (*changes*) is plural and thus requires a plural verb (*seem*).

However, the prepositional phrase inserted between the subject and the verb has as its last word a singular noun (*trade*), which, if you are not paying close attention, can easily appear to be the subject of the verb that follows.

Some sentences may also separate subjects and verbs through a combination of prepositional phrases and non-essential clauses, or include a compound subject followed by a prepositional phrase. In such cases, you must keep very careful track of which noun(s) a particular verb must agree with.

Incorrect: <u>The buildings</u> of Frank Gehry, including Gehry's private residence, **attracts** thousands of visitors annually because critics frequently praise his designs for embodying the most important principles of contemporary architecture.

This is a more complicated sentence than the ones we've looked at so far in this chapter, so we're going to deconstruct it one piece at a time.

The commas around *including Gehry's private residence* signal a non-essential clause, so we're going to start by crossing that clause out.

Incorrect: <u>The buildings</u> of Frank Gehry, ~~including Gehry's private residence,~~ **attracts** thousands of visitors annually because critics frequently praise his designs for embodying the most important principles of contemporary architecture.

Next, we can notice that the beginning of the sentence contains the word *of*, which signals a prepositional phrase. We're going to cross that out as well.

Incorrect: <u>The buildings</u> ~~of Frank Gehry, including Gehry's private residence,~~ **attracts** thousands of visitors annually because critics frequently praise his designs for embodying the most important principles of contemporary architecture.

Now the error is clear. The subject, *the buildings*, is plural, whereas the verb *attracts* is singular. A plural verb must therefore be provided.

Correct: <u>The buildings</u> of Frank Gehry, including Gehry's private residence, **attract** thousands of visitors annually because critics frequently praise his designs for embodying the most important principles of contemporary architecture.

D. Prepositional Phrase – Verb – Subject

In this structure, which is typically used only in very formal writing, the normal word order (or **syntax**) of a sentence is reversed so that the prepositional phrase appears at the beginning of a sentence, followed by the verb and then subject, always in that order.

In the examples below, the subject is underlined, the prepositional phrase is italicized, and the verb is in bold.

Incorrect: *Along the Loup Canal in Nebraska* **extends** <u>parks, lakes, and trails</u> owned and operated by the Loup power district.

Correct: *Along the Loup Canal in Nebraska* **extend** <u>parks, lakes, and trails</u> owned and operated by the Loup power district.

When this structure is used, the preposition is usually the first word of the sentence, but occasionally it may appear slightly later. In such cases, it will typically be preceded by a participle (*–ing* or *–ed*).

Incorrect: Running *along the Loup Canal in Nebraska* **is** <u>parks, lakes, and trails</u> owned and operated by the Loup power district.

Correct: Running *along the Loup Canal in Nebraska* **are** <u>parks, lakes, and trails</u> owned and operated by the Loup power district.

Although the reversed syntax may make the sentence sound odd to you, it is important to understand that the syntax itself is not what makes the sentence incorrect. Rather, the problem is that the subject and the verb disagree.

Let's break down the construction.

Usual: A park and a lake **runs** *along the Loup Canal*, a hydroelectric and irrigation canal located in eastern Nebraska.

Unusual: *Along the Loup Canal* **runs** a park and a lake, both of which are owned and operated by the Loup Power District.

Note that in the second version, the error is much more difficult to hear.

Occasionally, a verb may come before a subject <u>without</u> being preceded by a prepositional phrase.

Incorrect: Radioactivity is generally not considered harmful when people are exposed to it at low levels for brief periods, but less clear **is** <u>its long-term effects</u>.

Correct: Radioactivity is generally not considered harmful when people are exposed to it at low levels for brief periods, but less clear **are** <u>its long-term effects</u>.

Again, this type of phrasing is only used in very formal writing, and it is unlikely to be a major concern for you in your own papers.

Exercise: Subject-Verb Agreement 1

Directions: In the following sentences, underline the subject, and conjugate the verb in parentheses so that it agrees in number. Remember that singular verbs end in –s, and plural verbs do not end in –s. (Answers p. 283)

Example: Easy <u>communication</u> between speakers of different languages _____**is**_____ (*to be*) a lovely ideal, but in reality it could lead to eternal confusion.

1. The process of living vicariously through a fictional character in order to purge one's emotions _____ (*to be*) known as catharsis.

2. Near the border between China and Tibet _____ (*to lie*) the Himalaya Mountains, which include some of the highest peaks in the world.

3. Although drivers are required to purchase automobile insurance, levels of coverage often _____ (*to vary*) depending on the driver's age and state of residence.

4. In the eighteenth century, the first public library in the United States and the first fire department in the state of Pennsylvania _____ (*to be*) founded by Benjamin Franklin.

5. Tropical waves in the Atlantic basin frequently _____ (*to develop*) from disturbances that begin in east Africa and drift over the continent into the Atlantic Ocean.

6. Playboating, a discipline of whitewater rafting or canoeing in which players stay in one spot while performing certain maneuvers, _____ (*to involve*) specialized canoes designed for the sport.

7. Opposition to rodeos from animal-rights workers _____ (*to focus*) primarily on the poor treatment and living conditions of the horses used in competitions.

8. A natural thief and spy, the jay, along with the crow and the raven, _____ (*to belong*) to a highly intelligent group of birds called the corvids.

9. Among the finds from a recent archaeological dig in London _____ (*to be*) earthenware knobs originally used for "pay walls": boxes into which Elizabethan theater-goers deposited their admission fees.

10. Researchers have hypothesized that whales sing by pumping air into pouches, which then
    _____ (*to release*) vibrations into the surrounding water.

11. The highly textured bark and distinctive silhouette of the Dutch Elm tree _____
    (*to distinguish*) it from the equally common English Elm tree.

12. Possible explanations for the suspicion surrounding Shakespeare's Macbeth
    _____ (*to include*) the superstition that the witches' song is an actual incantation
    and the belief that theaters only mount the play when they are in need of money.

13. According to the law of diminution, the pitches of notes sounded by an orchestra
    _____ (*to remain*) the same even as the amount of sound diminishes.

14. Along the deepest part of the ocean floor _____ (*to sit*) the Mariana Trench and the
    HMRG Deep, the two lowest spots ever identified on earth.

15. Louise Erdrich's fiction and poetry _____ (*to draw*) on their author's Chippewa
    heritage to examine complex familial relationships among Native Americans as they reflect on
    issues of identity.

In addition:

There is/There are, etc.

When *there* is used as a subject, the verb must agree with the noun (complement) that follows the verb.

There is
There was   } go with **singular** nouns
There has been

There are
There were   } go with **plural** nouns
There have been

Incorrect: In recent months, there **has been** <u>many questions</u> raised about the handling of the company's finances.

Correct: In recent months, there **have been** <u>many questions</u> raised about the handling of the company's finances.

(N)either...(N)or

When *(n)either...(n)or* is followed by a verb, the verb must take the number of the noun that follows *nor*.

Incorrect: Neither the senator nor her <u>aide</u> **are** expected to appear at the press conference.

Correct: Neither the senator nor her <u>aide</u> **is** expected to appear at the press conference.

BUT:

Incorrect: Neither the <u>senator</u> nor her <u>aides</u> **is** expected to appear at the press conference.

Correct: Neither the <u>senator</u> nor her <u>aides</u> **are** expected to appear at the press conference.

When *(n)either* appears without *(n)or* and is used with two singular nouns, a singular verb should also be used. *Neither* is short for *neither <u>one</u>*, so this word is singular by definition.

Incorrect: Both the senator and her aide appeared at the press conference, but <u>neither</u> **were** willing to speak to reporters.

Correct: Both the senator and her aide appeared at the press conference, but <u>neither</u> **was** willing to speak to reporters.

Collective Nouns = Singular

Collective nouns refer to groups of people, e.g., *family, agency, institution, school, committee, council, jury, city, country, company, university,* and *team*. In American English (unlike British English), they are considered **singular**.

Incorrect: After many days of deliberation, <u>the jury</u> **have** finally returned with a verdict.

Correct: After many days of deliberation, <u>the jury</u> **has** finally returned with a verdict.

A number of = Plural
The number = Singular

Correct: <u>A number of</u> workers **are** beginning to protest the economic policies instituted by the new administration.

Correct: <u>The number</u> of workers beginning to protest the new administration's economic policies **is** unexpectedly high.

One of the = Singular
One of the Xs who/that = Plural

When the phrase *one of the...* is used as a subject, the prepositional phrase begun by *of* often contains a plural noun (*mysteries* below). Don't be fooled: the subject is *one*, and a singular verb is required.

Incorrect: <u>One of the biggest *mysteries*</u> surrounding ancient Peru **involve** khipus, the knotted strings used to keep records.

Correct: <u>One of the biggest *mysteries*</u> surrounding ancient Peru **involves** khipus, the knotted strings used to keep records.

When the phrase *one of those Xs who/that...* is used, however, a plural verb is technically necessary. *Who* and *that* are used to refer to the noun that immediately precedes them. In this construction, the noun is always plural, so a plural verb should be used.

Incorrect: He is <u>one of those **students**</u> *who* always **waits** until the last minute to turn in assignments but still **manages** to receive excellent grades.

Correct: He is <u>one of those **students**</u> *who* always **wait** until the last minute to turn in assignments but still **manage** to receive excellent grades.

Gerunds when used as subjects = Singular

Incorrect: <u>Playing</u> parlor games such as charades **were** a popular pastime in the early twentieth century, before the invention of radio and television.

Correct: <u>Playing</u> parlor games such as charades **was** a popular pastime in the early twentieth century, before the invention of radio and television.

That, *Whether*, and *What* = Singular

Correct:	**That (= The fact that)** <u>Mark Twain made substantial contributions to nineteenth century literary theory</u> **is** no surprise given his importance in the world of letters.
Correct:	**What** <u>has been criticized</u> **is** the author's refusal to discuss her work publicly, not the content of her novels.
Correct:	**Whether (= The question whether)** <u>*The Tale of Genji* was actually written entirely by Murasaki Shikibu</u> **is** unlikely to ever be determined unless a major archival discovery is made.

Indefinite Pronouns

Indefinite pronouns refer to unspecified quantities. They can be singular or plural depending on context.

Singular*	Plural	Singular or Plural
(N)either	Few	Any
No one	Both	None
Anybody/one	Several	Some
One	Many	More
Each	Others	Majority
Every		Most
Everybody/one		All

If the pronouns in the right-hand column are paired with singular nouns, they are singular.

Incorrect:	**Most** of the Colorado River's <u>water</u> **come** from rainfall and melting snow.
Correct:	**Most** of the Colorado River's <u>water</u> **comes** from rainfall and melting snow.

If they are paired with plural nouns, they are plural.

Incorrect:	**Most** of the manufacturer's new safety <u>regulations</u> **has** now been put into effect.
Correct:	**Most** of the manufacturer's new safety <u>regulations</u> **have** now been put into effect.

The noun(s) may also come before the pronoun.

Correct:	Clinical trials may be run by <u>pharmaceutical companies, universities, or hospitals</u>; **all are** required to disclose their results on ClinicalTrials.gov.

Sometimes an additional phrase may also be placed between the noun and the verb.

Correct:	**Most** of the new safety <u>regulations</u> *adopted by the manufacturer* **have** now been put into effect.

Exercise: Subject-Verb Agreement 2

In the following sentences, underline the subject or word that determines the number of the verb, and conjugate the verb in parentheses so that it agrees in number. (Answers p. 284)

Example: There _____ **have** _____ (*to have*) been many objections made to the hospital's plan to construct its new infectious disease laboratories so close to the town center.

1. The number of natural materials being replaced by synthetics _____ (*to appear*) to be growing because unlike wood, leather, and ceramics, plastic is enormously versatile and inexpensive to produce.

2. According to researchers, knowing two or more languages _____ (*to improve*) one's ability to focus in the face of distraction and to ignore irrelevant information.

3. Each of the Taino's five chiefdoms, which inhabited the Bahamas before the arrival of Europeans, _____ (*to be*) ruled by a leader known as a cacique.

4. For the past several years, the theater company _____ (*to have*) traveled to various schools throughout the city in order to expose students to classic works.

5. Whether the first birds evolved from arboreal or terrestrial ancestors _____ (*to remain*) a source of ongoing debate among paleontologists.

6. *The Catcher in the Rye* is one of those books that _____ (*to tend*) to polarize readers, who typically find the protagonist, Holden Caulfield, either refreshingly honest or unbearably whiny and self-involved.

7. Having an excessive amount of confidence in one's personal beliefs frequently _____ (*to lead*) to poor decision-making, especially in organizational or political contexts.

8. A number of works by Mary Shelley _____ (*to contain*) the notion that cooperation between individuals, especially women, could represent a means to improve society.

9. That Jane Goodall became the world's foremost expert on chimpanzees _____ (*to be*) hardly a surprise to those who observed her childhood fascination with animals.

10. One of *The Tale of Genji*'s most extraordinary features _____ (*to be*) its ability to maintain coherency while describing the actions of more than 400 characters.

11. Delphi, home of the Delphic Oracle, contains a wide range of artifacts as well as many prestigious dedications, but neither _____ (*to prove*) that Delphi was a focus of attention for the general population in ancient Greece.

12. Every one of the illuminated manuscripts in the library's collection _____ (*to be*) unique, although most _____ (*to contain*) similar groups of texts accompanied by vividly colored decorations.

13. There _____ (*to be*) many prominent economists in the United States who consider changes in the demand for goods to be one of the fundamental causes of inflation.

14. Some of the passages in the book _____ (*to describe*) the physical realities of the Middle Ages in great detail, while others reflect the dazzling debates that would later lead to the Renaissance.

15. While reactions to the exhibition were mixed, neither the artist's exceptional showmanship nor his innovative techniques _____ (*to be*) questioned by the spectators.

Chapter Seventeen

Verb Tense

As a general rule, verbs should remain consistent (or **parallel)** in tense or form throughout a sentence. Unless there is information to indicate that a change in tense is necessary, a sentence that begins in the past should stay in the past, and a sentence that begins in the present should stay in the present.

Incorrect: Jane Austen's novel *Pride and Prejudice* **charts** the emotional development of the protagonist, Elizabeth Bennet, who **learns** the error of making hasty judgments and **came** to appreciate the difference between the superficial and the essential.

Correct: Jane Austen's novel *Pride and Prejudice* **charts** the emotional development of the protagonist, Elizabeth Bennet, who **learns** the error of making hasty judgments and **comes** to appreciate the difference between the superficial and the essential.

Although much of the writing you do will require you to apply this basic principle—in a history paper, for example, most of the verbs will obviously need to be in the past tense—English does contain a wide variety of tenses, and to maximize the clarity and effectiveness of your writing, you should have an understanding of the ways in which they are constructed and used.

Principle Parts

Every verb has four principle parts:

1) **Infinitive** or *to* form

2) **Present participle**, or *–ing* form

3) **Past participle**. Regular verbs end in *–ed*. Irregular verbs commonly end in *–ung, –unk, –en, –awn*, or *–own*, e.g., *sung, sunk, broken, drawn, grown*. This form is used after any form of *to be* or *to have*.

4) **Simple past**, also known as the **preterit**. The simple past of regular verbs ends in *–ed* and is identical to the past participle. Irregular verbs commonly end in *–ang, –ank, –oke*, or *–ew*, e.g., *sang, sank, broke, grew*, although some do not follow any pattern.

	Infinitive	Present Participle	Past Participle	Simple Past
Regular	to walk	walking	walked	walked
Irregular (-eak)	to speak	speaking	spoken	spoke
Irregular (-ow)	to grow	growing	grown	grew
Irregular (-ing)	to ring	ringing	rung	rang
Irregular (-ink)	to sink	sinking	sunk(en)	sank

For a complete list of irregular verbs, see the chart on the following page.

Simple vs. Compound Tenses

There are two main types of tenses: simple and compound.

Simple tenses are called "simple" because they consist of a single verb, either present or past.

> Examples: *she goes, they work, it begins, we thought*

Compound tenses involve two verbs:

1) A main verb

2) A "helping" verb, or auxiliary (ox-ill-uh-ree) verb, a form of *to be* or *to have*

> Examples: *she <u>will</u> go, they <u>would</u> work, it <u>has</u> begun, we <u>had</u> thought*

Note that when *be* or *have* is used as the helping verb, the past participle, not the simple past, must be used.

Incorrect	Correct
He has sang	He has sung
They have grew	They have grown
She had rose	She had risen
It was spoke	It was spoken
Having flew	Having flown

Likewise, the past participle should not be used immediately after a noun, when no helping verb is present.

Incorrect	Correct
He sung	He sang
They grown	They grew
She risen	She rose

Irregular Verbs: Principle Parts

Infinitive	Simple Past	Past Participle
To (a)rise	(A)rose	(A)risen
To (a)waken	(A)woke	(A)woken
To be	Was	Been
To become	Became	Become
To begin	Began	Begun
To blow	Blew	Blown
To break	Broke	Broken
To choose	Chose	Chosen
To do	Did	Done
To draw	Drew	Drawn
To drink	Drank	Drunk
To drive	Drove	Driven
To fly	Flew	Flown
To freeze	Froze	Frozen
To get	Got	Gotten*
To give	Gave	Given
To go	Went	Gone
To grow	Grew	Grown
To hide	Hid	Hidden
To know	Knew	Known
To ride	Rode	Ridden
To ring	Rang	Rung
To run	Ran	Run
To see	Saw	Seen
To sew	Sewed	Sewn
To shrink	Shrank	Shrunk(en)
To sing	Sang	Sung
To sink	Sank	Sunk(en)
To speak	Spoke	Spoken
To spring	Sprang	Sprung
To steal	Stole	Stolen
To stink	Stank	Stunk
To swim	Swam	Swum
To take	Took	Taken
To tear	Tore	Torn
To throw	Threw	Thrown
To wear	Wore	Worn
To write	Wrote	Written

*Although *got* is used as the past participle of *get* in British English, *gotten* is standard in American English.

Exercise: Irregular Verbs and Past Participles

In the following sentences, write the correct form of the past participle. (Answers p. 284)

Example: Although the restaurant was _____ (*to give*) stellar reviews when it opened last year, the quality of the food has declined considerably since then.

1.   Since 1896, the Kentucky Derby — arguably the most famous horse race held in the United States — has _____ (*to take*) place on a track measuring one-and-a-quarter miles.

2.   Unusual sequences of rocks discovered in a geological formation in Namibia indicate that for millions of years, the entire earth was _____ (*to freeze*) over.

3.   Although prairie dogs were once on the verge of extinction, their numbers have _____ (*to rise*) to pre-twentieth century levels over the past few years.

4.   Only one ship remaining in the Navy's fleet has ever _____ (*to sink*) an enemy vessel: the USS Constitution, which earned the nickname "Old Ironsides."

5.   Over the past few years, the ballet troupe has _____ (*to become*) one of the few eminent dance companies to promote choreographic innovation.

6.   There are about 570 marathons held in the United States every year, and approximately 0.5% of the U.S. population has _____ (*to run*) in one.

7.   Michael J. Rosen has _____ (*to write*) works ranging from picture books to poetry, and he has also edited several anthologies varying almost as broadly in content.

8.   In 1911, the *Mona Lisa* was _____ (*to steal*) from the Louvre by a museum employee, Vincenzo Peruggia, who believed that the painting belonged in an Italian gallery.

9.   While the popularity of rooftop solar systems has _____ (*to grow*) rapidly over the past decade, wind energy has generally remained the province of industrial-scale operations.

10.   In several recent instances, vacationers have discovered cameras that were _____ (*to hide*) in rental properties — findings that have raised questions about the safety of staying in a stranger's home.

A. Present

Present = Infinitive minus *to*; adds *-s* in the third person singular

Examples: *it is, they go, he plays*

Words such as *now, currently,* and *presently* indicate that the present tense is required.

Correct: Although critics initially expressed skepticism about Emily Dickinson's literary abilities, they <u>now</u> **consider** Dickinson as a major poet.

It is also conventional to use the present tense when discussing works of fiction (the **literary present**). Their characters and events are considered "timeless" and viewed as existing in a sort of eternal present.

Incorrect: The protagonist of Harper Lee's 1960 novel *To Kill a Mockingbird* **was** a six-year old girl named Jean Louise Finch, better known as Scout.

Correct: The protagonist of Harper Lee's 1960 novel *To Kill a Mockingbird* **is** a six-year old girl named Jean Louise Finch, better known as Scout.

The present is often used to describe laws, treaties, etc. instituted in the past but still relevant.

Correct: Some companies have argued that the Unlawful Internet Gambling Enforcement Act, which illegalized online gambling when it was passed in 2006, **includes** an exception for fantasy sports.

The present is also used for commands (the **imperative**), in which *to* is removed from the infinitive.

Correct: **Stop** wasting money on Internet gambling!

B. Present Perfect vs. Simple Past

Present Perfect = *Has/Have + Past Participle*

Examples: *it has been, they have gone, he has played*

The present perfect is used to describe actions that **began in the past and continue into the present**. Tip-offs for this tense include *for** and *since*, and phrases such as *over the past few years* or *in recent months*.

Correct: <u>Since</u> the start of the twentieth century, scientists **have made** hundreds, if not thousands, of groundbreaking discoveries.

Correct: Photovoltaic cells **have been** the dominant solar power source <u>for</u> the past five decades, but the use of concentrating solar power is increasing.

Correct: <u>Over the last decade</u>, the rising popularity of internet news sources **has forced** many local newspapers to shut down.

---

*Note that *for* can also be used to indicate the duration of **completed** actions in the past, e.g., *The storm <u>lasted</u> for many hours*. In such cases, the simple past is required.

The present perfect can also be used to describe actions that **occurred recently**. Very often, this use involves references to studies and research.

Correct: Studies **have shown** that naps lasting approximately half an hour can boost job performance by up to 34% by enhancing attention to detail and decreasing stress.

Simple Past or **Preterit** = *Verb + -ed* (regular verbs)

Examples: *it was, they went, he played*

The simple past is used to describe actions that both began and ended in the past. Sentences requiring this tense often include a date or time indicating that an entire action is complete.

Correct: During the <u>nineteenth century</u>, Charles Dickens **was** renowned as one of the most famous British novelists.

Correct: Tropical Storm Edouard **became** the first of eight named storms to form in September <u>2002</u>, the most such storms for any month in the Atlantic at the time.

Note that some sentences can be written correctly in either the present perfect or the simple past. The connotation simply shifts according to which tense is used.

He **has written** several novels.
=   He may write more novels.

He **wrote** several novels.
=   He will not write any more novels.

In response to a series of scandals, the council **has adopted** new ethics rules.
=   The rules are still in the process of being adopted, or more rules may be adopted in the future.

In response to a series of scandals, the council **adopted** new ethics rules.
=   The rules are finished being adopted and are considered final.

When specific context is provided, however, then only the present perfect or simple past is typically acceptable.

Incorrect: In the 1880s new steamships **have brought** cheap grain and meat to Europe, bankrupting family farms and causing mass migration to cities such as London and Paris.

Correct: In the 1880s new steamships **brought** cheap grain and meat to Europe, bankrupting family farms and causing mass migration to cities such as London and Paris.

The above sentences describe an event that occurred at one particular point in time: the 1880s. As a result, only the simple past can be used.

Now consider these sentences.

Incorrect: South Africa experienced a series of massive and devastating blackouts in 2008, and consequently, the country's electricity **was rationed** ever <u>since</u> that time.

Correct: South Africa experienced a series of massive and devastating blackouts in 2008, and consequently, the country's electricity **has been rationed** ever <u>since</u> that time.

In order to imply that electricity is still being rationed, the present perfect must be used.

C. Past Perfect

Past Perfect = *Had + Past Participle*

Examples: *it had been, they had gone, he had played*

Sometimes a sentence will describe two events or actions that occurred in the past. The **past perfect** can be used to refer to the action that occurred **first**.

Correct: When Thomas Jefferson returned from France, where he **had served** as the American ambassador, he brought with him a variety of foods and cooking styles that soon became dietary staples in the United States.

In the above sentence, the use of the past perfect is correct because logically, Jefferson must have served as the American ambassador to France (action #1) before he returned from that country and brought with him a variety of foods and cooking styles (action #2).

The past perfect cannot, however, refer to a completed action that came **after** another action.

Incorrect: Descended from a long line of university professors, Nobel physics laureate Maria Goeppert Mayer <u>received</u> the majority of her training in Germany and <u>later</u> **had taught** at several universities in the United States.

Correct: Descended from a long line of university professors, Nobel physics laureate Maria Goeppert Mayer <u>received</u> the majority of her training in Germany and <u>later</u> **taught** at several universities in the United States.

In the above example, the word *later* makes it clear that Goeppert Mayer taught at several universities in the United States <u>after</u> she received the majority of her training in Germany. As a result, the past perfect cannot be used.

Important: the phrase *by the time* is often a tip-off that the past perfect is required.

Incorrect: <u>By the time</u> the committee members adjourned the meeting, they **made** several important decisions about the budget.

Correct: <u>By the time</u> the committee members adjourned the meeting, they **had made** several important decisions about the budget.

Logically, the committee members must have made several important decisions (action #1) before they made the decision to adjourn (action #2); therefore, the past perfect is required.

There are, however, instances when either the past perfect or the simple past is acceptable.

Correct: <u>Before</u> a complete version of Louisa May Alcott's novel *Little Women* appeared in 1880, the book **had been published** in two separate volumes.

Correct: <u>Before</u> a complete version of Louisa May Alcott's novel *Little Women* appeared in 1880, the book **was published** in two separate volumes.

In the first sentence, the past perfect is used to emphasize the appearance of the book in two volumes before its appearance in one.

In the second sentence, the simple past is also correct because it describes two actions that took place in the past and keeps the tense of the sentence consistent.

Exercise: Present Perfect, Simple Past, and Past Perfect

For each sentence, decide whether the tense of each underlined verb is correct or incorrect. If there is an error, write the correct tense. (Answers p. 285)

1. Beginning in the eleventh century, reviving economic development **has allowed** Pamplona to recover its urban life after suffering repeated Viking invasions.

    Correct   **Incorrect**   **Correction:** _____

2. Despite its status as a regional capital, eighteenth century Quebec City **was** essentially a small colonial outpost that maintained close ties to its rural surroundings.

    Correct   **Incorrect**   **Correction:** _____

3. Since the 1920s, most major motion picture studios **accumulated** tangled lists of owners and corporate ancestors, and none more so than Paramount Pictures.

    Correct   **Incorrect**   **Correction:** _____

4. In 1915, the Dutch government approved the proposal for new ships to protect its holdings in the East Indies, not realizing that the request **has been** withdrawn because of the start of the First World War.

    Correct   **Incorrect**   **Correction:** _____

5. Abu Dhabi is full of archeological evidence indicating that civilizations, beginning with the Umm an-Nar Culture, **have been** located there for over 4,000 years.

    Correct   **Incorrect**   **Correction:** _____

6. By the time Pearl S. Buck was awarded the Nobel Prize for Literature in 1938, she **was** a best-selling author in the United States for nearly a decade.

   Correct   **Incorrect**   **Correction:** _____

7. In 1847, Maria Mitchell **became** the first American astronomer to discover a comet; remarkably, she accomplished that feat using only a two-inch telescope.

   Correct   **Incorrect**   **Correction:** _____

8. During the 1950s, the Detroit area emerged as a metropolitan region with the construction of an extensive freeway system that **had continued** to expand over the next several decades.

   Correct   **Incorrect**   **Correction:** _____

9. The Arctic Council, a once-obscure body focused on issues such as monitoring Arctic animal populations, **has begun** to handle more important tasks in recent years.

   Correct   **Incorrect**   **Correction:** _____

10. An amateur scientist, Goethe was so impressed by the work of British chemist Luke Howard that he decided to publish, in German translation, an autobiographical letter that Howard **had sent** to him.

    Correct   **Incorrect**   **Correction:** _____

D. Would vs. Will

Future = *Will + Verb*

> Examples: *it will be, they will go, he will play*

The future is used to describe actions that have not yet occurred.

> Correct: Physicists hope that within the next 50 years, string theory or other new theoretical work **will provide** a solid understanding of quantum gravity, including an explanation of how the universe began.

Conditional = *Would + Verb*

> Examples: *it would be, they would go, he would play*

The conditional is used to describe **hypothetical** actions—actions that could occur but have not actually taken place.

> Correct: Clinical trials are the key to obtaining information about new medications: without volunteers to take part in them, there **would be** no new treatments for serious diseases such as cancer, multiple sclerosis, and arthritis.

Note that *would + verb* can also be used to describe recurring actions in the past.

> Correct: As a young child, Wolfgang Amadeus Mozart **would look** on in fascination while his older sister, Nannerl, received piano lessons from their father.

On their own, *would* and *will* are fairly straightforward; however, problems often arise when they are combined with other tenses within a sentence.

As a general rule, **you should not mix past and future in the same sentence** unless there is an extremely clear reason for doing so. That means:

- Sentences that contain verbs in the past tense should not contain the word *will*.

- Sentences that contain verbs in the present tense should not contain the word *would*.

You can also think of it this way: when a future action is discussed from the perspective of the past, *would* should be used—even when, from the perspective of the present, that action occurred long ago.

> Incorrect: William Shakespeare, who **will** become the greatest English dramatist, <u>was</u> born in Stratford-upon-Avon in 1564.

> Correct: William Shakespeare, who **would** become the greatest English dramatist, <u>was</u> born in Stratford-upon-Avon in 1564.

In the incorrect version of the above sentence, *was* (past) should not be combined with *will* (future). Because the sentence is describing Shakespeare's rise to fame from the perspective of the past, *would* should be used instead.

Likewise, a sentence containing a verb in the present tense should not contain *would*.

Incorrect:	If union members and company officials <u>reach</u> a compromise today, a labor crisis **would** most likely be averted.
Correct:	If union members and company officials <u>reach</u> a compromise today, a labor crisis **will** most likely be averted.

E. Would Have vs. Will Have

Past Conditional = *Would Have + Past Participle*

Examples: *it would have been, they would have gone, he would have played*

The past conditional describes an action that could have happened but that did not actually happen.

Correct:	When reporters asked the mayoral candidate to explain how he **would have responded** to the crisis, he seemed incapable of offering a coherent response.

One **very important** thing to know about this tense is that the construction *would have + past participle* **should not appear in a clause begun by *if*.** Even though this construction is common everyday speech, it is not correct: both *if* and *would have* are used to indicate hypothetical situations, and so it is redundant to include both. **The past perfect (*had + past participle*) should be used instead.**

Would have + verb can, however, appear in a **sentence** begun by *if*, as long as it is in the **main clause**.

Incorrect:	<u>If</u> the Washington Monument **would have been** constructed as originally designed, the National Mall <u>would have been</u> anchored by a pantheon of 30 columns.
Correct:	<u>If</u> the Washington Monument **had been** constructed as originally designed, the National Mall <u>would have been</u> anchored by a pantheon of 30 columns.

Future Perfect = *Will Have + Past Participle*

Examples: *it will have been, they will have gone, he will have played*

The future perfect describes an action in the future that will be finished **before** a second action. As is true for the past perfect, the phrase *by the time* is often associated with this tense.

Correct:	<u>By the time</u> construction on the GIFT Diamond Tower is complete, workers **will have spent** more than three years assembling the 87-story building.

183

F. Modal Verbs

Modal verbs are a class of conditional verbs. *Would, could,* and *might* are used for hypothetical situations, but modals can also be used to form requests and recommendations, and to ask or give permission.

Examples: *she would, you should, it could* (conditional of *can*), *one might* (conditional of *may*), *we ought*

Most of the confusion surrounding these verbs involves constructions in the past, particularly ones involving indirect speech (e.g., *he stated that*). If the reporting verb is in the past, a modal must follow.

Incorrect: Shortly after lasers were invented, the physicist and science fiction writer Robert Forward suggested that they **may** be used to push sails in space.

Correct: Shortly after lasers were invented, the physicist and science fiction writer Robert Forward suggested that they **might** be used to push sails in space.

The past tense of modals is formed by adding the word *have*, sometimes shortened to –*'ve*. Although –*'ve* is often pronounced identically to *of* in everyday speech, that word may not be substituted (*could have/could've,* NOT *could of*).

G. The Subjunctive

In the present, the subjunctive is used to indicate **necessity, demands**, and **requests**. It differs from the indicative (normal) form only in the third person singular (*s/he, it*), in which case no –*s* is added to the verb. Note that the present subjunctive form of *to be* is *be*, and the subjunctive form of *to have* is *have*.

Indicative	Subjunctive
The building **is** constructed.	City planners <u>recommend</u> that the building **be** constructed.
The committee **adopts** the proposal.	Some board members <u>insist</u> that the committee **adopt** the proposal.

The **past subjunctive** is used for **hypothetical situations**. It mainly affects the verb *to be*, which becomes *were* in both singular and plural forms.

Incorrect: <u>If</u> the committee **was** to adopt the proposal, construction on the building would begin later this year.

Correct: <u>If</u> the committee **were** to adopt the proposal, construction on the building would begin later this year.

H. The Progressive

Each tense has a **progressive** counterpart, which is used to emphasize that an action is in the process of taking place. The progressive is always formed by conjugating *to be* in the appropriate tense, then adding the present participle (–*ing* form), e.g., *it works* → *it is working, it would work* → *it would be working*.

Sequence of Tenses

A clause that describes a possible action or occurrence is known as an **"if" clause** or **hypothetical clause**. Because this type of clause cannot be a grammatically complete sentence, it must always be accompanied by a **main clause** (also known as a **result clause**) that can stand on its own as a full sentence.

The tenses that can be used in each type of clause and then combined within a sentence follow a strict pattern. Some tenses can only be used in "if" clauses, while other tenses can only be used in main clauses.

The chart below shows which tenses can be used in which clauses.

"If" Clause	Main Clause
Present If it rains, (main clause can be present or future) Should it rain, (main clause can only be future)	**Present** the coach cancels practice. **Future** the coach will cancel practice.
Simple Past If it rained, If it were to rain, Were it to rain,	**Conditional** the coach would cancel practice.
Past Perfect If it had rained, Had it rained, (**NOT**: If it would have rained)	**Past conditional** the coach would have canceled practice.

Note: either the "if" clause or the main clause can appear first. Clause order does not affect tense.

Correct: If economic resources were used to finance speculative activities, the risk of financial crisis would increase.

Correct: The risk of financial crisis would increase if economic resources were used to finance speculative activities.

Exercise: All Tenses

In the following exercises, identify any verb not in the proper tense, and write the correction on the line provided. Some of the sentences may not contain an error. (Answers p. 285)

Example: For all his claims about improving schools, the mayor **did** little to implement meaningful reforms since taking office.

_____**has done**_____

1. According to researchers, the Antarctic ice shelf **has shrank** by approximately 50 gigatons of ice each year since 1992.

    _____

2. In 1498, Dutch scholar Erasmus of Rotterdam moved from Paris to England, where he later **had become** a professor of ancient languages at Cambridge.

    _____

3. By 1900, McKim, Mead & White **had become** New York's largest architectural firm; today it remains among the most famous in the city's history.

    _____

4. Mahatma Gandhi, who was born in India, studied law in London and in 1893 went to South Africa, where he **has spent** twenty years opposing discriminatory legislation against Indians.

    _____

5. The country's economists speculated that thousands more jobs would have been lost if consumer demand for domestically manufactured products **would have continued** to decline.

    _____

6. NASA scientists have decided to delay the space shuttle's launch in order to determine whether recently repaired parts would cause damage if they **break** off in orbit.

   _____

7. Defying predictions that he **would fade** from the public eye, former Czech president Vaclav Havel reinvented himself as a film director after his retirement from office.

   _____

8. A Federal Aviation Administration task force has recommended that drone operators **are** required to register their aircrafts, paving the way for regulations intended to help reverse a surge in rogue drone flights.

   _____

9. During the Renaissance, glass products made on the island of Murano **could** only be crafted according to traditional techniques, and local artisans were forbidden to leave and sell their creations elsewhere.

   _____

10. After weeks of careful scrutiny, the consumer protection agency informed the public that a number of products **will be** recalled because of safety concerns.

    _____

11. Even before the beginning of the twentieth century, when the electronic age was still in its infancy, the first attempts to generate sound from electricity **had already began**.

    _____

12.   The Empire of Mali on the west coast of Africa **was founded** by King Sundiata Keita, a hero of the Mandinka people, during the Middle Ages.

_____

13.   Hardly a stranger to self-censorship, Mark Twain never hesitated to change his prose if he believed that the alterations **will improve** the sales of his books.

_____

14.   Some critics have argued that Dostoevsky was unique among nineteenth-century authors in that he surrendered fully to his characters and **allows** himself to write in voices other than his own.

_____

15.   For centuries, Norwegians **hang** dolls dressed as witches in their kitchens because they believe that such figures have the power to keep pots from boiling over.

_____

Chapter Eighteen

Adjectives vs. Adverbs

Adjectives modify nouns, pronouns, and other adjectives. They answer the question *what is x like?* They often take the following endings:

•	–al	critical
•	–ent	different
•	–ful	wonderful
•	–ible	incredible
•	–ic	enthusiastic
•	–ive	expensive
•	–ous	continuous

Adjectives can be placed before a noun or an adjective, or after a linking verb. Common linking verbs include *to be, to become/turn/grow, to say/remain, to seem/appear, to feel, to taste,* and *to smell.*

- I finished the **difficult** <u>assignment</u>. (Adjective modifies noun.)

- We're standing in front of the **big** <u>white</u> house. (Adjective modifies adjective.)

- We're standing in front of the big **white** <u>one</u>. (Adjective modifies pronoun.)

- The <u>waves</u> became **calm**. (Adjective modifies noun, after a linking verb.)

In addition, present participles (*–ing*) and past participles (typically end in *–ed*, but also *–en, –ung, –unk,* and *–own* for irregular verbs) can act as adjectives.

- The **singing** <u>bird</u> sat outside my window.

- The chicken was accompanied by **mixed** <u>vegetables</u>.

- The divers explored the **sunken** <u>ship</u>.

Nationalities, numbers, and professions can all act as adjectives.

- My dog is an **Italian** greyhound.

- There are **five** books on the table.

- **Architect** I.M. Pei is known for his use of glass.

Important: when a past participle of a regular verb either modifies a noun or is placed after a form of *to be*, it must end in *–ed*. Although these letters are not always pronounced clearly, they must be used in writing.

Incorrect:	When homeowners decide to undertake major renovations, they typically look for the most **experience** contractor they can find.
Correct:	When homeowners decide to undertake major renovations, they typically look for the most **experienced** contractor they can find.
Incorrect:	Complaining that a writer is **bias** is often a meaningless gesture that is simply intended to shut down discussion about a topic.
Correct:	Complaining that a writer is **biased** is often a meaningless gesture that is simply intended to shut down discussion about a topic.

Adverbs modify verbs, adjectives, and other adverbs. They answer the question *how is x done?*
They are usually formed by adding *–ly* to the adjective.

- When adjectives already end in *–l*, that letter is doubled before the *–y*.

- For adjectives that already end in *–y*, the adverb is formed by adding *–ily*.

Adjective	Adverb
clear	clearly
careful	carefully
lucky	luckily

- He walks **slowly**. (Adverb modifies verb.)

- Mr. Samson is a **highly** interesting conversationalist. (Adverb modifies adjective.)

- She runs **very** quickly. (Adverb modifies adverb.)

Note: the adverb form of *good* is *well*, and the adverb form of *fast* is also *fast*.

Incorrect:	He did **good** on the final exam.
Correct:	He did **well** on the final exam.
Correct:	She is a **fast** runner. (As adjective, modifying the noun *runner*)
Correct:	She runs **fast**. (As adverb, modifying the verb *runs*)

Exercise: Adjective or Adverb?

For the following sentences, determine whether the underlined word is an adjective or an adverb.
(Answers p. 286)

1.   Some of the largest rodents in the world, beavers construct dams in order to create **<u>deep</u>** waters that protect against predators.

      Adjective   **Adverb**

2.   While researchers **<u>initially</u>** believed that the disease originated in a single animal species, new evidence suggests that it arose simultaneously in various human and animal populations.

      Adjective   **Adverb**

3.   Even if conclusive evidence about the authorship of Shakespeare's plays were discovered, it is **<u>unlikely</u>** that popular speculation about their writer would permanently cease.

      Adjective   **Adverb**

4.   Philadelphia's Mural Arts Program takes in **<u>prosecuted</u>** graffiti vandals at the rate of over 100 per year and involves them in the creation of public art projects.

      Adjective   **Adverb**

5.   A gifted mimic, Rebecca is able to **<u>convincingly</u>** reproduce the voices and gestures of people she has met only a single time.

      Adjective   **Adverb**

6.   Physicist Michio Kaku has gained popularity in the mainstream media because of his deep knowledge and **<u>accessible</u>** manner of presenting complex scientific subjects.

      Adjective   **Adverb**

7.   The intensity with which the **Khmer** Empire pursued large-scale urbanization projects may have contributed to its collapse in the fifteenth century.

       Adjective   **Adverb**

8.   In contrast to what some critics have assumed, the author's adoption of a **pen** name occurred by chance and never held any particular significance for him.

       Adjective   **Adverb**

9.   Higher education in the United States has undergone numerous changes over the past hundred years: until the early twentieth century, it consisted **primarily** of rote memorization of Greek and Latin classics.

       Adjective   **Adverb**

10.   Critics have observed that the recently published collection of **English** poet John Donne's work is rewarding, if occasionally frustrating, to read.

       Adjective   **Adverb**

Order of Adjectives

When multiple adjectives modify each other in succession, they must follow a specific order:

- number
- size
- age
- shape
- color
- origin

Example: On the plate sat two **(size)** fresh **(age)** spiky **(shape)** red **(color)** Maine **(origin)** lobsters.

Of course, sentences will rarely require so many adjectives. In most cases, they'll involve two or three at most. Still, number must come before age, age before shape, and so on.

Incorrect: The lemur is a **brown small** mammal native to the island of Madagascar.

The above sentence is incorrect because adjectives of size (*small*) are required to come before adjectives of color (*brown*).

Correct: The lemur is a **small brown** mammal native to the island of Madagascar.

If you are a native English speaker, errors involving adjective order tend to be fairly easy to identify. Regardless of whether you know the formal rules, you'll generally be able to hear that something sounds "off." If English is not your first language, however, you will need to learn this order.

Adjective Replaces Adverb

Only adverbs can modify verbs.

Incorrect: Often, the term "Bollywood" is **incorrect** used to refer to the whole of Indian cinema; however, Bollywood is only a part of a larger film industry.

How is the term "Bollywood" used? *Incorrectly.*

Correct: Often, the term "Bollywood" is **incorrectly** used to refer to the whole of Indian cinema; however, Bollywood is only a part of a larger film industry.

Adverbs can also be used to modify adjectives, primarily to indicate **degree** or **intensity**: words like *really, very, slightly, extremely,* and *incredibly* serve this function. Adjectives cannot be used instead.

Incorrect: Although the southern part of Tunisia is covered by the Sahara Desert, the remaining area of the country contains hundreds of miles of coastline and **exceptional** <u>fertile</u> soil.

Correct: Although the southern part of Tunisia is covered by the Sahara Desert, the remaining area of the country contains hundreds of miles of coastline and **exceptionally** <u>fertile</u> soil.

Note that although errors involving adverbs replaced with adjectives are relatively easy to identify in short statements, they can be surprisingly tricky to catch in long ones.

In a sentence like the one below, for example, it is not uncommon for readers to mentally add an –(i)ly when none is present and continue to overlook the error even after seeing it multiple times.

Incorrect: Although the development of the Concorde required a significant economic loss, the aircraft became **increasing** important as a customer base developed for what was then the fastest commercial form of air travel in the world.

Correct: Although the development of the Concorde required a significant economic loss, the aircraft became **increasingly** important as a customer base developed for what was then the fastest commercial form of air travel in the world.

Adverb Replaces Adjective

Although the incorrect replacement of an adjective with an adverb is less common than the opposite error, it is also the source of much confusion. When sentences involve verbs of feeling and appearing (e.g., *to seem*, *to appear*, *to feel*, and *to look*), many people are unsure which form to use.

The key to forming these constructions correctly is to know that **"perception" verbs are linking verbs,** which take **adjectives** as complements.

Incorrect: Because the man <u>looked</u> somewhat **oddly**, he received a number of suspicious glances from people who passed him on the street.

Correct: Because the man <u>looked</u> somewhat **odd**, he received a number of suspicious glances from people who passed him on the street.

The incorrect version of the above sentence means that the man was performing the act of looking in an odd manner, not that other people perceived his appearance as odd. While this version is grammatically acceptable, it is also highly illogical.

Are You Good...Or Are You Well?

One extremely common point of confusion involves the adjective/adverb pair *good* and *well*.

In everyday speech, it is exceedingly common for the question *How are you?* to be answered with *I'm good, thanks*. Then, of course, there are those people who say *I'm well*. But are they actually correct? Or are they just being pretentious?

In reality, both versions are grammatically acceptable.

Let's start with the fact that *am* is a form of *to be*, which is a linking verb and thus is followed by an adjective. Based on that fact, *good* (adjective) would seem to be the correct option.

In reality, however, *well* is both the adverb form of *good* **and** an adjective meaning the opposite of *ill*. Thus, when people say *I'm well, thanks*, they're actually forming a grammatically correct statement. But if you think *I'm good* sounds too casual, and *I'm well* sounds too fussy, you can always just stick with *I'm fine*.

Exercise: Adjectives vs. Adverbs

For the following exercises, fix any error in adjective or adverb usage. Some of the sentences may not contain an error. (Answers p. 286)

Example: Just who or what inspired the painter John Constable's wonderfully mysterious cloud studies has never been ~~entire~~ clear.

        entirely

1. In many countries that lack medical workers, citizens with little or no professional preparation have been successfully trained to substitute for doctors and nurses.

2. Consumed for its energizing effects, caffeine is also a psychoactive drug that, according to research, can cause people to feel sickly and exacerbate a variety of stress-related ailments.

3. First produced in 1908, the Ford Model T (nicknamed the "Tin Lizzie") was a black big car that revolutionized Americans' relationship with the automobile.

4. Although the room initially seemed tidy, we saw upon closer inspection that books, pens, and pieces of paper had been scattered haphazard beneath a desk.

5. When examined under a microscope, the beaker of water revealed a hodgepodge of microscopic drifters that looked quite differently from other sea creatures.

6. Though few people believe that human beings are entirely rational, a world governed by anti-Enlightenment principles would surely be infinite worse than one governed by Voltaire and Locke.

7. During an era noted for its barbarity, the ancient city of Persepolis, located in modern-day southern Iran, was a relatively cosmopolitan place.

8. When Mt. Vesuvius first began to show signs of eruption, many of the people living at the base of the volcano hasty abandoned their villages to seek cover in nearby forests.

9. Italian nobleman Cesare Borgia was ruthless and vain, but he was also a brilliant Renaissance figure who was exceeding well-educated in the classics.

10. The upper basin of Utah's Lake Powell provides a minimum yearly flow of eight million tons of water to states across the southwestern United States.

11. Lake Pergusa, the only naturally occurring lake in Sicily, is surrounded by a well-known racing circuit that was created in the 1960s and that has hosted many sporting international events since that time.

12. Even when his theme is the struggle to find a place in a seeming irrational cosmos, Oscar Wilde writes with lively sympathy and hopefulness.

13. Although many children want to read digitized books and would read for fun more frequently if they could obtain them, most claim that they would feel bad about giving up print books completely.

14. The origin of the senators' proposal dates back nearly three-quarters of a century, making it one of the most eager anticipated pieces of legislation this year.

15. Because the officer was able to present himself in an unthreatening manner, the suspect remained calmly for the duration of the interview.

Chapter Nineteen

Comparatives vs. Superlatives

Comparative = *–er* form of adjective or *more + adjective*. Used to compare **two** things.

Examples: smaller, larger, faster, brighter, more interesting, more exciting

Incorrect: Between the rhino and the hippo, the rhino is the **heavier** creature, while the hippo is the **most** ferocious.

Correct: Between the rhino and the hippo, the rhino is the **heavier** creature, while the hippo is the **more** ferocious.

Superlative = *–est* form of adjective or *most + adjective*. Used to compare **three or more** things.

Examples: smallest, largest, fastest, brightest, most interesting, most exciting

Incorrect: The executive interviewed <u>five</u> candidates for the position and ultimately decided that Sergei was the **more** qualified.

Correct: The executive interviewed <u>five</u> candidates for the position and ultimately decided that Sergei was the **most** qualified.

Forming Comparatives and Superlatives

As indicated above, comparatives and superlatives can be formed with *–er/–est* or *more/most + adjective*.

Type of Adjective	Ending
1-syllable	–ER
2-syllable ending in –Y or –OW	–ER
All other adjectives with 2 or more syllables*	More/Most + Adjective

*A few adjectives can take either *–er/-est* or *more/most*. For example *most sincere* and *sincerest* are both acceptable.

The chart below shows the formation of some sample comparative and superlative adjectives.

Simple	Comparative	Superlative
Clear	Clearer	Clearest
Funny	Funnier	Funniest
Narrow	Narrower	Narrowest
Interesting	More interesting	Most interesting

Comparative and Superlative Adverbs: Quicker...Or More Quickly?

Some adverbs also have a comparative form.

- When the adverb form is identical to the adjective (rare), add –er.

- When the adverb is formed by adding –ly, use more/most + adverb.

Adjective	Adverb	Comparative	Superlative
Fast	Fast	Faster	Fastest
Quick	Quickly	More quickly	Most quickly
Interesting	Interestingly	More interesting	Most interesting

Incorrect: Sweden is tilting toward a cashless future **quicker** than almost any other country; its residents, accustomed to the convenience of paying by app and credit card, rarely use cash.

Because *quickly* is the adverb form of *quick*, *more + adverb* must be used.

Correct: Sweden is tilting toward a cashless future **more quickly** than almost any other country; its residents, accustomed to the convenience of paying by app and credit card, rarely use cash.

Other adjectives that have identical adverb forms include the following:

- Close
- Early
- Far
- Hard
- High
- Late
- Likely
- Low
- Near
- Right
- Wrong

Exercise: Comparatives and Superlatives

For the following sentences, identify and correct any error involving comparatives or superlatives. (Answers p. 287)

Example: Asked to choose between the gorilla and the chimpanzee, experienced primate researchers would not hesitate to declare the chimpanzee the ~~smartest~~ animal.

smarter

1. Between the black leopard and the snow leopard, the black leopard possesses the more effective camouflage while the snow leopard has the most striking tail.

2. When the influenza virus, one of the commo[nest diagnosed diseases in the United States, was formally recognized in 1933, many doctors believed that a cure would be found shortly.

3. In assessing the skills of Garry Kasparov versus those of Bobby Fischer, most chess experts would declare Fischer to be the better player.

4. Once restricted to a single season, forest fires are now a constant threat in some locations, beginning more early in the year and lasting later than they previously did.

5. Although many viewers find his work on color and geometric shapes to be excessively abstract and inaccessible, Paul Klee is nonetheless regarded as one of the most innovative artists of the early twentieth century.

6. Confronted with two equally qualified finalists, the awards committee is struggling to determine which one is most deserving of the top prize.

7. Tests on the germination rates of *Salsola imbricata* seeds show that the plant sprouts quicker and more consistently at 20°C than at higher temperatures.

8. Though London has a longstanding reputation as a city whose weather is defined by rain and fog, in reality Paris receives the highest amount of rainfall each year.

9. Both poodles and pugs are known for making excellent pets, but between the two breeds, pugs have the sweetest disposition while poodles are smarter.

10. Although puzzles such as Sudoku can help people keep their minds nimble as they age, studies show that physical exercise such as biking or running has a more strong effect on mental acuity.

Double Positives and Double Negatives

Never use *more* or *most* in addition to the comparative or superlative form of an adjective.

Comparative

Incorrect: When traveling over large distances, most people choose to go by airplane rather than by train because the airplane is the **more faster** option.

Correct: When traveling over large distances, most people choose to go by airplane rather than by train because the airplane is the **faster** option.

Superlative

Incorrect: The Indian sub-continent was home to some of the **most earliest** civilizations, ranging from the urban society of the Indus Valley to the classical age of the Gupta Dynasty.

Correct: The Indian sub-continent was home to some of the **earliest** civilizations, ranging from the urban society of the Indus Valley to the classical age of the Gupta Dynasty.

Double Negative

Do not use *no* with the words *scarcely* and *hardly*. However, *any* may be used.

Incorrect: The economist John Maynard Keynes predicted a society so prosperous that people would **not scarcely/not hardly** need to work.

Correct: The economist John Maynard Keynes predicted a society so prosperous that people would **scarcely/hardly** need to work.

Correct: The economist John Maynard Keynes predicted a society so prosperous that people would have **scarcely/hardly any** need to work.

Exercise: Double Positives and Double Negatives

For the following sentences, identify and correct any error involving double positives or double negatives. (Answers p. 288)

Example: Throughout the Middle Ages, one of knights' ~~most~~ largest concerns was how to protect themselves in battle.

1.   When selecting a host city from among dozens of contenders, Olympic officials must take into consideration which one is most likeliest to benefit from the legacy of the games.

2.   Although the plays of Lillian Hellman and Bertolt Brecht were met with great popularity during the 1920s, they are scarcely never performed anymore in the United States.

3.   Since the advent of commercial flight and high-speed rail in the twentieth century, hardly no significant technological changes have affected the traveling public.

4.   During its early years, the Ford Motor Company didn't produce scarcely more than a handful of cars a day, but within a decade it led the world in the expansion of the assembly line.

5.   Though the Panama Canal is hardly new, having opened nearly a hundred years ago, the idea of a waterway connecting the Atlantic and Pacific Oceans is significantly older than the canal itself.

6.   Imitation, long considered the most sincerest form of flattery, may carry evolutionary benefits for both model and mimic.

7.   During the early days of cable television, many viewers were only able to access four channels, with reception being weakest in rural areas and most clearest in large cities.

8.   The Industrial Revolution, which began in the late 1700s and lasted more than fifty years, was the period when machine power became more stronger than hand power.

9.   Although many people have attempted to solve the mystery of Stonehenge, its purpose is hardly any clearer than it was centuries ago.

10.   To thoroughly understand historical figures, we must study them not only in the bright light of the present but also in the more cloudier light of the circumstances of their own lifetimes.

Chapter Twenty

Comparisons and Amounts

As a general rule, comparisons should be formed as simply and concisely as possible.

Awkward	Clear
In similarity to	(Un)like
Opposing	Similar to
Opposite (to)	In comparison to
In opposition to	Compared to
Contrasting with	In contrast to

Incorrect: **Contrasting with** household surveys, store surveys can be used to compare prices of similar items across many different locations and types of stores.

Correct: **In contrast to** household surveys, store surveys can be used to compare prices of similar items across many different locations and types of stores.

Like vs. As

Both *like* and *as* are used to indicate similarities between two items, but they are not interchangeable.

Like is a preposition primarily used to compare **nouns** and **pronouns**: *noun x is like noun y*, NOT *noun x is as noun y*.

Incorrect: Health insurance, **as** other forms of insurance, allows people to pool their risk of incurring expenses for unforeseen illness or other medical emergencies.

Correct: Health insurance, **like** other forms of insurance, allows people to pool their risk of incurring expenses for unforeseen illness or other medical emergencies.

As is a conjunction used to join **clauses**. Unlike prepositional phrases, clauses contain subjects and verbs.

Incorrect: **Like** <u>is</u> true for other forms of insurance, health insurance allows people to pool their risk of incurring expenses for unforeseen illness or other medical emergencies.

Correct: **As** <u>is</u> true for other forms of insurance, health insurance allows people to pool their risk of incurring expenses for unforeseen illness or other medical emergencies.

The construction *as adjective…as* can also be used to indicate that two people or things are equal.

Correct: It is almost **as** difficult to find consistent information about the Fort Pillow incident during the Civil War **as** it is to determine its significance.

Note, however, that *as* <u>can</u> be followed by a noun or pronoun when it is used idiomatically.

Correct: Sold for lower prices than their name-brand counterparts, medications that are distributed without patent protection are known **as** <u>generic drugs</u>.

Faulty Comparisons

Use *than*, not *then*, to form comparisons.

Incorrect: Cleopatra's Needle, the obelisk that stands in Manhattan's Central Park, was created more **then** a thousand years before Cleopatra was born.

Correct: Cleopatra's Needle, the obelisk that stands in Manhattan's Central Park, was created more **than** a thousand years before Cleopatra was born.

Otherwise, the rule for forming comparisons is as follows: **compare things to things and people to people.**

Incorrect: In the United States during the mid-twentieth century, Norman Rockwell's **art** was better known than **Russian painter Wassily Kandinsky**.

In the above sentence, art (thing) is illogically compared to Wassily Kandinsky (person). Most students will instinctively correct the above sentence as follows:

Correct: In the United States during the mid-twentieth century, Norman Rockwell's **art** was better known than **Russian painter Wassily Kandinsky's** <u>art</u>.

The above version is perfectly acceptable; however, an alternate (and more sophisticated) fix for the sentence involves replacing the noun *art* with a pronoun.

Correct: In the United States during the mid-twentieth century, Norman Rockwell's **art** was better known than **that (= the art) of** Russian painter Wassily Kandinsky**.**

BUT NOT: In the United States during the mid-twentieth century, Norman Rockwell's **art** was better known than **that of** Russian painter **Wassily Kandinsky's. (= the art of Wassily Kandinsky's** *art***)**

A **plural** faulty comparison can be corrected with either a noun or the phrase *those of*.

Incorrect: In Victorian England, Charles Dickens' **novels** were more widely read than **Victor Hugo**.

Correct: In Victorian England, Charles Dickens' **novels** were more widely read than **the novels of** Victor Hugo.

Correct: In Victorian England, Charles Dickens' **novels** were more widely read than **those (= the novels) of** Victor Hugo.

BUT NOT: In Victorian England, Charles Dickens' **novels** were more widely read than **those of Victor Hugo's. (= the novels of Victor Hugo's *novels*)**

Make sure that the pronouns reflect the number of the nouns they replace: singular nouns must be replaced by singular pronouns, and plural nouns must be replaced by plural pronouns.

Incorrect: The maker of the 2011 documentary *Summer Pastures* suggests that for all the hardships they endure, Tibetan nomads lead <u>lives</u> no more stressful than **that** of most city dwellers.

Correct: The maker of the 2011 documentary *Summer Pastures* suggests that for all the hardships they endure, Tibetan nomads lead <u>lives</u> no more stressful than **the lives** of most city dwellers.

Correct: The maker of the 2011 documentary *Summer Pastures* suggests that for all the hardships they endure, Tibetan nomads lead <u>lives</u> no more stressful than **those** of most city dwellers.

Comparing Equivalent Things

When two things are being compared, they must be equivalent.

Incorrect: Unlike **a train**, <u>the length</u> of a tram is usually limited to one or two cars, which may run either on train tracks or directly on the street.

What is being compared here?

1) A train

2) The length of a tram

Even though both *train* and *length* are nouns, they are not equivalent. We must either compare a train to a train or a length to a length.

Correct: Unlike **the length of** a train, <u>the length</u> of a tram is usually limited to one or two cars, which may run either on train tracks or directly on the street.

Correct: Unlike **that of** a train, <u>the length</u> of a tram is usually limited to one or two cars, which may run either on train tracks or directly on the street.

Any vs. Any Other

When two things from the same category are compared, the phrase *any other* should be used to indicate that one of the things is better, faster, more difficult, etc. than the other items in that category.

Incorrect: A source of intense fascination for both art historians and museum patrons, Leonardo da Vinci's *Mona Lisa* is perhaps more famous than **any** painting in the world.

Because the *Mona Lisa* is itself a painting, it is illogical to say that is more famous than *any painting*.

Correct: A source of intense fascination for both art historians and museum patrons, Leonardo da Vinci's *Mona Lisa* is perhaps more famous than **any** <u>other</u> painting in the world.

Can It Be Counted?

Some modifiers commonly used in comparisons can only be placed before singular (non-countable) or plural (countable) nouns.

Singular	Plural
Less	Fewer
Much	Many
Amount	Number

Note: errors involving these modifiers generally involve the use of a singular form before a plural noun (e.g., *a large <u>amount</u> of trees* rather than *a large <u>number</u> of trees*), so I am providing examples of only this error.

Incorrect: As a result of its extreme temperatures and harsh living conditions, Antarctica supports **less** <u>animal species</u> than any other continent does.

Correct: As a result of its extreme temperatures and harsh living conditions, Antarctica supports **fewer** <u>animal species</u> than any other continent does.

Incorrect: Moving between industries can be unsettling, but new jobs can sometimes offer workers **much** more <u>opportunities</u> than their existing jobs can.

Correct: Moving between industries can be unsettling, but new jobs can sometimes offer workers **many** more <u>opportunities</u> than their existing jobs can.

Incorrect: In comparison to New York City, London is home to a much higher **amount** of historical <u>sites</u>.

Correct: In comparison to New York City, London is home to a much higher **number** of historical <u>sites</u>.

Exercise: Faulty Comparisons and Amounts

For the following sentences, correct any error involving comparisons or amounts. (Answers p. 288)

Example: Though no longer a household name, the nineteenth-century English biologist Richard Owen published more than 600 articles and made discoveries that rivaled ⌄Charles Darwin.
                                                                                                                those of

1. The writings of John Locke, opposing the writings of Thomas Hobbes, emphasize the idea that people are by nature both reasonable and tolerant.

2. In response to protests against unfair labor practices, the company issued an official statement encouraging skeptics to compare the organization's pay, benefits, and workplace conditions to other major employers.

3. As part of its application, the university asks students to compose a short essay in which they compare their educational interests and goals to that of other students.

4. Archaeologists have long been far more puzzled by members of the Saqqaq culture, the oldest known inhabitants of Greenland, than by those of other prehistoric North American cultures.

5. Doctors in Norway prescribe less antibiotics than those in any other country, so people do not have a chance to develop resistance to many kinds of drug-resistant infections.

6. Today's neuroscientists, contrasting those of thirty years ago, have access to sophisticated instrumentation that has only been developed over the past decade.

7. Unlike dyslexia, people with dysgraphia often suffer from fine motor-skills problems that leave them unable to write clearly.

8. In contrast to merchants in coastal regions of central Asia, merchants in landlocked regions had a smaller amount of trade options because of their distance from maritime routes of commerce.

9. The reproduction of ciliates, unlike other organisms, occurs when a specimen splits in half and grows a completely new individual from each piece.

10. The hands and feet of Ardi, the recently discovered human ancestor who lived 4.4 million years ago, are much like those of other primitive extinct apes.

11. At the age of twenty-four, playwright Thornton Wilder was balding and bespectacled, and his clothes were like a much older man.

12. In ancient Greece, women were not allowed to vote or hold property, their status differing from slaves only in name.

13. Although birds are not generally known for their intelligence, recent findings have established that parrots often possess skills similar to human toddlers.

14. People waste an unfathomable amount of food: in fact, according to a recent report, roughly 50% of all produce in the United States is thrown away.

15. One major difference between lowland Mayan rituals and that of other ancient peoples, some scholars believe, is that the former developed in relative isolation.

Chapter Twenty-One

Word Pairs

Word pairs (formally known as **correlative conjunctions**) can be used to indicate comparisons, causes and effects, and sequences of events. When one half of a word pair is used, the other half must also be present.

A. (N)either...(n)or

Either the company's president **or** her assistant will be present at the press conference scheduled for later this afternoon.

According to the politician, **neither** the recent crisis **nor** any other period of economic turmoil had been caused by environmental protection policies.

B. Not only...but (also)

Apples **not only** taste very good, **but** they **also** contain numerous essential vitamins and minerals.

C. Both / Between / At once } and

The news station trails its competitor in **both** the morning **and** the evening news broadcast.

Many people find it difficult to decide **between** buying a Mac **and** buying a PC.

The politician is **at once** controversial because of his refusal to compromise **and** beloved because of his personal charisma.

D. From...to

In Russia, the shift **from** monarchy **to** totalitarianism occurred at a remarkably rapid pace.

E. Just as...so

Just as Thomas Edison is known for inventing the electric light bulb, **so** is Albert Einstein known for developing a theory of general relativity.

F. So
Such } that

The first lesula monkey seen by researchers bore a strong resemblance to the owl-faced monkey, but **so** unusual was the lesula monkey's coloring **that** they suspected it was a new species.

The first lesula monkey seen by researchers bore a strong resemblance to the owl-faced monkey, but the lesula monkey had **such** unusual coloring **that** they suspected it was a new species.

G. The –er...the –er

The **longer** the reporters pressed the candidate, the **greater** his refusal to answer questions became.

H. As
Not so much } as

Although she began training later than many other gymnasts, Jessica is just **as** good an athlete **as** most of her competitors.

Although her plays have garnered praise from many critics, Toni Morrison is known **not so much** for her theatrical works **as** she is for her novels.

I. More
Less
No sooner } than

Although Jane Austen's novels are **more** widely read **than** those of her contemporaries, Austen was hardly the only female author in nineteenth-century England.

No sooner had the senator announced her intention not to run for re-election **than** the media began to speculate about the next stage of her political career.

J. Only when
   Only after } did
   Not until*

Only when/after negotiations over the new contract began **did** workers and managers realize the extent of their conflicts.

Not until negotiations over the new contract began **did** workers and managers realize the extent of their conflicts.

K. It was only when
   It was only after } that
   It was not until

It was only when/after negotiations over the new contract began **that** workers and managers realized the extent of their conflicts.

It was not until negotiations over the new contract began **that** workers and managers realized the extent of their conflicts.

---

*A form of *to be* or *to have* can also be used with a passive construction (e.g., *Not until the police arrived at the museum <u>was</u> it discovered that the thief had escaped with several paintings,* OR: *Not until now <u>have</u> the effects of the chemical truly been understood*).

Exercise: Word Pairs

For the following sentences, fill in the missing half of the word pair. (Answers p. 289)

Example: In his novel *Parallel Stories*, Peter Nadas is concerned not only with historical events _____but also_____ with their role in influencing people's lives.

1. Known for his designs inspired by natural principles, architect Michael Pawlyn was initially torn between studying architecture _____ studying biology, but he eventually chose the former.

2. Long Island was the setting for *The Great Gatsby*, but finding traces of the world Fitzgerald depicted there is as much a job for the imagination _____ it is for a map and a guidebook.

3. Once stereotyped as savants because of their depictions in movies such as *Rain Man*, people on the autistic spectrum are typically neither superhuman memory machines _____ incapable of performing everyday tasks.

4. Obedience to authority is not only a way for rulers to keep order in totalitarian states, _____ the foundation on which such states exist.

5. In the Middle Ages, the term "arts" referred to a wide range of fields including geometry, grammar, and astronomy; only in the nineteenth century _____ it come to denote painting, drawing, and sculpting.

6. Audiences find the play at once amusing because of the comedic skills of its leading actors _____ tedious because of its excessive length.

7. So great was the surplus of food created by the ancient Mesopotamians _____ it led to the establishment of the first complex civilization in human history.

8. Dumping pollution in oceans not only adds to the unsightliness of the formerly pristine waters _____ destroys the marine life that inhabits them.

9. Because the Articles of Confederation did not provide for the creation of either executive agencies _____ judiciary institutions, they were rejected in favor of the Constitution.

10. Just as moral intelligence, an innate sense of right and wrong, allowed human societies to flourish, _____ did a strong sense of hierarchy allow canine societies to thrive.

11. One of the main effects of industrialization was the shift from a society in which women worked at home _____ one in which women worked in factories and brought home wages to their families.

12. Over the past decade, Internet usage has become so pervasive _____ many psychologists are beginning to study its effects on the lives of children and adolescents.

13. It was not until the late seventeenth century _____ some English writers began to challenge the traditional view of commerce, which held that money-making was a source of moral corruption to be avoided at all cost.

14. Just as the Machine Age transformed an economy of farm laborers and artisans into one of assembly lines, _____ the technology revolution is replacing factory workers with robots, and clerks with computers.

15. Although Voltaire wrote a number of tragedies and believed he would be remembered as a dramatist, he is known today not so much for his theatrical works _____ for his satires.

Chapter Twenty-Two

Parallel Structure

Parallel structure is used to indicate that multiple items in a sentence are equally important. In any list, each item should appear in the same format: noun, noun, and noun; verb, verb, and verb; or gerund, gerund, and gerund.

List with nouns

Incorrect: <u>Changes</u> in wind circulation patterns, <u>runoff</u> from sewage, and **using** chemical fertilizers can lead to the creation of ocean waters that are inhospitable to marine life.

Correct: <u>Changes</u> in wind circulation patterns, <u>runoff</u> from sewage, and **use** of chemical fertilizers can lead to the creation of ocean waters that are inhospitable to marine life.

List with verbs

Incorrect: In their works, Impressionist painters <u>emphasized</u> the interplay of light and dark, <u>used</u> rapid brushstrokes, and **conveying** a sense of immediacy.

Correct: In their works, Impressionist painters <u>emphasized</u> the interplay of light and dark, <u>used</u> rapid brushstrokes, and **conveyed** a sense of immediacy.

List with gerunds

Incorrect: Because they have a highly developed sense of vision, most lizards communicate by <u>gesturing</u> with their limbs, <u>changing</u> their colors, or **to display** their athletic abilities.

Correct: Because they have a highly developed sense of vision, most lizards communicate by <u>gesturing</u> with their limbs, <u>changing</u> their colors, or **displaying** their athletic abilities.

Exercise: "List" Parallel Structure

For the following sentences, make the items in each list parallel in structure. (Answers p. 290)

Example: Most parrot species spend their time perching on tree limbs, climbing onto rocks and branches, or ~~they forage~~ for seeds and flowers.
    foraging

1. Lady Jane Grey, known as the nine-day queen, was renowned for her sweetness, her beauty, and being subjected to the whims of her mother.

2. Mediterranean cooking is best known for its reliance on fresh produce, whole grains, and it uses significant amounts of olive oil as well.

3. The biggest beneficiaries of the Grateful Dead archive may prove to be business scholars who are discovering that the Dead were visionaries in the way they created customer value, promoted networking, and how they implemented strategic business planning.

4. The term "single-family house" describes how a house is built and who is intended to live in it, but it does not indicate the house's size, shape, or where it is located.

5. Seeing the Grand Canyon, standing in front of a beautiful piece of art, and to listen to a beautiful symphony are all experiences that may inspire awe.

6. Neighbors of the proposed park argue that an amphitheater would draw more traffic, disrupt their neighborhood, and their only patch of open space would diminish.

7. Evidence suggests that the aging brain retains and even increases its capacity for resilience, growth, and having a sense of well-being.

8. Antiques are typically objects that show some degree of craftsmanship or attention to design, and they are considered desirable because of their beauty, rarity, or being useful.

9. Spiders use a wide range of strategies to capture prey, including trapping it in sticky webs, lassoing it with sticky bolas, and to mimic other insects in order to avoid detection.

10. According to medical authorities at the Mayo Clinic, building muscle can boost metabolism, aiding in weight loss, and increase stamina and focus.

Two-Part Parallel Structure

When only two items are present, **the construction on one side of a conjunction or comparison must match the construction on the other side of the conjunction as closely as possible.**

Most often, the conjunction used to separate parallel items will be *or*, *and*, or *but*; however, any transition or word pair (e.g., *not only…but also, both…and*) can be used to signal that a parallel construction is necessary.

For example:

> Incorrect: More than simply providing badly needed space in cramped cities, skyscrapers **connect** people <u>and</u> **fostering** creativity.

> Incorrect: More than simply providing badly needed space in cramped cities, skyscrapers **connect** people <u>and</u> **creativity is fostered** in them.

The presence of the conjunction *and* indicates that the constructions on either side of it must match.

> Correct: More than simply providing badly needed space in cramped cities, skyscrapers **connect** people <u>and</u> **foster** creativity.

In some cases, parallel structure can involve longer phrases.

> Incorrect: The researchers called for <u>the enforcement</u> of existing cigarette-sale regulations **as well as** <u>investigating</u> teenagers' motivations for smoking.

In the above sentence, the construction on either side of the conjunction *as well as* must be the same. So next, we want to look at the specific construction of those two pieces of information.

What did the researchers call for?

1) **enforcement** of existing cigarette-sale regulations

2) **investigating** teenagers' motivations for smoking

When we examine the two sides, we see that their constructions do not match.

- The first side contains *noun + of + noun* (*enforcement of…regulations*).

- The second side contains *gerund + noun* (*investigating…motivations*).

To make the two sides parallel, we must replace the gerund *investigating* with its noun form, *investigation*, and add the preposition *of*.

> Correct: The researchers called for <u>the enforcement</u> of existing cigarette-sale regulations **as well as** <u>an investigation</u> of teenagers' motivations for smoking.

Parallel Structure with Adjectives

In some cases, a single verb can "apply" to two adjectives, making it unnecessary to include the verb a second time.

> Correct: After waiting more than an hour for the candidate to make his scheduled appearance, the voters **grew** impatient and the reporters irritated.

In the above sentence, the verb *grew* applies to the second adjective, *irritated*, as well as the first, *impatient*. Most people's inclination, however, would be to rewrite the sentence as follows:

> Correct: After waiting more than an hour for the candidate to make his scheduled appearance, the voters **grew** impatient and the reporters **grew** irritated.

While this version of the sentence is correct, it is not inherently more correct than the first version.

Parallel Structure with Prepositions

When parallel structure involves word pairs, the construction after the first half of the word pair must match the construction after the second half.

Often, each half of the word pair will be followed by a preposition. When this is the case, the **same preposition** should be used both times.

> Incorrect: As one of the greatest American dancers and choreographers of the twentieth century, Martha Graham was praised **not only** **for** the brilliance of her technique **but also** **in** the vividness and intensity of her movements.

The verb *praised* applies to the two items that follow: (1) *the brilliance of her technique*, (2) *the vividness and intensity of her movements*. The correct expression is *praised for*, so the preposition *for* should appear before the second item.

> Correct: As one of the greatest American dancers and choreographers of the twentieth century, Martha Graham was praised **not only** **for** the brilliance of her technique **but also** **for** the vividness and intensity of her movements.

When doing so does not result in confusion or disrupt the flow of a sentence, it is also acceptable to omit the preposition in the second item.

> Correct: As one of the greatest American dancers and choreographers of the twentieth century, Martha Graham was praised both **for** the brilliance of her technique and **(no preposition)** the vividness and intensity of her movements.

In the above sentence, the preposition *for* then automatically applies to the nouns on both sides of the word pair (*the brilliance, the vividness and intensity*).

When a sentence involves two verbs that require different prepositions, the appropriate preposition must follow each verb. A preposition cannot apply to a verb that it does not idiomatically follow.

Incorrect: In general, car dealers have shown little **interest or enthusiasm <u>for</u>** electric cars, despite widespread popular support for these vehicles.

Because the idiomatic phrase is *interest in*, not *interest for*, the preposition *in* must be added after *interest*.

Correct: In general, car dealers have shown little **interest <u>in</u>** or **enthusiasm <u>for</u>** electric cars, despite widespread popular support for these vehicles.

Multiple Sentences

In some cases, you may also find it useful to employ a parallel construction across multiple sentences, as a tool for creating suspense or emphasis. Note that this type of writing is much more common in journalism than it is in academic writing.

Not parallel: <u>An actor stands</u> on the stage and delivers a monologue **as** an audience hangs onto his every word. <u>A singer performs</u> a ballad **as** listeners fall silent. **As a group of spectators** watch in awe, a dance troupe glides across the stage.

The first two sentences begin with *a noun + verb...as*, so the third sentence should begin that way as well.

Parallel: <u>An actor stands</u> on the stage and delivers a monologue <u>as</u> an audience hangs onto his every word. <u>A singer performs</u> a ballad **as** listeners fall silent. **A dance troupe glides** across the stage **as** a group of spectators watch in awe.

Exercise: Two-Part Parallel Structure

In the following sentences, identify the conjunction or comparison indicating that parallel structure is required, and rewrite the relevant portion of the sentence to include a parallel construction.
(Answers p. 290)

Example: Hans Holbein was one of the most exquisite draftsmen of all time, renowned for the precise rendering of his drawings **and** <u>his portraits were compellingly realistic</u>.

> **the compelling realism of his portraits**

1. A staple of Louisiana's culinary tradition, Cajun cuisine is predominantly rustic: it relies on local ingredients and preparation of it is simple.

2. The university is installing a more detailed course-evaluation system so that students can decide whether they should register for certain classes or should they avoid them altogether.

3. Known for her musical compositions as well as in her poems and letters, Hildegard of Bingen was just as renowned in the twelfth century as she was in the twentieth.

4. While the novel has many detractors, it also has many admirers who argue that its popularity is based on its gripping storyline and its characters' motives are believable.

5. The majority of rebellions that occurred in Tudor England did not achieve their objectives because of weakness of the rebels and the reigning monarchs were extremely powerful.

6. For fans of the legendary food writer Charles H. Baker, the contents of a dish are less compelling than what the story is behind it.

_____

7. During the sixteenth century, an outbreak of fighting in Europe led to the invention of new weapons and to old weapons growing and evolving.

_____

8. The time publishing companies devote to books has been reduced by financial constraints as well as increasing the emphasis on sales and marketing considerations.

_____

9. In contemporary education, there is a disturbing contrast between the enormous popularity of certain approaches and credible evidence for their effectiveness is lacking.

_____

10. At its peak, the Roman army was nearly unconquerable not only because of the hard and effective training of its commanders but also because of its troops being exceptionally well-organized.

_____

Chapter Twenty-Three

Dangling, Misplaced, and Squinting Modifiers

As a rule, modifiers should be placed as close as possible to the nouns, pronouns, or phrases they modify; sentences that separate modifiers from the items they modify are often unclear and sometimes downright absurd.

There are three main types of modification errors.

   1) Dangling Modifiers

   2) Misplaced Modifiers

   3) Squinting Modifiers

Dangling Modifiers

Sentences that include dangling modifiers are typically characterized by an introductory phrase that describes the subject and is set off by a comma.

Whenever a sentence contains such an introductory statement, the subject must appear immediately after the comma. If the subject does not appear there, the modifier is dangling, and the sentence is incorrect.

   Incorrect: <u>An elementary school teacher from Arkansas,</u> increased funding and support
                   for public libraries were what **Bessie Boehm Moore** worked for.

The first thing we can note about the above sentence is that it contains an introductory phrase (*An elementary school teacher from Arkansas*) that does not name the subject—it does not tell us who the elementary school teacher from Arkansas *is*.

We must therefore ask ourselves whom or what it is referring to. When we look at the rest of the sentence, it is clear that this description can only refer to Bessie Boehm Moore. The words *Bessie Boehm Moore* do not appear immediately after the comma, so the modifier is dangling.

In order to fix the sentence, we must place Bessie Boehm Moore's name after the comma.

Correct: An elementary school teacher from Arkansas, **Bessie Boehm Moore** worked to increase funding and support for public libraries.

One potentially tricky construction to watch out for involves the possessive form of a subject placed after an introductory phrase.

Incorrect: An elementary school teacher from Arkansas, **Bessie Boehm Moore's goal** was to increase funding and support for public libraries.

At first glance, this sentence looks and sounds correct. But who is the elementary school teacher from Arkansas? *Bessie Boehm Moore.*

Here, however, the *goal* is the subject—not *Bessie Boehm Moore.* As a result, the modifier is dangling.

Correct: An elementary school teacher from Arkansas, **Bessie Boehm Moore** worked to increase funding and support for public libraries.

When fixing dangling modifiers, it is most important that you identify the subject because that word must follow the introductory phrase. The rest of the sentence can then be rearranged as necessary.

Note that it is acceptable to begin the main clause with a modifier describing the subject; the description is considered part of the **complete subject**.

Correct: An Arkansas native, <u>**elementary school teacher**</u> Bessie Boehm Moore worked to increase funding and support for public libraries.

In the above sentence, the phrase *elementary school teacher* functions not as a noun but as a modifier describing Bessie Boehm Moore. As a result, it can be correctly placed after the comma.

Note that sentences that begin with participles, both present (ending in *–ing*) and past (*–ed, –ung, –unk, –own*), are particularly vulnerable to the creation of dangling modifiers.

Present Participle

Incorrect: **Stretching** from one end of the city to the other, the efficiency of <u>the new tram system</u> often surprises both tourists and city residents.

Correct: **Stretching** from one end of the city to the other, <u>the new tram system</u> often surprises both tourists and city residents with its efficiency.

Past Participle

Incorrect: **Raised** in a small town in Missouri, the majority of <u>singer and actress Josephine Baker</u>'s career was spent performing throughout Europe.

Correct: **Raised** in a small town in Missouri, <u>singer and actress Josephine Baker</u> spent the majority of her career performing throughout Europe.

Exercise: Dangling Modifiers

Rewrite each sentence to remove the dangling modification. (Suggested answers p. 291)

Example: Though very sturdy, full protection from an opponent's weapons was not offered by chain mail, so medieval knights would often wear a helmet and carry a shield as well.

<u>**Though very sturdy, chain mail did not offer full protection from an opponent's weapons,**</u>

<u>**so medieval knights would often wear a helmet and carry a shield as well.**</u>

1. Often advertised to promote health and reduce stress, harmful side effects can be produced by dietary supplements, even though they are easy to purchase.

2. Born in St. Lucia in the West Indies, author Derek Walcott's work includes a number of plays and poems, most notably *Omeros*.

3. Despite winning several architectural awards, the impractical layout of the university's new dormitory has been criticized by students.

4. One of the earliest authorities to take a stand against pollution, it was proclaimed by King Edward I in 1306 that sea coal could not be burned because its smoke was hazardous to people's health.

5. Predicting renewed interest in their country's natural resources, a plan has been established by political leaders to create mines in the most underdeveloped regions.

    _____

    _____

6. Though educated and well mannered, the status of Jane Eyre remains low throughout the majority of the novel of which she is the protagonist.

    _____

    _____

7. Projecting an image of pain and brutality that has few parallels among advanced paintings of the twentieth century, Pablo Picasso created *Guernica* in the aftermath of a World War II bombing.

    _____

    _____

8. Believing that real estate prices would not rise indefinitely, it was argued by the economist that the housing bubble would eventually burst.

    _____

    _____

Misplaced Modifiers

Unlike dangling modifiers, misplaced modifiers do not necessarily involve introductory phrases and can occur anywhere in a sentence. They do, however, involve modifiers that are separated from the words or phrases they are intended to modify—a construction that often produces unintentionally ridiculous or illogical statements.

Some errors involve single words:

> Incorrect: Hersheypark was opened in 1907 as **only** a leisure park for employees of the Hershey Chocolate Company, but Hershey executives later decided that members of the public should be given access as well.

The placement of the word *only* in the above version of the sentence implies that Hersheypark was exclusively a leisure park when it opened, but that it later became something else.

The statement that members of the public were later given access to the park suggests an alternate meaning, however—namely, that when Hersheypark was opened, employees of the Hershey Chocolate Company were the sole people given access to it.

Logically, then, the word *only* should modify *employees of the Hershey Chocolate Company*.

> Correct: Hersheypark was opened in 1907 as a leisure park for employees of the Hershey Chocolate Company **only**, but Hershey executives later decided that members of the public should be given access as well.

This version of the sentence makes it clear that *only* refers to the employees rather than to the park itself.

Other errors involve entire phrases, often involving relative pronouns (*which, that, who*):

> Incorrect: Paul Conrad was a cartoonist known for his political satires that spent nearly three decades on staff at *The Los Angeles Times*.

Even though it's pretty obvious what the sentence is *trying* to say, what it's actually saying is that *political satires* spent three decades on staff at the newspaper, when it was clearly *Paul Conrad* who did so.

Note that this type of construction illustrates the perils of using *that* to refer to people. Because *that* can also refer to things, the potential to create ambiguous or misleading constructions is much higher.

In order to correct the sentence, we must make it clear Conrad worked at the newspaper.

> Correct: Paul Conrad, a cartoonist known for his political satires, spent nearly three decades on staff at *The Los Angeles Times*.

> Correct: Known for his political satires, Paul Conrad spent nearly three decades on staff at *The Los Angeles Times*.

224

Squinting Modifiers

"Squinting" modifiers are so named because they look in both directions. Whereas dangling and misplaced modifiers describe the wrong thing, squinting modifiers create ambiguity by modifying two things.

For example, consider the following statement:

Incorrect: Writing papers at the last minute **quickly** leads to grammatical errors.

In the above sentence, the word *quickly* can modify either *writing* or *leads*.

- If it modifies *writing*, then the sentence is referring to the act of writing quickly at the last minute.

- If it modifies *leads*, then the sentence is saying that grammatical errors quickly appear when papers are written at the last minute.

To fix the error, we must rearrange the sentence to make it clear which word *quickly* is intended to modify.

Correct: **Quickly** writing papers at the last minute leads to grammatical errors.

Correct: When students write papers at the last minute, they **quickly** make grammatical errors.

Split Infinitives

Split infinitives are created when an adverb is placed between *to* and the verb itself, e.g., *to **boldly** go where no man has gone before*. Traditionally, this construction has been considered incorrect; however, like the prohibition against ending sentences with prepositions, this is a rule rooted in the desire to make English more like Latin.

Latin infinitives consist of just one word, and so it is impossible to split them. In contrast, English infinitives consist of two words (*to + verb*), and there is no logical reason why an adverb should not be placed between them—particularly if placing it elsewhere in a sentence would result in an awkward construction.

That said, if you're writing for a grammar purist, you may want to play it safe and avoid splitting infinitives. Otherwise, there's no compelling reason to worry about them.

Exercise: Misplaced and Squinting Modifiers

Rewrite each of the following sentences to remove the misplaced or squinting modification.
(Answers p. 291)

Example: In 1820, Thomas Jefferson brought the first tomatoes to the United States from France, but they did not catch on immediately, having served as the American ambassador.

> **In 1820, Thomas Jefferson brought the first tomatoes to the United States from France,**
>
> **having served as the American ambassador, but they did not catch on immediately.**

1. A recent discovery suggests that for the past 2.5 billion years, a B-flat has been continuously emitted by a black hole 250 million light years from Earth, the lowest note ever detected.

2. Claude McKay was one of the most important poets of the Harlem Renaissance that moved to New York after studying agronomy in Kansas.

3. The California Street Cable Railroad is an established public transit company in San Francisco, which was founded by Leland Stanford.

4. Some studies indicate that consuming small amounts of chocolate frequently is correlated with good health.

_____

_____

5. Only after joining Miles Davis's Second Great Quintet did Herbie Hancock, who professionally had performed as a musician since the age of seven, succeed in finding his voice as a pianist.

_____

_____

6. Some of the world's fastest trains run between the cities of Tokyo and Kyoto, which can reach speeds of up to 200 miles per hour.

_____

_____

7. When economic activity weakens, monetary policymakers can push interest rate targets below the economy's natural rate, lowering the cost temporarily of borrowing.

_____

_____

8. Many ancient cities were protected from bands of invaders by fortresses that roamed in search of settlements to plunder.

_____

_____

Chapter Twenty-Four

Wordiness and Passive Voice

As William H. Strunk famously commanded in *The Elements of Style*, writers should strive to *omit unnecessary words*, and it remains as good a rule of thumb as any. To be clear, it does not mean that good writing is composed exclusively of short, robotic utterances. It does, however, mean that you should consider whether your words actually add anything to your argument or explanation, or whether you are throwing in lots of extra verbiage simply because you like the way it sounds.

Admittedly, when you're writing a paper at 2 a.m. on the day it's due, your primary goal is probably just to hit the minimum number of pages. But what's good for your word count can be very bad for your writing. Besides, another person (your teacher/professor/TA) will actually read that paper and exert some degree of effort in an attempt to cut through all those words and understand what you are trying to say. You'll probably make that person's life—not to mention your grade—considerably better if you just come out and say it. It is possible to be simple and straightforward without being simplistic.

There are, of course, countless ways in which writing can be made unnecessarily wordy and awkward. In this chapter, however, we're going to look at a few of the top offenders.

Redundancy

One of the most straightforward ways to reduce wordiness is simply to make sure that you do not use multiple words and phrases that have the same meaning.

Incorrect: Although the city of Troy, described by Homer in his epic poem *The Iliad*, was long believed to be **an imaginary city that did not exist**, recent excavations have revealed remains consistent with some of the locations depicted in the book.

By definition, an "imaginary city" is one that does not exist, and so it is unnecessary to specify that fact.

Better: Although the city of Troy, described by Homer in his epic poem *The Iliad*, was long believed to be **an imaginary city**, recent excavations have revealed remains consistent with some of the locations depicted in the book.

If we wanted to pare the sentence down even further, we could eliminate the repetition of *city*. In addition, a reader who knew that *The Iliad* was an epic poem would not need to be reminded of that fact.

> Even better: Although Troy, described by Homer in *The Iliad*, was long believed to be an imaginary city, recent excavations have revealed remains consistent with some of the locations depicted in the book.

Excessive repetition across sentences should also be avoided.

> In *The Great Gatsby*, Fitzgerald writes a story with **a main character that is considered "larger than life." This main character is considered "larger than life"** because he lives in a luxurious mansion, throws expensive parties, and **goes by the made-up name of Jay Gatsby.** Nick Carraway is the narrator who sees a different side of **this man that goes by the name of Jay Gatsby.** Nick sees **this man** as "great" aside from all his wealth and corruption.

When the repetition is eliminated, the paragraph becomes much cleaner and considerably easier to read.

> In *The Great Gatsby*, Fitzgerald writes a story with a main character that is **considered "larger than life"** because he lives in a luxurious mansion, throws expensive parties, and goes by the made-up name of Jay Gatsby. Nick Carraway is the narrator who sees a different side of **Gatsby.** Nick sees **this man** as "great" aside from all his wealth and corruption.

Another form of redundancy involves **over-explaining** or **defining** basic pieces of information. While knowing how to gauge a reader's level of background knowledge and adjust an explanation accordingly is a very real challenge for most student writers, some terms are so common that it can be safely assumed that readers will already be familiar with them.

> Wordy: Natural resources, **which are found within nature in their actual shape and form,** can be preserved through recycling.

It is fair to assume that most readers are familiar with the phrase "natural resources," and so the bolded phrase adds nothing to the sentence. In fact, it serves no purpose other than to give the impression that the writer is attempting to fill up space because s/he has nothing substantial to say about the topic.

> Concise: Natural resources can be preserved through recycling.

In this version, the writer simply states the thesis and can move on to the important work of supporting it.

Modifiers

Yet another common source of wordiness involves the use of lengthy modifiers. Often, it involves using multiple adjectives—often with very similar meanings—to create unnecessarily flowery and dramatic descriptions.

Wordy: Fate is **unquestionably and undeniably** the **most controlling** influence for Romeo and Juliet's **distressing tragedy**. (It is hard to imagine a non-distressing tragedy!)

Concise: Fate is **clearly the most important** element in Romeo and Juliet's tragedy.

These modifiers can also take the form of "that" or "what" clauses.

Wordy: George Orwell's novel *1984* is set in a society **that is dystopian** and where people can be tortured for thinking things **that are different** from **what the government allows**.

Concise: George Orwell's novel *1984* is set in a **dystopian society** where people can be tortured for thinking things **the government does not allow**.

You should also avoid devoting large swaths of text emphasizing the importance of the prompt or topic in an exaggerated way.

> For decades, the question of whether students should be taught grammar in school has been **one of the most significant controversies** for educators of English and Language Arts. While there are many inlets and outlets to this **most pressing of topics**, this **tedious yet ever important question** deserves to be considered with the **utmost seriousness**.

The paragraph above sounds like it was written by a college student trying desperately to sound like an adult (and win points with an instructor). In contrast, the version below sounds like it was actually written by an adult.

> The question of whether students should be taught grammar in school is a longstanding debate in American education. While the issue has been examined from many angles over the last several decades, it continues to merit further study.

Notice how much simpler and clearer the language is here; the writer simply introduces the topic without any fuss.

Exercise: Eliminating Redundancies

In the following sentences, identify and cross out any redundancy that appears. (Answers p. 292)

Example: When Alexander Fleming arrived in his laboratory one morning in 1928, he had no idea he was about to <u>permanently</u> alter the course of medical history ~~forever~~.

1. Economics is classified as and has been called a social science, one that is concerned with fair distribution, level of production, and the overall consumption of goods.

2. Although the students in the auditorium were silent throughout the entire lecture, the professor spoke so softly that his voice was nearly inaudible and could hardly be heard.

3. Scuba divers usually move around underwater by using fins attached to their feet, but external propulsion can be provided from an outside source by a specialized propulsion vehicle or a sled pulled from the surface.

4. Accused of purposefully neglecting to follow crucial steps in the laboratory's safety protocol, the researcher insisted that the oversight was inadvertent and accidental.

5. Faced with reports of a breaking scandal, company executives deliberately concealed the news from both shareholders and consumers on purpose because they feared the inevitable financial consequences.

6. Both the raw ingredients and distillation technology used by early perfumers significantly influenced and had an important effect on the development of chemistry.

7. The upper basin of Utah's Lake Powell provides a minimum annual flow of eight million tons of water each year to states across the Southwest.

8. Vietnam became independent from Imperial China in 938 A.D., with consecutive Vietnamese royal dynasties flourishing one after the other as the nation expanded geographically and politically.

9. Hydrothermal vents, fissures in a planet's surface from which heated water spurts, are commonly found near volcanoes and areas where tectonic plates diverge, coming apart from one another.

10. Historically, only a small number of educated elites were taught to write in the past, so written records tend to reflect the assumptions and values of a limited range of individuals.

Transitions

Very often, students rewrite transitional words and phrases such as *so*, *because*, and *in order to* in an excessively wordy manner, often because they believe doing so will make their writing sound more sophisticated. In most cases, however, the extra words end up weighing the writing down and making it harder for the reader to follow.

Wordy: Every year, modern cowboys hunt down thousands of wild stallions in the southwestern United States, **the reducing of the horse population to more sustainable levels being their goal**.

Concise: Every year, modern cowboys hunt down thousands of wild stallions in the southwestern United States **(in order) to reduce** the horse population to more sustainable levels.

Below are some common phrases in both their wordy and concise versions:

Wordy	Concise
Being that it was Due to the fact of it(s) being Because of it(s) being	Because it was
The reason is because Because x is the reason why	Because it was The reason is that
Despite its being In spite of it(s) being	Although it was
For the purpose of going	(In order) to go

Wordy: **Due to the fact of her being** a divorced woman whose academic qualifications did not even include a bachelor's degree, psychologist Melanie Klein (1882-1960) was an outsider within her profession.

Wordy: **Because** she was a divorced woman whose academic qualifications did not even include a bachelor's degree **is the reason why** psychologist Melanie Klein (1882-1960) was an outsider within her profession.

Concise: **Because** she was a divorced woman **(or: As a divorced woman)** whose academic qualifications did not even include a bachelor's degree, psychologist Melanie Klein (1882-1960) was an outsider within her profession.

Wordy: **In spite of its lacking** traditional circus elements such as animals and clowns, Cirque du Soleil is an exciting spectacle.

Concise: **Although it lacks** traditional circus elements such as animals and clowns, Cirque du Soleil is an exciting spectacle.

Good -ING, BAD -ING

As we saw in the previous section, *–ing* words tend to create constructions that are somewhat wordy and awkward. That does not mean, however, that these words should uniformly be avoided. On the contrary, there are many instances in which they are perfectly acceptable. But this is where the participle vs. gerund distinction becomes important.

Participles act as adjectives or modifiers. They can describe nouns and pronouns, and join clauses.

In the sentence below, for example, the participle *exciting* simply modifies the noun *spectacle*.

> Participle: Although it lacks traditional circus elements such as animals and clowns, Cirque du Soleil is an **exciting** spectacle.

Used this way, the *–ing* word functions as a normal adjective and is not a cause for concern.

Participles also begin participial phrases, joining clauses smoothly and providing stylistic variety.

> Correct: **Rejecting** a quiet life in Norway, Roald Amundsen chose to seek his fortune at sea and became the first person to reach both the North and South Poles.

> Correct: Artists are not frequently associated with domestic serenity, **making** literary families cells of both inspiration and psychological investigation.

Gerunds act as nouns, and they're a little more complicated than participles.

They are frequently used with possessive pronouns.

> Correct: I was irritated by <u>his</u> **whistling**.

They can also be used after object pronouns. Although this usage is commonly believed to be incorrect, it is in fact acceptable—it merely changes the emphasis.

> Correct: I was irritated by <u>him</u> **whistling**.

The first version places the focus on the whistling itself, whereas the second version places the focus on *him*.

When gerunds are present in short, isolated statements such as the ones above, there is nothing particularly wrong with them; rather, problems occur when gerunds are used as an alternative to verbs. In such cases, they often lead to wordy and ungrammatical constructions. Whenever possible, *subject + verb* should be used instead.

> Gerund: The renowned physicist's book has been praised **because of making** difficult concepts accessible to an audience with little mathematical knowledge.

> Verb: The renowned physicist's book has been praised **because it makes** difficult concepts accessible to an audience with little mathematical knowledge.

Another common problem involves using **a gerund in place of a standard noun or adjective form**.

Gerund: The **depicting** of everyday subjects in art has a long history, although scenes from daily life were often squeezed into the edges of compositions.

Noun: The **depiction** of everyday subjects in art has a long history, although scenes from daily life were often squeezed into the edges of compositions.

Gerund: In *The Great Gatsby*, the symbol of the green light is **deceiving** at first, tricking the reader into thinking it is merely a symbol of hope.

Adjective: In *The Great Gatsby*, the symbol of the green light is **deceptive** at first, tricking the reader into thinking it is merely a symbol of hope.

The second example is less problematic than the first, but this construction should still be used sparingly.

Although it is acceptable to use **gerunds as subjects**, this construction also facilitates the creation of wordy and awkward phrases. Frequently, these take the form of *acting as x is something that y does*.

Wordy: **Regarding** the citizens of Oceania as expendable **is something that** the totalitarian government in George Orwell's novel *1984* **does**.

Concise: The totalitarian government in George Orwell's novel *1984* **regards** the citizens of Oceania as expendable.

So When Is It Okay to Use a Gerund...?

When standard usage requires one

Incorrect: The Spanish city of Cádiz held the distinction **to be** the only city in continental Europe to survive a siege by Napoleon.

Correct: The Spanish city of Cádiz held the distinction **of being** the only city in continental Europe to survive a siege by Napoleon.

To preserve parallel structure

Incorrect: The panelists at the conference are responsible both for presenting original research and **they respond** to questions about its potential applications.

Correct: The panelists at the conference are responsible both for presenting original research and **for responding** to questions about its potential applications.

To indicate method or means

Transition: The nineteenth-century French novelist Gustave Flaubert reputedly sought to achieve stylistic perfection in his novels, **and he rewrote** each sentence ten times.

Gerund: The nineteenth-century French novelist Gustave Flaubert reputedly sought to achieve stylistic perfection in his novels **by rewriting** each sentence ten times.

Exercise: Eliminating Unnecessary Gerunds

Rewrite the underlined portion of each sentence to eliminate the gerund. (Answers p. 292)

Example: At the ceremony marking the opening of the Washington Monument, crowds gathered to see Dolly Madison <u>because of her being</u> one of the few remaining public figures from the Revolutionary era.

because she was

1. It can hardly be considered a surprise that Incan emperors covered themselves in gold <u>because of holding</u> themselves to be the sun's human incarnation.

2. The museum's artistic director has arranged the exhibition thematically <u>with the purpose of this being to provide</u> a new understanding of the multifaceted complexity of Native American life.

3. The music of Cuba has been perhaps the most popular form of world music since the <u>introducing</u> of recording technology in the early twentieth century.

4. <u>In spite of its being</u> a smaller city than either London or New York, Dublin possesses a thriving theater scene whose productions regularly achieve international renown.

5. Contrary to popular belief, it is a good idea to alternate rooms while studying because the <u>retaining</u> of information is improved when people change their environments.

6. <u>Due to the fact of her experimenting</u> with stream of consciousness narratives and the underlying psychological motives of her characters, Woolf is considered a major innovator in English literature.

    _____

7. Although an array of government policies aim to support entrepreneurs through grants and tax breaks that facilitate the <u>acquiring</u> of capital, startup companies usually turn to private financing.

    _____

8. In scientific fields, scale models known as homunculi are often used <u>for the purpose of illustrating</u> physiological characteristics of the human body.

    _____

9. *Prince Jellyfish*, an unpublished novel by Hunter S. Thompson, was rejected by a number of literary agents <u>due to the fact of its lacking</u> popular appeal.

    _____

10. Astronaut Mae Jemison's <u>rejecting</u> of a career in ballet followed her decision to study engineering at Stanford University.

    _____

Passive Voice

In the **active** voice, the subject precedes the object. The emphasis is on the performer of the action.

William Shakespeare	wrote	Hamlet.
subject	**verb**	**object**

In the **passive** voice, the subject and the object are flipped: *x does y* becomes *y is done by x*. The emphasis is on the object of the action.

Hamlet	was written	by	William Shakespeare.
subject	**verb**	**preposition**	**object**

Compare the following sentences:

Active	Passive
Jamal **drinks** the water.	The water **is drunk by** Jamal.
The students in Professor Garcia's chemistry class **conducted** an experiment yesterday.	An experiment **was conducted by** the students in Professor Garcia's chemistry class yesterday.
A lack of concern for workers' environments **causes** some tensions between bosses and their employees.	Some tensions between bosses and their employees **are caused by** a lack of concern for workers' environments.

To form the passive in any given tense, flip the subject and the object. Then, conjugate *to be* in the appropriate tense, add the past participle of the main verb, and insert the word *by*. For example:

Active: **He will write the play.**

He is the subject, so it becomes the object (*him*) and is placed at the end of the sentence, along with *by*.

The play is the object, so it becomes the subject and is placed at the beginning of the sentence.

The sentence is in the future, so *to be* becomes *will be*, and the past participle (*written*) is added.

Passive: **The play will be written by him.**

"Half passive" constructions omit the word *by*, e.g., *Hamlet was written*.

A form of the verb *to be* can never be omitted, however.

Incorrect: *Hamlet* **written** by William Shakespeare.

Correct: *Hamlet* **was written** by William Shakespeare.

The following chart lists active vs. passive constructions in all of the major tenses.

Tense	Active	Passive
Present	We play the game.	The game is played by us.
Present Perfect	We have played the game.	The game has been played by us.
Past	We played the game.	The game was played by us.
Future	We will play the game.	The game will be played by us.
Future Perfect	We will have played the game.	The game will have been played by us.
Conditional	We would play the game.	The game would be played by us.
Past Conditional	We would have played the game.	The game would have been played by us.

Important: the passive should not be confused with the (active) present perfect tense, which is formed by combining *has* or *have* with a past participle. Unlike the passive, this construction does not include *by* or a form of *to be*.

Pres. Perfect: The students **have studied** two Shakespeare plays this year.

Passive: Two Shakespeare plays **have been studied** by the students this year.

Exercise: Active or Passive?

Determine whether each of the following sentences is active or passive. Underline any passive construction. (Answers p. 292)

1. Throughout the novel, the tapestry of local history is combined with more current themes by the author.

    Active   **Passive**

2. In the early 1920s, the music industry was already well on its way to becoming a major business because it was generating millions of dollars.

    Active   **Passive**

3. Robert Cornelius, an early American photographer, has been credited by historians of photography with taking the first selfie.

    Active   **Passive**

4. New research indicates that certain personal care products, such as shampoos and skin lotions, are a significant source of chemicals that contribute to urban air pollution.

    Active   **Passive**

5. As the crop varieties grown around the world have shrunk to just a handful of foods, regional and local crops have become scarce or disappeared altogether.

    Active   **Passive**

6. Contrary to popular myth, cities such as Syracuse and Troy were not named after their ancient counterparts by the land surveyor Simeon DeWitt.

    Active   **Passive**

7. Many of the items in the Grimms' first edition of fairy tales were taken not from a single source but from other pre-existing collections of stories.

   Active   **Passive**

8. The renowned contralto Marian Anderson was offered numerous contracts by opera companies, but she repeatedly declined because she preferred to appear in concert and recital only.

   Active   **Passive**

9. Over the past several decades, long-distance running has dramatically increased in popularity: the number of finishers in all US marathons has grown from fewer than 300,000 in 1995 to more than 500,000 in 2016.

   Active   **Passive**

10. The geologic instability known as the Pacific Ring of Fire has produced numerous faults, and approximately 10,000 earthquakes are caused by them annually.

    Active   **Passive**

Because passive constructions are by definition wordier than active ones, the indiscriminate use of them can create some very inelegant statements. As a result, the passive voice is commonly treated as something of a grammatical punching bag; some guides go so far as to offer what amounts to a blanket prohibition against it.

That said, there is nothing inherently wrong with it, and there are times when passive constructions do not pose a problem. **As a general rule, the passive voice is acceptable when it serves to emphasize that a person or object is on the receiving end of the action**; otherwise, the active voice should be the default.

For example, compare the following two statements.

Active: Shakespeare wrote *Hamlet* sometime between 1599 and 1602.

Passive: Hamlet was written sometime between 1599 and 1602.

In this case, the active version is not necessarily superior to the passive; the passive construction simply places the emphasis on the action of the writing itself. If the passive version were to appear, for example, in the context of an essay asserting that Shakespeare was not the true author of the plays normally attributed to him (a theory that has found a range of supporters over the centuries), it would be perfectly appropriate.

The passive can also be useful for describing a general situation.

Acceptable: The musician **is admired** for his ability to make instruments from a wide range of common objects.

It is also used to create impersonal constructions, or to imply a lack of responsibility.

Active: The company promised that **it would offer** compensation to those affected by the oil spill.

Passive: The company promised that **compensation would be offered** to those affected by the oil spill.

By saying that compensation *would be offered*, the company subtly downplays its responsibility. In contrast, the active statement implies that the company is stepping forward to accept responsibility.

The **overuse of passive constructions** can, however, seriously interfere with clarity and readability. Consider the sentence below.

Passive: In 1997, the internet **was accessed by** most users **by** the slow and inconvenient dial-up method; broadband connections **were had by** only a few homes.

This sentence contains multiple passive constructions, which bog the sentence down. Compare it to the active version, which is much easier to absorb.

Active: In 1997, **most users accessed the internet** by the slow and inconvenient dial-up method; only a few homes had broadband connections.

Now let's take a look at something longer:

> In George Orwell's *1984*, Big Brother **is** **utilized** **by** **the author** to showcase the immense power and influence the government has over its subordinates. The citizens of Oceania **are** **oppressed** **by** **the government**, **by** **which they** **are** **controlled** through fear, constant surveillance, and deprivation of knowledge. This is to prevent them from having ideas or behaviors that **are** **not permitted** **by** **the people in power**. Citizens **are** **expected** **by** **the government** to live as respectful Party members, forcefully having to dedicate their lives to serving Big Brother.

The above paragraph is absolutely jam-packed with passive constructions that serve the sole purpose of filling up space. This is exactly the kind of writing that gets students in trouble.

Compare it to the active version:

> In George Orwell's *1984*, **the author utilizes** Big Brother to showcase the immense power and influence the government has over its subordinates. The **government of Oceania oppresses its citizens** and controls them through fear, constant surveillance, and deprivation of knowledge. This is to prevent them from having ideas or behaviors that **the people in power do not permit**. **Citizens are expected** to live as respectful Party members, forcefully having to dedicate their lives to serving Big Brother.

Note that the last sentence remains half-passive. In this case, it makes sense to leave one such construction as a deliberate stylistic choice: the passive voice serves to emphasize the citizens' powerlessness—they are on the receiving end of the action in the most literal sense.

Exercise: Making Sentences Active

For the following sentences, rewrite passive constructions as active ones, or, if necessary, make active constructions passive. Note that some sentences may need to be substantially rearranged. (Answers p. 293)

Example: The risk of heart disease may be reduced by tai chi because its effects include decreasing levels of harmful triglycerides while increasing levels of "good" HDL cholesterol.

Tai chi may reduce the risk of heart disease because its effects include decreasing levels of

harmful triglycerides while increasing levels of "good" HDL cholesterol.

1. Only a handful of poems were published by Elizabeth Bishop during the course of her career, but each one was a model of perfection.

2. In the movie *The Killing Fields*, Cambodian photojournalist Dith Pran portrayed by first-time actor Haing S. Ngor, a role for which Ngor won an Academy Award.

3. Although paleontologists often find new dinosaur bones or footprints, the two types of fossils have not been found together by researchers until recently.

4. *Nereus*, a remotely operated underwater hybrid vehicle, was designed by scientists at the Woods Hole Oceanographic Institute to function at depths of up to 36,000 feet.

    _____

    _____

5. In the recent consumer report, it was indicated by market researchers that food prices in economically depressed neighborhoods are frequently higher than in wealthier ones.

    _____

    _____

6. The demand for foreign-language instruction has been acknowledged by the government, but funding for classes continues to be reduced.

    _____

    _____

7. Between the late 1970s and 1980s, nine albums were recorded by the Jamaican reggae musician Lone Ranger, born Anthony Alphanso Waldron.

    _____

    _____

8. Time Lapse Dance, a New York-based dance company whose mission is to provide modern reinterpretations of classic works, was founded by performance artist Jody Sperling in 2000.

    _____

    _____

9.   Murtabak, a dish composed of mutton, garlic, egg, onion, and curry sauce, is frequently eaten by people throughout the Middle East, Singapore, and Indonesia.

_____

_____

10.   Over the last several decades, many forms of meditation have been examined by researchers, and a number of them have been deemed ineffective.

_____

_____

Chapter Twenty-Five

Idioms and Diction

The term *diction* simply refers to a writer's choice of words. Diction errors involve words that are incorrect for a given situation, either because they have the wrong meaning or connotation, or because they are not **idiomatic** — that is, they do not obey the rules of standard written English.

Preposition-Based Idioms

Certain verbs and nouns must be followed by specific prepositions. **These idioms are not correct or incorrect for any logical reason; they simply reflect the fact that certain phrases have evolved to become standard usage.**

Incorrect: A familiarity **in** Latin is useful for anyone who wishes to pursue serious study of a modern Romance language.

Correct: A familiarity **with** Latin is useful for anyone who wishes to pursue serious study of a modern Romance language.

It is also incorrect to use a preposition where none is necessary.

Incorrect: Students have been **criticizing about** the administration's decision to begin classes half an hour earlier on most days.

Correct: Students have been **criticizing** the administration's decision to begin classes half an hour earlier on most days.

When two verbs require different prepositions, a separate preposition must follow each verb.

Incorrect: Gatsby tries to show to Daisy how rich he is, hoping that she will **approve** and be impressed **by** his lifestyle.

Correct: Gatsby tries to show to Daisy how rich he is, hoping that she will **approve of** and be impressed **by** his lifestyle.

A few common school-related errors to be aware of:

One does well or poorly **in** a subject.

Incorrect: I'm really happy for my friend: he got an A **on** Biology this semester.

Correct: I'm really happy for my friend: he got an A **in** Biology this semester.

One does well or poorly **on** a test.

Incorrect: I'm really happy for my friend: he scored a 97 **in** his test.

Correct: I'm really happy for my friend: he scored a 97 **on** his test.

One learns something **in** or **at** school.

Correct: We learned **in** school/**at** school today that Galileo was arrested for proposing that the earth revolved around the sun.

But one studies **at** (that is, attends) a school, college, or university.

Incorrect: My dream is to study **in** Harvard University.

Correct: My dream is to study **at** Harvard University.

This error is most likely due to the fact that most universities outside the United States are named after the cities in which they are located; thus, one can acceptably say *I want to study in Cambridge*, meaning that one wants to study in the city of Cambridge. This preposition, however, should not be used with actual university names.

And a note about *on*.

Recently, *on* has come to serve as a sort of all-purpose term that substitutes for a variety of prepositions, including *about*, *of*, and *for*. While some of these constructions are almost certainly here to stay, there are situations in which *on* is simply more ambiguous or less elegant than the standard preposition.

Informal	Better
Analysis on Critique on Disappointed on Discussion on A point on Review on Wait on*	Analysis of Critique of Disappointed at/about Discussion about/of A point about/regarding Review of Wait for
Wait on means "serve."	

Preposition-Based Idioms

Be curious about
Be particular about
Bring about
Complain about
Have qualms about
Set (ab)out
Think about
Wonder about
Worry about

Known as/to be
Recognized as
Serve as
Translate as

Accompanied by
Amazed by
Assisted by
Awed by
Confused by
Encouraged by
Followed by
Impressed by
Obscured by
Outraged by
Perplexed by
Puzzled by
Shocked by
Stunned by
Surprised by

Aptitude for
Celebrated for
Compensate for
Criticize for
Endure for
Famous for
Known for
Last for
Look (out) for
Named for/after
Necessary for
Prized for
Recognized for
Responsible for
Strive for
Wait for
Watch for

Across from
Apparent from
Defend from/against
Differ(ent) from
Draw inspiration from
Protect from/against
Refrain from

In itself

Adept in/at
Confident in
Engage in/with
Firm in
Interested in
Involved in
Succeed in/at
Take pride in

Enter into
Insight into

A native of
Analysis of
Appreciation of
Aware of
Characteristic of
Command of
Composed of
Consist of
Convinced of
Devoid of
(Dis)approve of
Family of
In recognition of
In the hope(s) of
(In)capable of
Knowledge of
Mastery of
Offer of
Principles of
Proponent of
Review of
Source of
Suspicious of
Take advantage of
Typical of

Understanding of
Use of
With the exception of

Based on
Confer on
Depend on
Draw (up)on
Dwell on
Focus on
Insist on
Reflect on
Rely on

Control over
Power over

Accepted to
Central to
Critical to
Devoted to
Explain to
Exposed to
In contrast to
Listen to
Native to
Point to
Prefer x to y
Recommend x to y
Relate to
Similar to
Threat(en) to
Unique to

Biased toward
Tendency toward

Take up

Contrast with
Correlate with
Identify with
(In)consistent with
(Pre)occupied with
Sympathize with
(Un)familiar with

To vs. –ING

Some verbs must be followed by the *to* form, while others must be followed by the *–ing* form.

Incorrect: Even brief exposure to words associated with money seems to cause people to become more independent and less inclined **in helping** others.

Correct: Even brief exposure to words associated with money seems to cause people to become more independent and less inclined **to help** others.

Sometimes, both forms are acceptable (although the infinitive tends to sound cleaner).

Correct: Although business titans and labor leaders were quickly able to negotiate a contract, workers soon <u>began</u> **to protest** the specifications of the agreement.

Correct: Although business titans and labor leaders were quickly able to negotiate a contract, workers soon <u>began</u> **protesting** the specifications of the agreement.

Exercise: Preposition-Based and TO/-ING Idioms

In the following sentences, identify and correct any error in the use of preposition, infinitives or -ING words. Some of the sentences may not contain an error. (Answers p. 293)

Example: In contrast ~~with~~ household surveys, store surveys can be used to compare prices of equivalent items across many different locations and types of stores.

1. In *The Odyssey*, certain characters are granted with the ability to make decisions for themselves, while others must confront fate and divine intervention.

2. As Secretary-General of the United Nations, Kofi Annan became a strong proponent for diplomatic intervention in humanitarian crises.

3. Although the author's diaries provide a wealth of information about her daily interests, they fail presenting a comprehensive picture of her life.

4. Over the last few decades, acceptance rates at many prestigious universities have sharply declined: only about 5-10% of students who apply to Ivy League universities are accepted in those schools, for example.

5. The Industrial Revolution, which began toward the end of the eighteenth century, marked the start of the modern era in both Europe and the United States.

6. Although it is indisputable that different people display varying levels of aptitude toward different subjects, academic abilities are most likely shaped by a complex interplay of genetic and cultural factors.

7. The choreographer Alvin Ailey, who integrated traditional African movements into his works, is credited to popularize modern dance.

8. A rebellion from the rigid academic art that predominated during the nineteenth century, the Art Nouveau movement was inspired by natural forms and structures.

9. Unlike his contemporaries, whose work he viewed as conventional and uninspiring, Le Corbusier insisted to use modern industrial techniques to construct buildings.

10. Both bizarre and familiar, fairy tales are intended to be spoken aloud rather than read silently, and they possess a truly inexhaustible power on children and adults alike.

11. The mineral azurite, a mineral produced by the weathering of copper deposits, has an exceptionally deep blue hue and thus has historically been associated to the color of winter skies.

12. Teachers have begun to note with alarm that the amount of time their students spend to play video games and surfing the Internet has severely impacted their ability to focus on single tasks for an extended period.

13. During the early decades of Japan's Heian Empire, a person who lacked a thorough knowledge on Chinese could never be considered fully educated.

14. Created in Jamaica during the late 1960s, reggae music emerged from a number of sources that ranged from traditional African songs and chants to contemporary jazz and blues.

15. In "Howl" as well as in his other poetry, Allen Ginsberg drew inspiration by the epic, free-verse style popularized by the nineteenth century poet Walt Whitman.

Commonly Confused Words

As an unwieldy mix of Germanic and Latinate languages, English has acquired many sets of words that are spelled differently and have different meanings, but that are pronounced the same. Such words are called **homophones**.

Incorrect: The **heroin** of Jane Austen's novel *Pride and Prejudice* is Elizabeth Bennet, a young woman who learns the consequences of judging people too quickly.

Correct: The **heroine** of Jane Austen's novel *Pride and Prejudice* is Elizabeth Bennet, a young woman who learns the consequences of judging people too quickly.

Heroin is an illegal substance; a *heroine*, on the other hand, is a female protagonist.

Unfortunately, there is no trick to learning homophone pairs; you must simply memorize which version of a word has a particular definition. Even more unfortunately, spell-check might not save you: if you type in a term that has the wrong meaning, there's no guarantee your computer will notice.

English contains dozens of homophone pairs, but the list on p. 254 targets some terms that are particularly likely to find their way into papers and other classwork. First, though, we're going to look at two of the very top offenders. (For confusion involving pronouns, e.g., *it's* vs. *its*, see Chapter 12.)

Affect vs. Effect

This set is exceptionally confusing because each word in the pair can function as both a verb and a noun.

Affect is most often used as a verb meaning "to influence," or "to have an effect on."

Correct: Consumer advocates caution that even seemingly low error rates in credit score calculations can **affect** millions of customers.

Less often, it is used as a verb meaning "to put on" or "to adopt in a pretentious manner."

Correct: Voiceover work often requires that quiz-show champion Arthur Chu **affect** a Chinese accent rather than speak in his naturally meticulous English.

Finally, it can be used as a noun meaning "outward expression of emotion."

Correct: According to researchers, the flat **affect** seen in some patients is characterized by an unchanging facial expression and a lack of response to external stimuli.

Effect is most often used as a noun meaning "an impact."

Correct: Benjamin Franklin collaborated on numerous studies demonstrating the protective **effects** of smallpox inoculation.

Less often, it is used as a verb meaning "to bring about a change."

Correct: Over the last few decades, the rise of e-commerce giants such as Amazon and eBay has **effected** enormous changes in consumers' shopping habits.

Lie vs. Lay

Lie – recline or remain; not followed by a noun or pronoun (direct object)
Lay – set down; followed by a noun or pronoun.

If you want to use this pair of words correctly, you must learn the chart below.

Infinitive	Simple Past	Past Participle
Lie	Lay	Lain
Lay	Laid	Laid

To determine whether *lie* or *lay* should be used, check to see whether the verb is followed by a direct object (noun or pronoun). If it isn't, then *lie* is the correct verb.

Correct: Some bacteria spores can **lie** dormant in soil for centuries because they have so thoroughly adapted to extreme weather conditions that neither intense heat nor bitter cold is capable of destroying them.

Since *dormant* is not a (pro)noun, *lie* is correct.

Now consider this sentence:

Correct: Ancient communities created the first bridges by taking planks from fallen trees and **laying** them across ravines and small bodies of water.

Because the verb is followed by the (object) pronoun *them*, the correct form is *laying*.

Unfortunately, things get a bit more complicated. Although *lie* and *lay* look and sound different in the present tense, the simple past of *lie* is also *lay*.

Correct: The bacteria spores **lay** dormant in the soil for centuries, having adapted so thoroughly to extreme weather conditions that neither intense heat nor bitter cold was capable of destroying them.

The **past participle** of *lie* (used after any form of *to be* or *to have*) is *lain*:

Correct: The bacteria spores **had lain** dormant in the soil for centuries, having adapted so thoroughly to extreme weather conditions that neither intense heat nor bitter cold was capable of destroying them.

In contrast, the **simple past** and **past participle** of *lay* are the same: *laid*.

Correct: Ancient communities created the first bridges when they took planks from fallen trees and **laid** them across ravines and small bodies of water.

Correct: Ancient communities created the first bridges when they took planks from fallen trees and, having **laid** them across ravines and small bodies of water, proceeded to walk across.

Commonly Confused Words

A part – n., a section or portion **Apart** – adj., adv., separate from	**Elicit** – v., to draw out **Illicit** – adj., illegal, not permitted
Adapt – v., to change for a new situation **Adopt** – v., to take as one's own	**Eminent** – adj., famous, renowned **Imminent** – adj., about to occur, unavoidable
Adverse – adj., difficult, challenging **Averse** – adj., having a strong dislike for	**Farther** – adv., used for physical distances **Further** – adv., used for discussions and situations
Advice – n., counsel **Advise** – v., to give advice	**Home (in)** – v., to zero in on **Hone** – v., to refine or sharpen
Allusion – n., a reference **Illusion** – n., something not real	**Imply** – v., to suggest; what an author does **Infer** – v., to draw a conclusion; what a reader does
Ambiguous – adj., unclear, subject to interpretation **Ambivalent** – adj., having mixed feelings	**Lead** – v., to show the way; n., a heavy element **Led** – v., simple past form of *lead*
Ascent/Descent – n., going up/down **Assent/Dissent** – n., agreement/disagreement	**Loose** – adj., the opposite of tight **Lose** – v., the opposite of win
Assure – v., to state positively and confidently **Ensure** – v., to make certain something will happen	**Persecute** – v., to harass or threaten **Prosecute** – v., to try someone in court
Capital – n., (1) main city; (2) money, funds **Capitol** – n., building occupied by a state legislature	**Perspective** – n., point of view **Prospective** – adj., potential
Cite – v., to attribute **Sight** – n., the ability to see; **Site** – n., location	**Principal** – adj., most important **Principle** – n., rule
Complement – n., something needed to make whole **Compliment** – n., kind words	**Precede** – v., to come before (pre = before) **Proceed** – v., to move along
Comprehensible – adj., understandable **Comprehensive** – adj., thorough, complete	**Simple** – adj., uncomplicated **Simplistic** – adj., superficial, overly simplified
Council – n., legislative group **Counsel** – v., to advise	**Tenant** – n., inhabitant of a dwelling **Tenet** – n., rule or principle
Discreet – adj., modest, not showy or flashy **Discrete** – adj., separate, distinct	**Use** – employ for a purpose **Utilize*** – put to an unintended use
Disinterested – adj., objective **Uninterested** – adj., not interested	**Waive** – v., dispense with, give up **Wave** – n., raise a hand in greeting

*The overuse of *utilize* as a replacement for *use* almost invariably comes off as pretentious. Try *employ* as an alternative.

Exercise: Commonly Confused Words

In the following sentences, correct any errors in spelling or usage. Some of the sentences may not contain an error. (Answers p. 294)

Example: The French Revolution of 1830, also known as the July Revolution, saw the overthrow of King Charles X and the ~~assent~~ of his cousin Louis-Philippe to the throne.
        ascent

1. To attract perspective students, the university has planned a series of lectures and open houses designed to exhibit its wide variety of academic programs and newly renovated facilities.

2. Although many traits are governed by a group of genes acting in concert, genes often have multiple functions, and altering a large amount of genetic material could have unforeseen affects on an organism.

3. Some global banks show an alarming willingness to facilitate the flow of illegal money; in certain cases, they even council financial institutions about how to evade regulators' grasp.

4. High-pressure sales practices by industry representatives have lead to predictions that regulators will increase oversight and prompted speculation about potential lawsuits.

5. The physics professor was awarded the university's top teaching award because of her ability to make a difficult subject unusually comprehensive to her students.

6. Nijinsky's genius as a dancer lay in his capacity to express through movement the emotions and subtleties of thoughts that others could express only through speech.

7. Early hearing aids were far from discrete: large and bulky, they required heavy batteries that had to be charged frequently and were frustrating for users.

8. Encouraged by his party's wins in recent state polls, the opposition leader has been putting pressure on the prime minister to wave interest on certain loans.

9. Intended to ease traffic and reduce air pollution, ride-sharing companies such as Uber and Lyft were founded as compliments to public transportation.

10. Government leaders and elected officials must take all the relevant parties' needs into account when attempting to address problems that effect the ability of different groups to live peacefully together.

11. Knowing the farmer who grows your food has become an important tenant of the modern agricultural movement, but little attention is paid to the people who actually pick the crops.

12. Istanbul was virtually depopulated when it fell to the Ottoman Turks, but the city recovered rapidly and by the mid-1600s had become the world's largest city as well as the new capitol of the Ottoman Empire.

13. The Free Basics service, a Facebook program that provides free access to certain online services, has drawn the ire of critics who insist that it runs contrary to principles of internet neutrality.

14. The large police presence at the international summit has had a chilling affect on protesters, even though it is unclear why such tight security measures are necessary.

15. One of the more frustrating aspects of the film is that its main character seems either incapable of or disinterested in conjuring traditional levels of empathy and self-awareness.

Connotation

"Connotation" refers to what a word implies, as opposed to what it literally states (i.e., **denotes**). Sometimes, words with the same literal meaning have different connotations that make them (in)appropriate in certain situations.

For example, the word *exhaust* literally means "to become very tired." Synonyms for it include *weaken*, *fatigue*, and *tire (out)*. In some situations, any of these options might be perfectly acceptable. For example, we could say *the patient grew exhausted*, or *the patient grew fatigued*, or *the patient grew tired*. Although they have slightly different implications, they are all idiomatically correct.

Now, however, consider the use of *exhaust* in the sentence below.

> Correct: Less than a year after they arrived on Roanoke Island, off the coast of North Carolina, Captain Ralph Lane and 108 colonists had **exhausted** their supplies and were forced to return to England.

In this case, *exhaust* has a very specific connotation: to "exhaust" supplies means to use them up completely. This is an idiomatic usage, and so *exhaust* cannot be replaced by another word with the same literal meaning. *Weaken, fatigue*, and *tire* would not be idiomatic here.

In other cases, a word may have the correct connotation but be used in an ungrammatical way.

> Incorrect: Throughout my internship, I valued the opportunity to work as part of a team and in a rapidly expanding media field because I felt that I was able to make important contributions while **progressing** my technical and personal skills.

It's clear what the writer intends to say here: his or her technical skills got better during the internship.

The problem is that people can *progress in* their ability to do something, but they cannot actually *progress* something. This is not a matter of style; the grammar is just wrong. The correct verb is *improve*.

> Correct: Throughout my internship, I valued the opportunity to work as part of a team and in a rapidly expanding media field because I felt that I was able to make important contributions while **improving** my technical and personal skills.

In addition, connotation often becomes a problem when new, challenging vocabulary words are involved. Although you may understand the literal definition, you may not have encountered the word sufficiently often to have a strong sense of how it is actually used. For example, consider the following sentence:

> Incorrect: In George Orwell's novel *1984*, the totalitarian government uses Big Brother to **streamline** the minds of its citizens so that they will be unable to think for themselves.

The word *streamline* means "make smoother or more efficient." On one hand, it's not an illogical choice of words: the writer clearly wants to imply that the totalitarian government in *1984* uses Big Brother to shape its citizens' minds and make them more compliant by ensuring they'll no longer need to think.

The problem in this case, however, is that the word doesn't have quite the right connotation. It's really a term used to describe processes or systems — it doesn't apply to things like government control.

In addition, *streamline* is almost always used in a positive context, to indicate that something became easier or required less effort to accomplish. That contrasts sharply with the distinctively negative context here.

Consider some alternatives:

Better: In George Orwell's novel *1984*, the totalitarian government uses Big Brother to **brainwash** its citizens so that they will be unable to think for themselves.

Better: In George Orwell's novel *1984*, the totalitarian government uses Big Brother to **warp** the minds of its citizens so that they will be unable to think for themselves.

In contrast to *streamline*, both *brainwash* and *warp* are clearly negative and more accurately convey the government's desire to achieve complete control over its citizens.

One more example:

Statistics show that an average of 27% of full-time college students who attend a four-year university actually graduate on time. This information was obtained from the website Complete College, where **an aggregate of states joined together** to make visible the declining rate of on-time graduations for different levels of post-high school education.

Clearly, the writer used the term *aggregate* in an attempt to sound more sophisticated, but it actually has the opposite effect. By definition, an aggregate is a group of people/organizations that have joined together, and so the phrase *aggregate of states joined together* is redundant as well as indicative of the fact that the writer does not really understand the connotation of the term. Although it may seem overly simple, the word *group* would actually have been a much better option here.

The moral of the story: Be careful when you use big words, especially ones you don't have a lot of experience with. Don't just go on thesaurus.com and pick some fancy terms at random. You're much better off with simpler ones you know how to use for sure.

Exercise: Connotation

In the following sentences, determine whether the underlined word is properly used. If not, provide a synonym (word or phrase) with the correct connotation. If necessary, you can use a thesaurus. (Suggested answers p. 295)

Example: Archaeologists have made a discovery that they hope could help ~~unfold~~ one of the most eunduring mysteries of ancient Peru: how to read the knotted string records kept by the Incas.

_____**unravel**_____

1. Foreign policies are known to change radically from one year to the next; the Cold War is perhaps the greatest testament to the <u>instantaneous</u> nature of international relations and foreign policy.

    _____

2. The prospect of free education does sound rather <u>obliging</u> for students planning to pursue higher education, but college still comes at a price for the government and teachers working for institutions.

    _____

3. Since the release of the Common Core State Standards, many issues in education have been called to the public's attention, and great debates have <u>derived</u>.

    _____

4. Because the benefits of free trade <u>oversee</u> its drawbacks, our society would ultimately be better off with free trade.

    _____

5. In his article "Don't Blame the Eater," David Zinczenko claims that he was overweight as a teenager because he only had fast food at his <u>disposal</u>.

    _____

6.   At the beginning of *The Odyssey*, Telemachus is completely unlike his father, but that situation quickly <u>overturns</u> when Telemachus begins to become an adult.

       _____

7.   Since the <u>inception</u> of the American children's literature industry in the 1820s, publishers have had to grapple with the question of who their primary audience should be.

       _____

8.   Some scientists believe there is no adequate alternative to animal testing, but new <u>enrichments</u> in medical research are providing options that would have been impossible just a few years ago.

       _____

9.   Many people do not take recycling seriously because they are poorly informed about the subject and do not consider it a <u>pressing</u> matter.

       _____

10.   Contrary to popular opinion, the employment of children in the early Industrial Revolution was not <u>ceased</u> by the Factory Acts; rather, they simply sped up a process of technological change that was making child labor obsolete.

       _____

Miscellaneous

Several

This word means "a few" — it should not be used as a synonym for *many*.

Incorrect: **Several** battles were fought during the course of World War II.

Correct: **Numerous** battles were fought during the course of World War II.

The Aforementioned

This term is an adjective and should precede a noun; it should not be used in isolation.

Correct: At 6.29 percent, Spain's interest rate is higher than those of Microsoft (4.83%), Wal-Mart (5.16%), and Verizon (5.49%). Investors have also signaled their skepticism toward the Greek economy by offering it an interest rate of 10.79%, roughly double the rate of any of the **aforementioned** <u>corporations</u>.

X is Because

An event can "begin" or "occur" or "take place" — it cannot "be because."

Awkward: <u>The beginning of the environmental movement</u> **was because** marine biologist Rachel Carson's book *Silent Spring* revealed the dangers of pesticides.

Clear: <u>The environmental movement</u> **began** when marine biologist Rachel Carson's book *Silent Spring* revealed the dangers of pesticides.

Alternatives to the Word *Say*

One thing to avoid when you are citing sources is the excessive repetition of the verb *says* (or *states*). Using a variety of synonyms for these terms is a relatively easy way to make your writing more engaging.

- Analyzes
- Argues
- Asserts
- Challenges
- Claims
- Contends
- Conveys
- Criticizes
- Critiques
- Debates
- Defends
- Depicts
- Deplores
- Describes
- Emphasizes
- Evokes
- Explores
- Expresses
- Implies
- Insists
- Invokes
- Laments
- Narrates
- Portrays
- Questions
- Rebukes
- Recounts
- Relates
- Relays
- Reinforces
- Reiterates
- Stresses
- Suggests
- Relates
- Tells
- Underlines

Chapter Twenty-Six

Register and Tone

Register refers to how **formal** or **informal** a writer's language is.

The type of language you use when talking to or texting your friends is most likely very different from the language you use when writing a paper for school. In the former situations, you're likely to speak **casually**, using slang phrases such as *really cool/really awesome* or *lots of stuff*, or to use abbreviations such as l8, LOL, or r u ok? If you were writing a paper, however, you'd be much more likely to employ **moderately formal language** and to use phrases such as *extremely interesting* or *many different possibilities*.

You also wouldn't—or at least shouldn't—write things like *a plethora of enthralling objects*. Used selectively and precisely, "ten-dollar words" are perfectly acceptable, but if you're just showing off, chances are you'll make it harder for readers to follow what you're actually saying. (Unless you read nonstop and have a phenomenal vocabulary, there's also a good chance that you will misuse words and end up sounding pretty silly.)

Roots

As discussed earlier, English is a hybrid language, half Germanic (Anglo-Saxon) and half Latin. Latin was the traditional language of the elite, and so words derived from it came to be associated with a more formal register. In contrast, words with Germanic roots tend to be associated with a more informal register.

This phenomenon can be observed particularly clearly in verbs: **phrasal verbs** (verb + preposition, e.g., *get in, take off, check out*) invariably have German roots.

In contrast, verbs ending in *–act, –ate, –ect, –el, –ire, –ize,* and *–ve* (e.g., *react, create, elect, propel, desire, criticize, revive*) are almost always derived from Latin. One way to make your writing more formal is to replace phrasal verbs with their single-word counterparts.

Informal: Forensic biology has been used to **check into** collisions between birds and wind turbines.

Formal: Forensic biology has been used to **investigate** collisions between birds and wind turbines.

Nouns can be similarly divided. Words ending in –*d*, –*f*, –*k*, –*t*, –*th*, –*ght*, and –*st* (e.g., *land, bluff, stock, hilt, truth, thought*) are often derived from Anglo-Saxon and considered more casual. Notice that these words are often short and blunt. In contrast, terms ending in –*a/ence*, –(*t*)*ion*, –*ity*, and –*ment* (e.g., *chance, notion, conformity, placement*) are typically derived from Latin or French, and are considered more elevated.

Informal: Immediately after liftoff, the rocket began moving at a very high **speed**.

Formal: Immediately after liftoff, the rocket began moving at a very high **velocity**.

Modifiers

Another common register problem area involves **modifiers** or **qualifiers** such as *totally, pretty,* and *completely*. While some of the less formal terms below may occasionally be appropriate, they quickly lose their impact and make writing seem immature.

Less Formal	More Formal
Kind of	Mildly
Sort of	Slightly
Pretty	Somewhat
A lot	Relatively
Completely	Quite
Incredibly	Firmly
Totally	Strongly
	Heavily
	Highly
	Entirely
	Exceedingly
	Extremely
	Remarkably
	Thoroughly
	Utterly

Informal: The Elizabethans **totally believed** in fate.

Better: The Elizabethans **firmly believed** in fate.

Informal: Romeo and Juliet's parents' fighting encourages the protagonists **to do some pretty risky things** so that they can still see each other.

Better: Romeo and Juliet's parents' fighting encourages the protagonists **to take a number of serious risks** so that they can still see each other.

Informal: Gatsby is looking to forget this burden on his plans by **totally** disregarding it and **completely** moving on with no remorse or regret.

Better: Gatsby is looking to forget this burden on his plans by **thoroughly** disregarding it and ~~**completely**~~ moving on with no remorse or regret.

This x of His/Hers

Another common construction that frequently makes its way into papers is *this x of his/hers*. In addition to being wordy and awkward, it is also too informal. Use *his/her + noun* instead.

Informal: Gatsby is looking to forget **this burden of his** by disregarding it and moving on with no remorse or regret.

Better: Gatsby is looking to forget **his burden** by disregarding it and moving on with no remorse or regret.

Hyperbole and Qualification

If you look at the chart on the previous page, you can notice that the list of "formal" modifiers is longer and contains a wider range of words. Notice also that the student examples we've looked at so far are heavily weighted toward extreme language, e.g., *totally*, *completely*. The result is a tone that can best be described as **hyperbolic**. (*Hyperbole* means "exaggeration," and *hyperbolic* is the adjective form.)

Many students mistakenly believe that in order to make a strong argument, they must use strong language. But in fact, the opposite is true: using overly strong language makes your argument *weaker*.

Indeed, one of the major differences between student writers and professional writers is that the professional writers are generally more neutral in tone and use far more **qualifying** words and phrases — terms such as *mildly*, *somewhat* and *relatively* — that are intended to make statements less harsh or extreme.

Although writers do sometimes state flat-out that a particular idea is wrong, just as often they will be far less direct. Instead of stating that their argument *absolutely, conclusively proves that x is true*, they're much more likely to imply skepticism by putting particular words or phrases in quotation marks, or ask rhetorical questions such as "But is this really the case"? They'll use words like *perhaps* and *suggest* and *somewhat*, not *completely* and *prove*.

In contrast, students are often so eager to convince the reader of their point that they get carried away, often to the point of making statements that are inconsistent with or out of proportion to their actual arguments.

This tendency is most often exhibited in introductions. You should, for example, avoid beginning your papers in the following ways:

- Throughout history…

- Since the beginning of time/the dawn of human existence…

- It is an eternal truth that…

Regardless of what class you are writing for, you are almost certainly NOT writing about all of history, nor are you sufficiently knowledgeable about the history of your topic to be able to make conclusive statements about it. Your opening sentence should be consistent with the **scope** of your paper: it should frame your topic in a specific way.

For example, compare two possible openings to a paper on *Romeo and Juliet*. Notice how much more specific the second option is: right away, it gives us a preview of what the essay will focus on.

Weak: Shakespeare's *Romeo and Juliet* is a play that has been acted, watched, and read by **millions of people for hundreds of years**.

Strong: **One of the most important lessons** Shakespeare's *Romeo and Juliet* teaches is that people can change dramatically in a short amount of time.

Now let's look at something more substantial. Consider the following excerpt from a *New York Times* opinion piece about the limits of satire, by the scholar Justin E.H. Smith:

> Over the past few years I have been made to see, in sum, that the nature and extent of satire is <u>not nearly as simple</u> a question as I had previously imagined. I am now prepared to agree that <u>some</u> varieties of expression that may have <u>some</u> claim to being satire should indeed be prohibited. I note this not with a plan or proposal for where or how such a prohibition might be enforced, but to acknowledge <u>something I did not fully understand</u> until I experienced it first hand — that even the most cherished and firmly-held values or ideals can change when the world in which those values were first formed changes.
>
> (https://www.nytimes.com/2019/04/08/opinion/the-end-of-satire.html)

Although Smith makes an extremely provocative assertion about the role of satire in society, he couches his language in very careful terms. He begins the paragraph, for example, by acknowledging that *the nature and extent of satire is <u>not nearly as simple a question</u> as [he] had previously imagined*—essentially, he is alerting the reader to the fact that he is going to be discussing a complex idea. It is the reader's job to pay attention to that warning, to make a sincere effort to follow his argument, and to not rush to oversimplify or infer a meaning more extreme than what is in fact present.

In the following sentence, the repetition of the qualifying words *some* and *may* (*<u>some</u> varieties of expression that <u>may</u> have <u>some</u> claim to being satire*) create a sense of tentativeness: Smith is well aware that he is wading into dangerous territory, and he is deliberately avoiding the trap of making overly broad statements. And because he maintains such a cautious tone initially, his later use of a stronger modifier, (*<u>most</u> cherished and firmly-held values*) is much more powerful, emphasizing the intensity of the stakes involved.

What often happens when students read this type of passage, however, is that they completely (!) miss these kinds of qualifiers—and thus all the nuances of the argument—and instead respond to it like this:

> Smith **clearly** believes that **all** satire should be **totally banned** from society. This kind of censorship is like something right out of Orwell's *1984*. It shows that Smith is someone that is **completely** unable to tolerate any sort of humor. Being able to laugh is the **only** way that people can survive life in a dictatorship, and Smith would take that away from them.

Not only does this response contain multiple intensifiers (*totally, completely, only*) that are wildly inconsistent with the moderate tone of the passage, but it also blatantly misinterprets Smith's words: he in no way implies that all satire should be banned, nor does he deny that it can be an important means of coping for people living under political oppression (in fact, he says nothing about the latter point at all).

On the contrary, Smith goes to great pains to make clear that he is only talking about specific types of (inflammatory) media that have the potential to be characterized as satire. There is no larger implication about his desire to impose widespread censorship. Regardless of how strongly you may disagree with his position, you have a responsibility to grapple with what is actually written, as opposed to what you assume or imagine he is saying.

Clichés and Jargon

Clichés are fixed phrases that express overused ideas. As a rule, you should do your best to avoid them because they make your ideas and analyses come across as simplistic and generic. They are also associated with a more casual register and can seem jarringly out of place when used in formal writing.

Weak:	Single-sex schools were **no stranger to us** even **back in the olden days**.
Better:	Single-sex schools **have been present** in the educational system **for decades**.
Weak:	The members of the Joad family experience many trials that **take a toll** on them.
Better:	The members of the Joad family experience many **exhausting** trials.
Weak:	In *Hamlet*, actions of betrayal hurt the people that are most loved and **at the end of the day** destroy them **where it hurts most**.
Better:	In *Hamlet*, characters betray the people they love most and **ultimately** destroy them by attacking them **at their most vulnerable points**.

The term **jargon** refers to specialized terminology associated with a particular field. There is nothing inherently wrong with jargon. There is sports jargon, scientific jargon, economic jargon, etc.

Then, there is **corporate** and **social media jargon**. While this type of language may be perfectly standard at an advertising agency or tech startup, it is associated with an informal register and comes off as glaringly out of place in an academic paper. It also flattens ideas and makes them seem stale and unoriginal.

Actionable	Circle back	Impactful	Move the needle	Reach out
At the end of the day	Dig/dive deep	Leverage	Move forward	Think outside the box
Best life	Empower	Low-hanging fruit	Optimize	Touch base

Exercise: Informal Language and Clichés

In the following sentences, rewrite the underlined portions to remove informal language, clichés, and jargon. (Suggested answers p. 296)

Example: In the beginning of *Frankenstein*, it seems that the protagonist is simply a scientist ~~chasing a pipe dream~~ of finding the key to eternal life, but closer analysis of the text reveals that he may not be sane.

     caught up in the impossible goal

1. Although it is often argued that people can become very successful without a college degree, millionaire college dropouts are actually <u>totally</u> rare.

2. Jhumpa Lahiri's *The Namesake* centers on Gogol Ganguli, the son of immigrant parents who <u>has a hard time with</u> his double identity and desire to rebel against his family.

3. Adrian Peterson, running back for the Minnesota Vikings, is a role model who has continued to show pride and courage, despite the <u>trials and tribulations</u> he has faced.

4. The protagonist of *The Great Gatsby* cares only about his dreams; as a result, his life <u>gets pretty</u> lonely.

5. Too much conformity within a society leads to citizens blindly accepting other people's opinions and <u>going along with</u> unjust laws.

6. Education is a wonderful asset for anyone: with a good one there is no limit to what people can achieve, and without one <u>opportunity may never come knocking</u>.

    _____

7. The Middle Ages were a period in which science <u>did really well</u> in the Islamic world, particularly in cities on the Iberian Peninsula such as Córdoba.

    _____

8. Because physical exercise allows people to calm and clear their minds, many students rely on it to help them manage <u>these stressful lives of theirs</u>.

    _____

9. Human rights organizations work to protect the rights of people all over the world and to <u>get rid of</u> abuses such as slavery, child labor, and political persecution.

    _____

10. Frederick Douglass's narrative describing his life as a slave allows the reader to experience the suffering of someone who lives in captivity and is unable <u>to become his best self</u>.

    _____

Answer Key

Parts of Speech (p. 16)

1. A: Adjective, B: Noun, C: Verb, D: Verb,
E: Adverb

2. A: Conjunction, B: Adjective, C: Pronoun,
D: Adverb, E: Preposition

3. A: Noun, B: Verb, C: Adverb, D: Preposition,
E: Noun

4. A: Adverb, B: Conjunction, C: Pronoun, D: Verb
(Infinitive), E: Adjective

5. A: Adjective, B: Preposition, C: Verb,
D: Verb (Infinitive), E: Verb

6. A: Noun, B: Verb, C: Verb, D: Noun, E: Preposition

7. A: Adjective, B: Noun (Singular), C: Verb,
D: Pronoun, E: Verb

8. A: Adjective, B: Verb, C: Adverb, D: Preposition,
E: Verb

9. A: Verb, B: Pronoun, C: Pronoun, D: Preposition,
E: Noun

10. A: Noun, B: Adjective (Adjectival Noun), C: Verb,
D: Preposition, E: Noun

11. A: Preposition, B: Verb, C: Adjective, D: Verb,
E: Verb

12. A: Verb, B: Preposition, C: Preposition, D: Adverb,
E: Preposition

13. A: Pronoun, B: Preposition, C: Preposition,
D: Adjective, E: Verb

14. A: Noun, B: Verb, C: Adjective, D: Adverb,
E: Pronoun

15. A: Adjective, B: Adverb, C: Verb, D: Adjective,
E: Pronoun

Capitalization (p. 25)

1. While competing at the **Olympics** in **Beijing**,
the **Japanese** sprinter Shingo Suetsugu set a record
for the 200-meter dash on **August** 22, 2008.

2. In Charles Beard's analysis, the **Constitution** is a
document that was created primarily to protect
the rights of wealthy landowners.

3. Throughout the **Anglo-Saxon** epic poem
Beowulf, vengeance plays a central role in the
actions of many of the characters.

4. Many early childhood experts have argued that
watching too much **TV** is dangerous for young
children because they have difficulty
distinguishing between fantasy and **reality**.

5. Civics was once a required class for students in
many **high schools**, but since the 1960s, the number
of students required to study how the **United States**
government works has declined dramatically.

6. As Odysseus and his crew journey home to the
island of **Ithaka**, they overcome many obstacles with
the help of the mythological **Greek** gods, yet they
also lose a number of crew members along the way.

7. In **September** of 2015, *Harper's* magazine
published William Deresiewicz's essay **"The
Neoliberal Arts: How Colleges Have Sold Their
Soul to the Market."**

8. After **Burberry** experienced a series of losses in the early 1980s, the **CEO**, Rose Marie Bravo, took steps to modernize the brand, and soon its popularity began to grow among celebrities.

9. According to Cowell, the court showdown between **Galileo** and the **Catholic Church** is quite possibly the greatest standoff between faith and science that **history** has ever seen.

10. Modern **communication** features such as caller **ID**, call waiting and voice mail help both companies and customers to save valuable time and calling charges.

Punctuating Titles (p. 26)

1. In his essay **"Why We Crave Horror Movies,"** Stephen King suggests that viewing paranormal acts on a screen can help people keep their own fears at bay.

2. Multiple readings of Oscar Wilde's novel **<u>The Picture of Dorian Gray</u>** reveal that the image of the painting referenced in the title can always be interpreted in new ways.

3. Rolled out on September 17, 1976, as the first orbiter in the space shuttle system, **<u>Endeavor</u>** was built to perform atmospheric test flights for NASA.

4. Chris Berg's article **"The Weight of the Word"** presents the argument that the United States government's attempts to close WikiLeaks were a fundamental breach of both free speech and freedom of the press.

5. Among Ike and Tina Turner's final joint hits were the cover version of **"Proud Mary"** (1971) and **"Nutbush City Limits"** (1973), with the former becoming one of Turner's most recognizable songs.

6. Set in sixteenth-century Venice, Shakespeare's play **<u>Othello</u>** was adapted from the Italian author Cinthio's short story "A Moorish Captain" (1565).

7. The narrator of Robert Browning's poem **"The Last Duchess"** recounts to a visitor that he keeps a painting of his former wife hidden behind a curtain that only he is allowed to draw back.

8. In the article **"Stuff Is Not Salvation,"** Anna Quindlen examines the American fixation with material possessions and offers a critique of consumer culture.

9. The director Nora Ephron, best known for her romantic comedy films, received an Academy Award nomination for **<u>Silkwood</u>** (1983), **<u>When Harry Met Sally...</u>** (1989), and **<u>Sleepless in Seattle</u>** (1993).

10. George Orwell's novel **<u>1984</u>** depicts a totalitarian society in which citizens are subject to constant surveillance from a leader known only as "Big Brother."

Is It a Sentence? (p. 27)

1. Sentence
2. Sentence
3. Fragment
4. Fragment
5. Sentence
6. Sentence
7. Sentence
8. Fragment
9. Sentence
10. Fragment
11. Fragment
12. Sentence
13. Sentence
14. Fragment
15. Fragment
16. Sentence
17. Sentence
18. Sentence

Sentences vs. Fragments (p. 37)

1. Fragment
2. Sentence
3. Fragment
4. Fragment
5. Fragment
6. Sentence
7. Fragment
8. Fragment
9. Sentence
10. Fragment
11. Fragment
12. Sentence
13. Sentence
14. Fragment
15. Fragment

Joining and Separating Independent Clauses (p. 44)

1. In large doses, many common substances found in household items have devastating **effects; however, (or: effects. However,)** many toxicologists insist that they are thoroughly innocuous in minuscule amounts.

2. Correct

3. The average family size in most countries has been steadily **decreasing, so** there are fewer children overall than there used to be.

4. Over the past several years, the country's food prices have increased **dramatically, and** they **(or: dramatically; they)** are now at their highest rate in two decades.

5. Correct

6. Correct

7. Medieval fairs often attracted uncontrollable crowds and led to **rioting. Therefore, (or: rioting; therefore,)** the right to hold one could only be granted by royal charter.

8. Lyme disease causes muscle aches in its early stages and nervous system problems in its later **ones; it (or: ones. It)** is so named because the first cases occurred in the town of Lyme, Connecticut.

9. Correct

10. During the nineteenth century, Detroit's roads and railways were **improved, but** its manufacturing sector remained weak until after the Industrial Revolution.

Punctuating Sentences with Dependent Clauses (p. 49)

1. Because domesticated canines do not naturally live in pack **structures, some** scientists scoff at dog-training approaches that require humans to act as pack leaders.

2. Freeways and transit systems have facilitated movement throughout the San Francisco metropolitan **area, with** millions of people taking up residence in the suburbs.

3. Since the city's government has curtailed spending on all non-essential services in an attempt to balance the **budget, the** new theater company has been forced to suspend several of its productions.

4. While many design movements have political or philosophical beginnings or **intentions, the** Art Deco style was invented for purely decorative purposes.

5. Whereas almost all general-interest books published in the United States are issued first in hardcover and then in **paperback, in** Europe the paperback is commonly the only version.

6. The Rosetta Stone provided the key to the modern understanding of hieroglyphs **because it** presented the same text in all three ancient Egyptian scripts.

7. Used as both food and medicine in many cultures for thousands of **years, garlic** dates to at least the time of the Giza Pyramids.

8. Former space shuttle commander Pamela Melroy retired from NASA in **2007, having** logged a total of nearly 40 days in orbit.

9. China was ruled by an emperor between the Qin Dynasty and the Qing **Dynasty, although** government bureaucracies were staffed by scholars selected by competitive examination and promoted according to merit.

10. The bowhead whale is thought to be the world's longest-living **mammal, sometimes** reaching up to 200 years in age.

Appositives and Participial Phrases (p. 50)

1. **Lacking vocal cords,** birds are thought to sing with their throat muscles.

2. Farmers in many parts of Brazil have successfully reduced the acidity of their soil, **substantially increasing food production**.

3. **A metal widely used by the ancient Greeks,** copper had great significance because it was associated with the sacred island of Cyprus.

4. During the 1970s, the demand for long-lasting foods caused manufacturers to add preservatives to simple dishes, **thus reducing the quality of the flavors**.

5. Science fiction is shaping the language companies use to market virtual reality technologies, **influencing the types of experiences for which headsets are designed**.

6. **An efficient source of transportation,** the electric cargo bicycle often outpaces its four-wheeled rivals for short-distance deliveries.

7. The earliest type of armor to be invented was chainmail, **a protective covering made from thousands of interlocking metallic rings**.

8. **Offering infinite possibilities for communication,** modern technology also provides endless opportunities for distraction.

9. **A leading figure in the Pop Art movement,** Andy Warhol was celebrated for his depictions of everyday objects.

10. **Measuring more than 250 square miles,** Lake Tahoe is larger than any other lake in North America.

Independent vs. Dependent Clauses (p. 58)

Note: If a correct answer is listed with a period, a semicolon can also be used. Because some answers already include multiple options, only the "period" version is provided.

1. *The Adventures of Huckleberry Finn* was originally intended for an adult **audience. Today,** it is widely read as part of the high school curriculum in the United States.

2. The Euphrates river receives most of its water in the form of rainfall and melting **snow. This results (or: snow, resulting)** in peak volumes during the spring months and low volumes during the summer ones.

3. African-American life during the 1920s was documented in great detail by the writers and artists of the Harlem **Renaissance. Far** less, however, is known about it during the 1930s.

4. Universities have historically offered a wide range of continuing education **classes. Some of them** are now offered over the Internet as well as in traditional classrooms.

5. In 1930, John Maynard Keynes predicted that technology would give rise to a 15-hour **workweek. Instead,** it gave rise to thousands of hours of pointless work.

6. Oils found in peanuts can provoke serious immune reactions in allergy **sufferers, most** of whom must be careful to avoid other types of nuts as well.

7. The First World War began in August of **1914. It** was directly caused by the assassination of Archduke Franz Ferdinand of Austria by the Bosnian revolutionary Gavrilo Princip.

8. Gwendolyn Knight painted throughout her life but did not start seriously exhibiting her work until relatively **late. Her** first retrospective occurred when she was nearly 80 years old. **(Note: because the second clause explains the first, a colon can be used here as well.)**

9. Black-backed woodpeckers live almost exclusively in severely burned **forests. They thrive** on insects that are adapted to fire and can detect heat up to 30 miles away.

10. Frederick Law Olmsted, who designed New York City's Central Park, also designed Montreal's Mount Royal **Park, most** of which is heavily wooded.

Transitions (p. 67)

1. In the past, coffees were blended to suit a homogenous popular taste, **but** that has changed in response to a growing awareness of regional differences.

2. People living in cities tend to eat more processed foods than those living in rural areas; **therefore/ thus/consequently**, city-dwellers experience higher rates of health problems.

3. The Taj Mahal is regarded as one of the eight wonders of the world; **indeed, (or: in fact,)** some historians have noted that its architectural beauty has never been surpassed.

4. Music serves no obvious evolutionary purpose; it has, **however/nevertheless**, played a role in every known civilization on earth.

5. There is no escaping the fact that most of the world's big cats are in serious trouble because of poaching, **and** tigers are no exception.

6. **Because** small companies generally lack the financial resources to upgrade their software and set up protective barriers, **[no transition]** their security systems can be hacked more easily than those of large ones.

7. No one truly knows where the pirate known as Blackbeard called home; **however/nevertheless**, author Daniel Defoe, a self-appointed piracy expert, claimed that he came from the English city of Bristol.

8. The correlation between bad moods and negative judgments is useful **because** it allows people to make informed guesses about how others are feeling from observing their actions and choices.

9. **Although** Frederic Chopin's charming and sociable personality drew loyal groups of friends and admirers, including the novelist George Sand, his private life was often painful and difficult.

10. Pyramids are most commonly associated with ancient Egypt, **so** it comes as a surprise to many people that Nubian civilization, located in modern-day Sudan, produced far more pyramids than Egyptian civilization ever did.

11. The two books recount the same series of events; **however**, they do so from different perspectives and are not intended to be read in any particular order.

12. **[No transition]** Eighteenth-century European sailors were convinced that citrus fruits could cure scurvy, a disease caused by a severe deficiency of vitamin C, but physicians dismissed that theory because it did not conform to prevailing beliefs.

13. **Because** the lemur shares some traits with other primates, it is frequently mistaken for an ancestor of modern monkeys and apes.

14. Modern chemistry keeps insects from ravaging crops, lifts stains from carpets, and saves lives, **but/yet** the constant exposure to chemicals is taking a toll on many people's health.

15. Thomas Jefferson believed that prisoners of war should be treated humanely; **therefore/thus/consequently**, during the American Revolution, he requested that British generals be held in private homes rather than behind bars.

Using Relative Clauses to Join Sentences (p. 71)

1. *Clueless* is a movie **that** was based on Jane Austen's classic novel *Emma*.

2. Ownership of the Arctic is governed by the 1958 Law of the Sea, **which** gives Arctic nations an exclusive economic zone 200 nautical miles from land.

3. The printing press was introduced in Europe by Johannes Gutenberg, **who** devised a hand mold to create movable metal type.

4. SpaceX was founded in June 2002 by Elon Musk, **whose** goal was to build a simple and relatively inexpensive reusable rocket.

5. Most volcanic activity occurs on the sea floor, **where** tectonic plates are spreading the earth apart.

Embedded Clauses (p. 78)

1. Frank Lloyd Wright, **who founded the Prairie School movement,** was one of the most renowned architects of the twentieth century.

2. Japan's bullet train, **which travels between the cities of Tokyo and Osaka,** is the world's fastest high-speed railway.

3. Sutter's Mill, **where gold was found in 1849,** was located on the South Fork American River in Coloma, California.

4. The design of Paris's Pompidou Center, **whose exterior is covered with brightly colored tubes,** marked a radical break with tradition.

5. Genetic diseases **that result from a mutation on only one gene** are known as single-gene or Mendelian disorders.

6. The Ottoman Empire, **whose capital was Constantinople,** remained at the center of interactions between Europe and Asia for 600 years.

7. Ray Dearlove, **who is the founder of the Australian Rhino Project,** has an ambitious plan to airlift 80 rhinos to Australia to save them from poachers.

8. Researchers have found that regular aerobic exercise, **the kind that gets your heart pumping,** may boost verbal memory and learning.

9. The last of the dense minerals **that make up much of the Earth's crust and upper mantle** has been found inside a meteorite.

10. Roald Dahl, **who was a member of Britain's Royal Air Force in his youth,** earned fame as the author of children's books such as *Matilda* and *The BFG*.

Punctuating Non-Essential and Essential Elements (p. 81)

1. As a general rule, species living on land, **particularly large species,** tend not to survive as long as those living in freshwater environments.

2. The disruptions in sleep **cycles that almost inevitably accompany movement across time zones** can be reduced if travelers are exposed to light before setting out on a trip.

3. Modern advertising, **which was introduced in the United States during the 1920s,** was created from techniques developed in the campaigns of Edward Bernays.

4. Some traditional assumptions about how to treat jellyfish stings have recently been called into question: rinsing the injured areas with seawater, **for example,** has been discovered to spread venom to other tissue.

5. Testing animal cognition is tricky, and comparing and contrasting across species lines, **especially when distinct species-specific tests are used,** is particularly challenging.

6. Proctor & Gamble, a multinational consumer goods **company headquartered** in Cincinnati, Ohio, produces a variety of household products, including soap, oil, and toothpaste.

7. Researchers have **determined that** about 66 million years ago, an asteroid came streaking out of the sky and crashed into what is now Mexico's Yucatán Peninsula.

8. Sweatshops were common in the early New York City garment industry; by the standards of the early 1900s, **however,** the Triangle Shirtwaist Company was not actually a sweatshop.

9. The destruction of American swamps and marshes, **long seen as wastelands that harbored deadly disease,** accelerated over the course of the twentieth century.

10. A new software called DXplain, **some hospitals report,** is helping doctors make diagnoses and avoid the types of errors that can sometimes cause harm to patients.

Correcting Non-Essential Clause Punctuation (p. 87)

1. Ant colonies can live for up to 30 years, the lifetime of the single queen who produces all the **ants, but** individual ants live at most a year.

2. Correct

3. The author Shirley Jackson, best known for her shocking short story **"The Lottery," was** born in San Francisco in 1916.

4. Correct

5. Chosen as young girls, the priestesses of Vesta (goddess of the **hearth) were** granted rights, privileges, and power unavailable to other women in ancient Rome.

6. Grand Staircase-Escalante National Monument is home to more than 650 bee species, most likely because it mirrors the range of habitats — from sandstone canyons and sagebrush-peppered deserts to aspen and pine **forests — in** which the insects live.

7. The scientific method — often presented as a fixed sequence of **steps — actually** represents a set of general principles. **(or: method, often presented as a fixed sentence of steps,)**

8. In the early sixteenth century, colonization attempts by the world's newest major power, **Spain,** were centered on the Caribbean islands and involved little contact with complex mainland civilizations.

9. Correct

10. Correct

11. Richard Rodgers and Oscar Hammerstein, having achieved success **independently, began** their collaboration with the musical *Oklahoma!* in 1943.

12. Human computers, who once performed basic numerical analysis for **laboratories, were** behind the calculations for everything from the first accurate prediction of the return of Halley's Comet to the success of the Manhattan Project.

13. Voyager 2—a space probe launched by NASA on August 20, **1977**—was actually launched 16 days before its twin, Voyager 1, on a trajectory that enabled encounters with Uranus and Neptune.

14. Batsford Arboretum, **a 55-acre garden that contains Great Britain's largest collection of Japanese cherry trees, is** open daily to the public for most of the year.

15. Early European settlers first called the Boston area **Trimountaine (after** its "three mountains," only traces of which remain today), but they later renamed it after Boston, England, the native city of several prominent colonists. **Note: the comma after the close parenthesis is correct because it precedes a FANBOYS conjunction (*but*) used to join two full sentences.**

Essential vs. Non-Essential Elements (p. 94)

1. Karl Marx, in collaboration with Frederich Engels, provides a detailed critique of capitalism in the **book** *The Communist Manifesto*.

2. Although the medieval **philosopher Peter Abelard** was expected to pursue a military career, he rejected that option, choosing to become a scholar instead.

3. Correct

4. Nearly a fifth of **researchers who work with mice** are estimated to become allergic to those animals; however, the real number may be higher because some people may not report their symptoms.

5. While working as an instructor for the U.S. Navy, George Lucas produced his first **film,** *Electronic Labyrinth: THX 1138 4EB*, which won first prize at the 1967–68 National Student Film Festival.

6. The original Olympics were banned in A.D. 393 by Roman **emperor Theodosius I**, but despite that prohibition, Europeans persisted in holding the Games during the Dark and Middle Ages.

7. Because the director harshly criticized **actors who dared to question his instructions,** he earned a reputation for being an exceptionally poor colleague.

8. Some scholars, including the historian **Niall Ferguson,** have suggested that populist governments are usually so incompetent that they prove short-lived.

9. Groundbreaking when it was released in 1990, the **documentary** *The Civil War* possessed a collage-like quality, presenting an incredible number of stories in rapid succession.

10. Correct

People vs. Things (p. 102)

1. For delicate patients **who** cannot handle the rigors of certain treatments, some doctors are now rejecting the assembly line of modern medical care for gentler, more traditional options.

2. Correct

3. In 1623, Galileo published a work **in which** he championed the controversial theory of heliocentrism, thus provoking one of the greatest scientific controversies of his day.

4. Correct

5. It has taken many decades for scientists to piece together the riddle of just where modern cats first became domesticated ~~at~~.

6. When readers **who** obtain their news from electronic rather than printed sources send articles to their friends, they tend to choose ones that confirm their pre-existing biases.

7. Correct

8. Most evidence points toward the deep past, approximately four billion years ago, as the era during which Mars could have held marine environments ~~in~~.

9. Correct

10. Ada Lovelace, for **whom** the programming language Ada is named, was a pioneer in computer science, foreseeing how an "analytical engine" could be built more than a century before the first such machine was constructed.

Colons and Dashes (p. 109)

1. In experiments on monkeys, mice, and dogs, as well as in multiple test-tube trials, a small number of Lyme Disease bacteria have been found to **survive a wide array of antibiotics**.

2. In creating psychoanalysis, Freud developed therapeutic techniques **such as free association** and transference, establishing their central role in the analytic process.

3. Correct

4. As inhabitants of the digital world, most people are exposed daily **to dozens** of photographs of friends, loved ones, celebrities, and strangers.

5. Correct

6. Correct

7. Correct

8. Crux is a constellation located in the southern part of the Milky **Way; it** is among the most easily identified star clusters because of its high visual magnitude.

9. As gaping holes of logic appear in Marc Antony's oration, we begin to see what sorts of artifices made his speech so **cunning: its** use of circumstantial evidence, its largely emotional pleas, and its desperate engagement of the citizens.

10. Correct

Forming Indirect Questions with "Whether" (p. 112)

1. When I am asked to write a blurb for the back cover of a novel, I don't spend a lot of time **wondering whether the book is** really worth readers' money.

2. Many people have argued that the medium in which journalists publish should have no bearing on **whether they receive** the protection of a state's law shielding them from lawsuits.

3. The philosopher Alex Rosenberg of Duke University has **asked whether neuroscience is** actually a bigger threat to humanity than artificial intelligence.

4. A recent GPS system failure has raised the **question (of) whether complex digital systems on earth could continue** to function if satellite clocks were wiped out.

5. Americans remain heavily split on the issue of **whether they should consume** genetically modified foods (GMOs) and organic products.

Question Mark or Period? (p. 113)

1. Although oil prices have begun to rebound, market analysts question whether a significant price recovery is truly about to **occur.**

2. Correct

3. Although the concept of debt dates to the ancient world, scholars still debate whether the Venetians were truly the inventors of corporate **stock.**

4. While most editors are concerned with how accurate a biography is, others are more interested in how fast it can be **published.**

5. Correct

6. The vast majority of American parents who pay an allowance tie the money to **whether their children have done chores around the house**.

7. Correct

8. The majority of experiments performed by cognitive psychologist Elizabeth Spelke have been designed to test how much babies and young children understand about the world around **them.**

9. When selecting shoes and equipment, mountain climbers must ask themselves the following question: will their chosen route take them over rock, snow, or **ice?**

10. Following his release from captivity, King Louis IX of France used his influence to show crusaders how **they could rebuild their defenses and conduct diplomacy.**

Punctuating Quotations (p. 120)

1. In *The Library: A Catalogue of Wonders*, Stuart Kells asserts **that libraries** represent people's attempts to impose order in a world of chaos.

2. Correct

3. As Fauvelle points out in *The Golden Rhinoceros: Histories of the African Middle Ages*, a ruler of Mali set out with 2,000 ships to **discover "the** furthest limit of the Atlantic Ocean" nearly 200 years before Columbus.

4. In his book *Toward a New Architecture*, the modernist architect Le Corbusier **states, "The** motor car is an object with a simple function (to travel) and complicated aims (comfort, resistance, appearance)."

5. Correct

6. When Mr. Darcy's feelings have grown too strong to repress, he approaches Elizabeth Bennet and proclaims, "You must allow me to tell you how ardently I love and admire **you" (Chapter 34).**

7. Correct

8. As one mother who successfully paid her children to complete their chores commented, "In behavioral psychology, this phenomenon is called **'positive reinforcement.'"**

9. "Social media stars are good at whatever made them **famous,"** says branding consultant Jeremiah Boehner, **"but** they're not always good businesspeople."

10. According to Joseph Campbell, the hero's journey features a descent into the "belly of the **beast";** during this phase, the hero is brought low, and his ego is diminished.

11. In the words of the writer and child psychologist Bruno Bettelheim, "Fairy tales can help children confront and resolve conflicts in their own **lives"** (*The Uses of Enchantment*, **72).**

12. Correct

13. The American Petroleum Institute has worked with many oil industry protection companies to stymie the renewable energy movement, in some cases **even "posing** as environmentalist groups in order to attract the support of environmentalists while simultaneously pushing their anti-renewable agenda."

14. While talking about the luncheon, Woolf admits that "it is part of the novelist's convention not to mention soup and salmon and ducklings," but "[she] shall take the liberty to defy that **convention" (723-724).**

15. "Our intention is to affirm this life," the composer John Cage wrote in the introductory remarks to a 1956 dance performance that he created with his partner Merce **Cunningham, "not** to bring order out of chaos."

Adding Commas (p. 126)

1. Emmy-winning actor André Braugher, the youngest of four children, was born **July 1, 1962,** in **Chicago, Illinois,** the son of a postal worker and a heavy-equipment operator.

2. **Large-scale social strife, economic stagnation, and an exploding population** all conspired to weaken the Qing Dynasty in nineteenth-century China.

3. A staff writer at *The New Yorker* and the Dina and Raphael Recanati Chair of Medicine at Harvard Medical School in **Boston, Massachusetts,** Jerome E. **Groopman, M.D., grew** up in **Queens, New York.**

4. The Battle of Antietam was fought on **September 17, 1862,** between Confederate General Robert E. Lee's Army of Northern Virginia and Union General George B. McClellan's Army of the Potomac near **Sharpsburg, Maryland,** and Antietam Creek.

5. As a result of **farming, deforestation, and other developments,** giant pandas have been driven out of the lowland areas where they once lived and now dwell in a few mountain ranges in **Sichuan, China.**

6. Long after ancient warriors had ceased to use chariots in warfare, ordinary citizens continued to rely on them for **traveling long distances, celebrating during festivals, and racing them in sporting events**.

7. Most modern brachiopods, also known as lamp shells, prefer **quiet, calm** water; they often attach to the undersides of stones or other hard objects.

8. British Prime Minister Winston Churchill was born at Blenheim Palace, his family's home in **Oxfordshire, England,** on 30 November 1874, a time when Britain was the dominant world power.

9. Among cities in the United States, **Philadelphia, Pennsylvania,** is unique in that it holds the title of UNESCO World Heritage City—an honor that was bestowed on it on **November 6, 2015.**

10. Based on the letters of Robert Gould Shaw, the film *Glory* premiered in limited release in the United States on **December 14, 1989,** and in wide release on **February 16, 1990.**

Eliminating Unnecessary Commas (p. 130)

1. Although it lacks traditional circus elements such as **animals and clowns**, Cirque du Soleil continues to draw thousands of spectators around the world each year.

2. Some of the most powerful telescopes in the world are now peering across vast distances of space, watching for the faintest dip of light or **wobble that** could suggest the presence of another world.

3. Although Tchaikovsky's music is popular with audiences around the world, early listeners often dismissed it as **vulgar and uninspired.**

4. Correct

5. Sherlock Holmes' creator, Arthur Conan Doyle, was a **physician himself,** and there is evidence that Holmes is modeled on Joseph Bell of the Royal Edinburgh Infirmary, one of the leading doctors of the day.

6. Because of the dearth of written records from the twelfth century, little factual information **exists about** the early life of Genghis Khan.

7. It is unclear whether caffeine actually helps people retain information, but early research suggests that it can increase the sensitivity of neurons involved in **learning and memory**.

8. Correct

9. New Zealand, one of the last lands to be settled by humans, developed fascinating, **distinctive forms** of wildlife during its long isolation.

10. Among the reforms introduced during Napoleon's reign were the abolition of all feudal privileges and the reorganization of **local administrative** systems.

Possessive vs. Plural (p. 136)

1. Like **today's (correct)** astronauts, future space colonists are likely to be selected on the basis of **their** suitability for long-duration spaceflight.

2. Fiction allows readers to understand other **people's actions** by entering into **characters' (correct)** minds and seeing situations from their interior points of view.

3. During the **1920s**, most of the works written by Langston Hughes focused on **African Americans'** struggle for equality.

4. Digital technology has become so embedded in our culture that we find it almost impossible to recognize that forms of computation without **algorithms** effectively control much of the world.

5. Recognized today as one of the **world's** leading authorities on the Sphinx, archaeologist Mark Lehner has conducted field research on the pyramids at Giza for nearly four decades.

6. Recent studies have suggested that if you consume a small amount of dark chocolate daily, **you're** more likely to be healthy overall.

7. Circadian rhythms dictate many of the **body's** most fundamental **processes**, including eating, sleeping, and producing hormones.

8. **It's** not yet clear how much plastic is consumed by corals in the wild, or what harm it might do to these important marine organisms, **whose (correct)** lives are already threatened by environmental dangers like warming seas and pollution.

9. In Sandra **Cisneros's (correct)** novel *The House on Mango Street*, the protagonist discovers that liberation can be found through creativity and literature.

10. News **stories (correct)** sometimes distort events in ways that create a negative perception of certain groups, leading to stereotypes, **biases**, and false assumptions.

Pronoun Agreement (p. 146)

1. Not until the early twentieth century did the city become capable of maintaining **its** population and cease to be dependent on rural areas for a constant stream of new inhabitants.

2. Correct

3. In 1294 Boniface VIII began his papacy, replacing St. Celestine V, who had declared that it was permissible for a pope to resign and then promptly **did so**.

4. The nitrogen cycle describes **nitrogen's movement (or: the movement of nitrogen)** from the air into organic compounds and then back into the atmosphere.

5. If you exercise to prevent diabetes, **you** may also want to avoid vitamins C and E since these antioxidants have been shown to correlate with it.

6. Correct

7. Once common across southwest Asia, the Indian cheetah was driven nearly to extinction during the late twentieth century and now resides in the fragmented pieces of **its** remaining habitat.

8. In **her** graphic novel *Persepolis*, a combination of comic-strip form and political commentary, **Marjane Satrapi** depicts her childhood and adolescence in Tehran and Vienna.

9. Always a site of contemplation, the art museum has lately seized on the wellness trend, marketing **itself** as a place of refuge from our frenzied lives.

10. Each of the chapters in Annie Dillard's *Pilgrim at Tinker Creek* has **its** own title, and so many readers mistakenly believe that the book is a compilation of essays.

11. **In the novel *1984*, George Orwell** depicts a totalitarian society in which people use a simplified form of English known as "newspeak."

12. The city's economy has weakened significantly in the past decade, **a decline that has led (or: leading)** to an overwhelming loss of manufacturing jobs.

13. Correct

14. As the son of an electrical worker, Einstein learned about physics not only by reading about it but also by observing the technology **its** applications could produce.

15. Japan's status as an island country means that **the Japanese** must rely heavily on other countries for the supply of natural resources that are indispensable to national existence.

Direct Object, Indirect Object, or Complement? (p. 150)

1. Direct object of the verb *stimulate*

2. Indirect object of the verb *crash*; separated by the preposition *to*

3. Complement of the verb *becoming*

4. Complement of the verb *remain*

5. Direct object of the verb *displayed*

6. Indirect object of the verb *led*; separated by the preposition *to*

7. Direct object of the verb *control*

8. Direct object of the verb *maintain*

9. Complement of the verb *was*

10. Indirect object of the verb *run*; separated by the preposition *on*

Noun Agreement (p. 152)

1. Both Wilfred Daniels and Leonard Chuene, who became powerful figures in South African sports, grew up as **promising athletes** who could never compete internationally because of apartheid.

2. Because they evolved in the warm climate of Africa before spreading into Europe, modern humans had **bodies** adapted to tracking prey over great distances.

3. Many of the great classical composers, including Mozart, Bach, and Mendelssohn, were born into musical families and began studying an instrument seriously when they were **children**.

4. Correct

5. Known for creating a unique sound through the use of non-traditional instruments, Miles Davis joined Louis Armstrong and Ella Fitzgerald as **one of** the greatest jazz musicians of the twentieth century.

6. Inscribed ostrich eggs and pieces of shell jewelry are **examples** of early human attempts to record thoughts symbolically rather than literally.

7. Joseph Charles Jones and George Bundy Smith, who fought for African Americans as **civil rights activists** during the early 1960s, were separated for nearly forty years after being arrested in Alabama in 1961.

8. The Opium Wars, which introduced the power of western armies and technologies to China, marked the end of Shanghai and Ningpo as **independent port cities**.

9. Although neither came from a literary family, novelists Amy Tan and Maxine Hong Kingston became **avid readers** while growing up near San Francisco.

10. Correct

Pronoun Case (p. 157)

1. Although our parents have little difficulty distinguishing between my twin sister and **me**, our teachers are much more easily fooled by our seemingly identical appearance.

2. It is exceedingly difficult **for us voters** to choose between the two candidates because their positions on so many issues are so similar that they are effectively indistinguishable.

3. After listening patiently to their admittedly flimsy excuses, the principal decided to sentence **her** and Akiko to a week of detention.

4. Along with our project, the professor handed Sabrina and **me** a note requesting that we remain after class in order to discuss our research methods.

5. Though extremely long, the meeting between **them** and their advisor was unusually productive because it provided many new ways of thinking about a familiar subject.

6. Correct

7. When the gubernatorial candidate arrived at the auditorium to give a speech, we found it nearly impossible to distinguish between **her** and her assistant, so similar were they in height and appearance.

8. My lab partner and **I** were awarded first prize in the science fair for our work on the breakdown of insulin production in people who suffer from diabetes.

9. Correct

10. An unfamiliar subject when the class began, Roman history became increasingly fascinating to **him** and Alexis over the course of the semester.

Subject-Verb Agreement 1 (p. 165)

1. The process of living vicariously through a fictional character in order to purge one's emotions **is** known as catharsis.

2. Near the border between China and Tibet **lie** the Himalaya Mountains, which include some of the highest peaks in the world.

3. Although drivers are required to purchase automobile insurance, levels of coverage often **vary** depending on the driver's age and state of residence.

4. In the eighteenth century, the first public library in the United States **and** the first fire department in the state of Pennsylvania **were** founded by Benjamin Franklin.

5. Tropical waves in the Atlantic basin frequently **develop** from disturbances that begin in east Africa and drift over the continent into the Atlantic Ocean.

6. Playboating, a discipline of whitewater rafting or canoeing in which players stay in one spot while performing certain maneuvers, **involves** specialized canoes designed for the sport.

7. Opposition to rodeos from animal-rights workers **focuses** primarily on the poor treatment and living conditions of the horses used in competitions.

8. A natural thief and spy, the jay, along with the crow and the raven, **belongs** to a highly intelligent group of birds called the corvids.

9. Among the finds from a recent archaeological dig in London **were** earthenware knobs originally used for "pay walls": boxes into which Elizabethan theater-goers deposited their admission fees.

10. Researchers have hypothesized that whales sing by pumping air into pouches, which then **release** vibrations into the surrounding water.

11. The highly textured bark **and** distinctive silhouette of the Dutch Elm tree **distinguish** it from the equally common English Elm tree.

12. Possible explanations for the suspicion surrounding Shakespeare's Macbeth **include** the superstition that the witches' song is an actual incantation and the belief that theaters only mount the play when they are in need of money.

13. According to the law of diminution, the pitches of notes sounded by an orchestra **remain** the same even as the amount of sound diminishes.

14. Along the deepest part of the ocean floor **sit** the Mariana Trench **and** the HMRG Deep, the two lowest spots ever identified on earth.

15. Louise Erdrich's fiction **and** poetry **draw** on their author's Chippewa heritage to examine complex familial relationships among Native Americans as they reflect on issues of identity.

Subject-Verb Agreement 2 (p. 170)

1. The number of natural materials being replaced by synthetics **appears** to be growing because unlike wood, leather, and ceramics, plastic is enormously versatile and inexpensive to produce.

2. According to researchers, knowing two or more languages **improves** one's ability to focus in the face of distraction and to ignore irrelevant information.

3. Each of the Taino's five chiefdoms, which inhabited the Bahamas before the arrival of Europeans, **was** ruled by a leader known as a cacique.

4. For the past several years, the theater company **has** traveled to various schools throughout the city in order to expose students to classic works.

5. Whether the first birds evolved from arboreal or terrestrial ancestors **remains** a source of ongoing debate among paleontologists.

6. *The Catcher in the Rye* is one of those books that **tend** to polarize readers, who typically find the protagonist, Holden Caulfield, either refreshingly honest or unbearably whiny and self-involved.

7. Having an excessive amount of confidence in one's personal beliefs frequently **leads** to poor decision-making, especially in organizational or political contexts.

8. A number of works by Mary Shelley **contain** the notion that cooperation between individuals, especially women, could represent a means to improve society.

9. That Jane Goodall became the world's foremost expert on chimpanzees **was** hardly a surprise to those who observed her childhood fascination with animals.

10. One of *The Tale of Genji*'s most extraordinary features **is** its ability to maintain coherency while describing the actions of more than 400 characters.

11. Delphi, home of the Delphic Oracle, contains a wide range of artifacts as well as many prestigious dedications, but neither **proves** that Delphi was a focus of attention for the general population in ancient Greece.

12. Every one of the illuminated manuscripts in the library's collection **is** unique, although most **contain** similar groups of texts accompanied by vividly colored decorations.

13. There **are** many prominent economists in the United States who consider changes in the demand for goods to be one of the fundamental causes of inflation.

14. Some of the passages in the book **describe** the physical realities of the Middle Ages in great detail, while others reflect the dazzling debates that would later lead to the Renaissance.

15. While reactions to the exhibition were mixed, neither the artist's exceptional showmanship nor his innovative techniques **were** questioned by the spectators.

Irregular Verbs and Past Participles (p. 175)

1. Since 1896, the Kentucky Derby — arguably the most famous horse race held in the United State — has **taken** place on a track measuring one-and-a-quarter miles.

2. Unusual sequences of rocks discovered in a geological formation in Namibia indicate that for millions of years, the entire earth was **frozen** over.

3. Although prairie dogs were once on the verge of extinction, their numbers have **risen** to pre-twentieth century levels over the past few years.

4. Only one ship remaining in the Navy's fleet has ever **sunk** an enemy vessel: the USS Constitution, which earned the nickname "Old Ironsides."

5. Over the past few years, the ballet troupe has **become** one of the few eminent dance companies to promote choreographic innovation.

6. There are about 570 marathons held in the United States every year, and approximately 0.5% of the U.S. population has **run** in one.

7. Michael J. Rosen has **written** works ranging from picture books to poetry, and he has also edited several anthologies varying almost as broadly in content.

8. In 1911, the *Mona Lisa* was **stolen** from the Louvre by a museum employee, Vincenzo Peruggia, who believed that the painting belonged in an Italian gallery.

9. While the popularity of rooftop solar systems has **grown** rapidly over the past decade, wind energy has generally remained the province of industrial-scale operations.

10. In several recent instances, vacationers have discovered cameras that were **hidden** in rental properties—findings that have raised questions about the safety of staying in a stranger's home.

Present Perfect, Simple Past, and Past Perfect (p. 180)

1. Incorrect: Beginning in the eleventh century, reviving economic development **allowed** Pamplona to recover its urban life after suffering repeated Viking invasions.

2. Correct

3. Incorrect: Since the 1920s, most major motion picture studios **have accumulated** tangled lists of owners and corporate ancestors, and none more so than Paramount Pictures.

4. Incorrect: In 1915, the Dutch government approved the proposal for new ships to protect its holdings in the East Indies, not realizing that the request **had been** withdrawn because of the start of the First World War.

5. Correct

6. Incorrect: By the time Pearl S. Buck was awarded the Nobel Prize for Literature in 1938, she **had been** a best-selling author in the United States for nearly a decade.

7. Correct

8. Incorrect: During the 1950s, the Detroit area emerged as a metropolitan region with the construction of an extensive freeway system that **continued** to expand over the next several decades.

9. Correct

10. Correct

All Tenses (p. 186)

1. According to researchers, the Antarctic ice shelf **has shrunk** by approximately 50 gigatons of ice each year since 1992.

2. In 1498, Dutch scholar Erasmus of Rotterdam moved from Paris to England, where he later **became** a professor of ancient languages at Cambridge.

3. Correct

4. Mahatma Gandhi, who was born in India, studied law in London and in 1893 went to South Africa, where he **spent** twenty years opposing discriminatory legislation against Indians.

5. The country's economists speculated that thousands more jobs would have been lost if consumer demand for domestically manufactured products **had continued** to decline.

6. NASA scientists have decided to delay the space shuttle's launch in order to determine whether recently repaired parts would cause damage if they **broke** off in orbit.

7. Correct

8. A Federal Aviation Administration task force has recommended that drone operators **be** required to register their aircrafts, paving the way for regulations intended to help reverse a surge in rogue drone flights.

9. Correct

10. After weeks of careful scrutiny, the consumer protection agency informed the public that a number of products **would be** recalled because of safety concerns.

11. Even before the beginning of the twentieth century, when the electronic age was still in its infancy, the first attempts to generate sound from electricity **had already begun**.

12. Correct

13. Hardly a stranger to self-censorship, Mark Twain never hesitated to change his prose if he believed that the alterations **would improve** the sales of his books.

14. Some critics have argued that Dostoevsky was unique among nineteenth-century authors in that he surrendered fully to his characters and **allowed** himself to write in voices other than his own.

15. For centuries, Norwegians **have hung** dolls dressed as witches in their kitchens because they believe that such figures have the power to keep pots from boiling over.

Adjective or Adverb? (p. 191)

1. Adjective
2. Adverb
3. Adjective
4. Adjective
5. Adverb
6. Adjective
7. Adjective
8. Adjective
9. Adverb
10. Adjective

Adjectives vs. Adverbs (p. 195)

1. Correct

2. Consumed for its energizing effects, caffeine is also a psychoactive drug that, according to research, can cause people to feel **sick** and exacerbate a variety of stress-related ailments.

3. First produced in 1908, the Ford Model T (nicknamed the "Tin Lizzie") was a **big black** car that revolutionized Americans' relationship with the automobile.

4. Although the room initially seemed tidy, we saw upon closer inspection that books, pens, and pieces of paper had been scattered **haphazardly** beneath a desk.

5. When examined under a microscope, the beaker of water revealed a hodgepodge of microscopic drifters that looked quite **different** from other sea creatures.

6. Though few people believe that human beings are entirely rational, a world governed by anti-Enlightenment principles would surely be **infinitely** worse than one governed by Voltaire and Locke.

7. Correct

8. When Mt. Vesuvius first began to show signs of eruption, many of the people living at the base of the volcano **hastily** abandoned their villages to seek cover in nearby forests.

9. Italian nobleman Cesare Borgia was ruthless and vain, but he was also a brilliant Renaissance figure who was **exceedingly** well-educated in the classics.

10. Correct

11. Lake Pergusa, the only naturally occurring lake in Sicily, is surrounded by a well-known racing circuit that was created in the 1960s and that has hosted many **international sporting** events since that time.

12. Even when his theme is the struggle to find a place in a **seemingly** irrational cosmos, Oscar Wilde writes with lively sympathy and hopefulness.

13. Correct

14. The origin of the senators' proposal dates back nearly three-quarters of a century, making it one of the most **eagerly** anticipated pieces of legislation this year.

15. Because the officer was able to present himself in an unthreatening manner, the suspect remained **calm** for the duration of the interview.

Comparatives vs. Superlatives (p. 199)

1. Between the black leopard and the snow leopard, the black leopard possesses the more effective camouflage while the snow leopard has the **more** striking tail.

2. When the influenza virus, one of the **most commonly** diagnosed diseases in the United States, was formally recognized in 1933, many doctors believed that a cure would be found shortly.

3. Correct

4. Once restricted to a single season, forest fires are now a constant threat in some locations, beginning **earlier** in the year and lasting later than they previously did.

5. Correct

6. Confronted with two equally qualified finalists, the awards committee is struggling to determine which one is **more** deserving of the top prize.

7. Tests on the germination rates of *Salsola imbricata* seeds show that the plant sprouts **more quickly** and more consistently at 20°C than at higher temperatures.

8. Though London has a longstanding reputation as a city whose weather is defined by rain and fog, in reality Paris receives the **higher** amount of rainfall each year.

9. Both poodles and pugs are known for making excellent pets, but between the two breeds, pugs have the **sweeter** disposition while poodles are smarter.

10. Although puzzles such as Sudoku can help people keep their minds nimble as they age, studies show that physical exercise such as biking or running has a **stronger** effect on mental acuity.

Double Positives and Double Negatives (p. 201)

1. When selecting a host city from among dozens of contenders, Olympic officials must take into consideration which one is **likeliest** to benefit from the legacy of the games. (**Note: "most likely" is also an idiomatically acceptable alternative**)

2. Although the plays of Lillian Hellman and Bertolt Brecht were met with great popularity during the 1920s, they are scarcely **ever** performed anymore in the United States.

3. Since the advent of commercial flight and high-speed rail in the twentieth century, hardly **any** significant technological changes have affected the traveling public.

4. During its early years, the Ford Motor Company **produced** scarcely more than a handful of cars a day, but within a decade it led the world in the expansion of the assembly line.

5. Correct

6. Imitation, long considered the **most sincere/sincerest** form of flattery, may carry evolutionary benefits for both model and mimic.

7. During the early days of cable television, many viewers were only able to access four channels, with reception being weakest in rural areas and **clearest** in large cities.

8. The Industrial Revolution, which began in the late 1700s and lasted more than fifty years, was the period when machine power became **stronger** than hand power.

9. Correct

10. To thoroughly understand historical figures, we must study them not only in the bright light of the present but also in the **cloudier** light of the circumstances of their own lifetimes.

Faulty Comparisons and Amounts (p. 206)

1. The writings of John Locke, **unlike/in contrast to** the writings of Thomas Hobbes, emphasize the idea that people are by nature both reasonable and tolerant.

2. In response to protests against unfair labor practices, the company issued an official statement encouraging skeptics to compare the organization's pay, benefits, and workplace conditions to **those of** other major employers.

3. As part of its application, the university asks students to compose a short essay in which they compare their educational interests and goals to **those of** other students.

4. Correct

5. Doctors in Norway prescribe **fewer** antibiotics than those in any other country, so people do not have a chance to develop resistance to many kinds of drug-resistant infections.

6. Today's neuroscientists, **in contrast to** those of thirty years ago, have access to sophisticated instrumentation that has only been developed over the past decade.

7. Unlike **people/those with** dyslexia, people with dysgraphia often suffer from fine motor-skills problems that leave them unable to write clearly.

8. In contrast to merchants in coastal regions of central Asia, merchants in landlocked regions had a smaller **number** of trade options because of their distance from maritime routes of commerce.

9. The reproduction of ciliates, unlike **the reproduction/that of** other organisms, occurs when a specimen splits in half and grows a completely new individual from each piece.

10. Correct

11. At the age of twenty-four, playwright Thornton Wilder was balding and bespectacled, and his clothes were like **the clothes/those of** a much older man.

12. In ancient Greece, women were not allowed to vote or hold property, their status differing from **the status/that of** slaves only in name.

13. Although birds are not generally known for their intelligence, recent findings have established that parrots often possess skills similar to **the skills/those of** human toddlers.

14. Correct

15. One major difference between lowland Mayan rituals and **those of** other ancient peoples, some scholars believe, is that the former developed in relative isolation.

Word Pairs (p. 211)

1. Known for his designs inspired by natural principles, architect Michael Pawlyn was initially torn **between** studying architecture **and** studying biology but eventually chose the former.

2. Long Island was the setting for *The Great Gatsby*, but finding traces of the world Fitzgerald depicted there is **as** much a job for the imagination **as** it is for a map and a guidebook.

3. Once stereotyped as savants because of their depictions in movies such as *Rain Man*, people on the autistic spectrum are typically **neither** superhuman memory machines **nor** incapable of performing everyday tasks.

4. Obedience to authority is **not only** a way for rulers to keep order in totalitarian states, **but also** the foundation on which such states exist.

5. In the Middle Ages, the term "arts" referred to a wide range of fields including geometry, grammar, and astronomy; **only in** the nineteenth century **did** it come to denote painting, drawing, and sculpting.

6. Audiences find the play **at once** amusing because of the comedic skills of its leading actors **and** tedious because of its excessive length.

7. **So** great was the surplus of food created by the ancient Mesopotamians **that** it led to the establishment of the first complex civilization in human history.

8. Dumping pollution in oceans **not only** adds to the unsightliness of the formerly pristine waters **but also** destroys the marine life that inhabits them.

9. Because the Articles of Confederation did not provide for the creation of **either** executive agencies **or** judiciary institutions, they were rejected in favor of the Constitution.

10. **Just as** moral intelligence, an innate sense of right and wrong, allowed human societies to flourish, **so did** a strong sense of hierarchy allow canine societies to thrive.

11. One of the main effects of industrialization was the shift **from** a society in which women worked at home **to** one in which women worked in factories and brought home wages to their families.

12. Over the past decade, Internet usage has become **so** pervasive **that** many psychologists are beginning to study its effects on the lives of children and adolescents.

13. It was **not until** the late seventeenth century **that** some English writers began to challenge the traditional view of commerce, which held that money-making was a source of moral corruption to be avoided at all cost.

14. **Just as** the Machine Age transformed an economy of farm laborers and artisans into one of assembly lines, **so** the technology revolution is replacing factory workers with robots, and clerks with computers.

15. Although Voltaire wrote a number of tragedies and believed he would be remembered as a dramatist, he is known today **not so much** for his theatrical works **as** for his satires.

Parallel Structure: Lists (p. 214)

1. Lady Jane Grey, known as the nine-day queen, was renowned for her sweetness, her beauty, and **her subjection** to the whims of her mother.

2. Mediterranean cooking is best known for its reliance on fresh produce, whole grains, and **significant amounts of olive oil**.

3. The biggest beneficiaries of the Grateful Dead archive may prove to be business scholars who are discovering that the Dead were visionaries in the way they created customer value, promoted networking, and **implemented** strategic business planning.

4. The term "single-family house" describes how a house is built and who is intended to live in it, but it does not indicate the house's size, shape, or **location**.

5. Seeing the Grand Canyon, standing in front of a beautiful piece of art, and **listening** to a beautiful symphony are all experiences that may inspire awe.

6. Neighbors of the proposed park argue that an amphitheater would draw more traffic, disrupt their neighborhood, and **diminish** their only patch of open space.

7. Evidence suggests that the aging brain retains and even increases its capacity for resilience, growth, and **sense of well-being**.

8. Antiques are typically objects that show some degree of craftsmanship or attention to design, and they are considered desirable because of their beauty, rarity, or **usefulness/utility**.

9. Spiders use a wide range of strategies to capture prey, including trapping it in sticky webs, lassoing it with sticky bolas, and **mimicking** other insects in order to avoid detection.

10. According to medical authorities at the Mayo Clinic, building muscle can boost metabolism, **aid** in weight loss, and increase stamina and focus.

Two-Part Parallel Structure (p. 218)

1. A staple of Louisiana's culinary tradition, Cajun cuisine is predominantly rustic: it relies on local ingredients <u>and</u> **simple preparation**.

2. The university is installing a more detailed course-evaluation system so that students can decide whether they should register for certain classes <u>or</u> ~~should they~~ **avoid** them altogether.

3. Known for her musical compositions <u>as well as</u> **for** her poems and letters, Hildegard of Bingen was just as renowned in the twelfth century as she was in the twentieth.

4. While the novel has many detractors, it also has many admirers who argue that its popularity is based on its gripping storyline <u>and</u> **the believability of its characters' motives.**

5. The majority of rebellions that occurred in Tudor England did not achieve their objectives because of weakness of the rebels <u>and</u> **the extreme power of reigning monarchs**.

6. For fans of the legendary food writer Charles H. Baker, the contents of a dish are <u>less</u> compelling <u>than</u> **the story behind it**.

7. During the sixteenth century, an outbreak of fighting in Europe led to the invention of new weapons <u>and</u> to **the growth and evolution of old ones**.

8. The time publishing companies devote to books has been reduced by financial constraints <u>as well as</u> **an increased emphasis** on sales and marketing considerations.

9. In contemporary education, there is a disturbing contrast between the enormous popularity of certain approaches <u>and</u> **the lack of credible evidence for their effectiveness**.

10. At its peak, the Roman army was nearly unconquerable because of <u>not only</u> the hard and effective training of its commanders <u>but also</u> **the exceptional organization of its troops**.

Possible Answers: Dangling Modifiers (p. 222)

1. Often advertised to promote health and reduce stress, **dietary supplements** can produce harmful side effects, even though they are easy to purchase.

2. **Derek Walcott** was born in St. Lucia in the West Indies; his work includes a number of plays and poems, most notably *Omeros*.

3. Despite winning several architectural awards, **the university's new dormitory** has been criticized by students for its impractical layout.

4. One of the earliest authorities to take a stand against pollution, **King Edward I** proclaimed in 1306 that sea coal could not be burned because its smoke was hazardous to people's health.

5. Predicting renewed interest in their country's natural resources, **political leaders** have established a plan to create mines in the most underdeveloped regions.

6. Though **Jane Eyre** is educated and well mannered, her status remains low throughout the majority of the novel of which she is the protagonist.

7. Projecting an image of pain and brutality that has few parallels among advanced paintings of the twentieth century, *Guernica* was created by Picasso in the aftermath of a World War II bombing.

8. Believing that real estate prices would not rise indefinitely, **the economist** argued that the housing bubble would eventually burst.

Possible Answers: Misplaced and Squinting Modifiers (p. 226)

1. A recent discovery suggests that for the past 2.5 billion years, <u>a B-flat</u>, **the lowest note ever detected**, has been continuously emitted by a black hole 250 million light years from Earth.

2. <u>Claude McKay</u>, one of the most important poets of the Harlem Renaissance, **moved** to New York after studying agronomy in Kansas.

3. <u>The California Street Cable Railroad</u>, **which was founded by Leland Stanford**, is an established public transit company in San Francisco.

4. Some studies indicate that **frequently** <u>consuming</u> small amounts of chocolate is correlated with good health.

5. Only after joining Miles Davis's Second Great Quintet did Herbie Hancock, who had <u>performed</u> **professionally** as a musician since the age of seven, succeed in finding his voice as a pianist.

6. Some of <u>the world's fastest trains</u>, **which can reach speeds of up to 200 miles per hour**, run between the cities of Tokyo and Kyoto.

7. When economic activity weakens, monetary policymakers can push interest rate targets below the economy's natural rate, **temporarily** <u>lowering</u> the cost of borrowing.

8. **Fortresses** <u>protected many ancient cities</u> from bands of invaders that roamed in search of settlements to plunder.

Eliminating Redundancies (p. 231)

1. Economics is **classified as** ~~and has been called~~ a social science, one that is concerned with fair distribution, level of production, and the overall consumption of goods.

2. Although the students in the auditorium were silent throughout the entire lecture, the professor spoke so softly that his voice was **nearly inaudible** ~~and could hardly be heard~~.

3. Scuba divers usually move around underwater by using fins attached to their feet, but **external** propulsion can be provided ~~from an outside source~~ by a specialized propulsion vehicle or a sled pulled from the surface.

4. Accused of purposefully neglecting to follow crucial steps in the laboratory's safety protocol, the researcher insisted that the oversight was **inadvertent** ~~and accidental~~.

5. Faced with reports of a breaking scandal, company executives **deliberately** concealed the news from both shareholders and consumers ~~on purpose~~ because they feared the inevitable financial consequences.

6. Both the raw ingredients and distillation technology used by early perfumers **significantly influenced** ~~and had an important effect on~~ the development of chemistry.

7. The upper basin of Utah's Lake Powell provides a minimum **annual** flow of eight million tons of water ~~each year~~ to states across the Southwest.

8. Vietnam became independent from Imperial China in 938 A.D., with consecutive Vietnamese royal dynasties **flourishing** ~~one after the other~~ as the nation expanded geographically and politically.

9. Hydrothermal vents, fissures in a planet's surface from which heated water spurts, are commonly found near active volcanoes as well as areas where tectonic plates **diverge,** ~~coming apart from one another~~.

10. **Historically**, only a small number of educated elites were taught to write ~~in the past~~, so written records tend to reflect the assumptions and values of a limited range of individuals.

Eliminating Unnecessary Gerunds (p. 235)

1. because they held
2. (in order) to provide
3. introduction
4. Although it is
5. retention
6. Because she experimented
7. acquisition
8. to illustrate
9. because it lacked
10. rejection

Active or Passive? (p. 239)

1. Passive: Throughout the novel, the tapestry of local history **is combined with more current themes by the author**.

2. Active

3. Passive: Robert Cornelius, an early American photographer, **has been credited by historians of photography** with taking the first selfie.

4. Active

5. Active

6. Passive: Contrary to popular myth, **cities such as Syracuse and Troy <u>were</u> not named after their ancient counterparts <u>by</u> the land surveyor Simeon DeWitt**.

7. (Half-)Passive: Many of the items in the Grimms' first edition of fairy tales <u>**were**</u> **taken** not from a single source but from other pre-existing collections of stories.

8. Passive: The renowned contralto Marian Anderson <u>**was**</u> **offered numerous contracts <u>by</u> opera companies**, but she repeatedly declined because she preferred to appear in concert and recital only.

9. Active

10. Passive: The geologic instability known as the Pacific Ring of Fire has produced numerous faults, and approximately **10,000 earthquakes <u>are</u> caused <u>by</u> them** annually.

Making Sentences Active (p. 243)

1. **Elizabeth Bishop published only a handful of poems** during the course of her career, but each one was a model of perfection.

2. In the movie *The Killing Fields*, Cambodian photojournalist Dith Pran **was** portrayed by first-time actor Haing S. Ngor, a role for which Ngor won an Academy Award.

3. Although paleontologists often find new dinosaur bones or footprints, **researchers have not found the two types of fossils together until recently**.

4. **Scientists at the Woods Hole Oceanographic Institute designed** *Nereus*, a remotely operated underwater hybrid vehicle, to function at depths of up to 36,000 feet.

5. In the recent consumer report, market researchers **indicated** that food prices in economically depressed neighborhoods are frequently higher than in wealthier ones.

6. **The government has acknowledged the demand for foreign language instruction**, but funding for classes continues to be reduced.

7. Between the late 1970s and 1980s, **the Jamaican reggae musician Lone Ranger, born Anthony Alphanso Waldron, recorded nine albums**.

8. **Performance artist Jody Sperling founded Time Lapse Dance**, a New York-based dance company whose mission is to provide modern reinterpretations of classic works, in 2000.

9. **People throughout the Middle East, Singapore, and Indonesia frequently eat murtabak**, a dish composed of mutton, garlic, egg, onion, and curry sauce.

10. Over the last several decades, **researchers have examined many forms of meditation and deemed a number of them ineffective**.

Preposition-Based and TO/-ING Idioms (p. 250)

1. In *The Odyssey*, certain characters are granted ~~with~~ the ability to make decisions for themselves, while others must confront fate and divine intervention.

2. As Secretary-General of the United Nations, Kofi Annan became a strong proponent **of** diplomatic intervention in humanitarian crises.

3. Although the author's diaries provide a wealth of information about her daily interests, they fail **to present** a comprehensive picture of her life.

4. Over the last few decades, acceptance rates at many prestigious universities have sharply declined: only about 5-10% of students who apply to Ivy League universities are accepted **to** those schools, for example. **(Note: "into" and "at" are also used but are less standard.)**

5. Correct

6. Although it is indisputable that different people display varying levels of aptitude **for** different subjects, academic abilities are most likely shaped by a complex interplay of genetic and cultural factors.

7. The choreographer Alvin Ailey, who integrated traditional African movements into his works, is credited **with popularizing** modern dance.

8. A rebellion **against** the rigid academic art that predominated during the nineteenth century, the Art Nouveau movement was inspired by natural forms and structures.

9. Unlike his contemporaries, whose work he viewed as conventional and uninspiring, Le Corbusier insisted **on using** modern industrial techniques to construct buildings.

10. Both bizarre and familiar, fairy tales are intended to be spoken aloud rather than read silently, and they possess a truly inexhaustible power **over** children and adults alike.

11. The mineral azurite, a mineral produced by the weathering of copper deposits, has an exceptionally deep blue hue and thus has historically been associated **with** the color of winter skies.

12. Teachers have begun to note with alarm that the amount of time their students spend **playing** video games and surfing the Internet has severely impacted their ability to focus on single tasks for an extended period.

13. During the early decades of Japan's Heian Empire, a person who lacked a thorough knowledge **of** Chinese could never be considered fully educated.

14. Correct

15. In "Howl" as well as in his other poetry, Allen Ginsberg drew inspiration **from** the epic, free verse style popularized by the nineteenth century poet Walt Whitman.

Commonly Confused Words (p. 255)

1. To attract **prospective** students, the university has planned a series of lectures and open houses designed to exhibit its wide variety of academic programs and newly renovated facilities.

2. Although many traits are governed by a group of genes acting in concert, genes often have multiple functions, and altering a large amount of genetic material could have unforeseen **effects** on an organism.

3. Some global banks show an alarming willingness to facilitate the flow of illegal money; in certain cases, they even **counsel** financial institutions about how to evade regulators' grasp.

4. High-pressure sales practices by industry representatives have **led** to predictions that regulators will increase oversight and prompted speculation about potential lawsuits.

5. The physics professor was awarded the university's top teaching award because of her ability to make a difficult subject unusually **comprehensible** to her students.

6. Correct

7. Early hearing aids were far from **discreet**: large and bulky, they required heavy batteries that had to be charged frequently and were frustrating for users.

8. Encouraged by his party's wins in recent state polls, the opposition leader has been putting pressure on the prime minister to **waive** interest on certain loans.

9. Intended to ease traffic and reduce air pollution, ride-sharing companies such as Uber and Lyft were founded as **complements** to public transportation.

10. Government leaders and elected officials must take all the relevant parties' needs into account when attempting to address problems that **affect** the ability of different groups to live peacefully together.

11. Knowing the farmer who grows your food has become an important **tenet** of the modern agricultural movement, but little attention is paid to the people who actually pick the crops.

12. Istanbul was virtually depopulated when it fell to the Ottoman Turks, but the city recovered rapidly and by the mid-1600s had become the world's largest city as well as the new **capital** of the Ottoman Empire.

13. Correct

14. The large police presence at the international summit has had a chilling **effect** on protesters, even though it is unclear why such tight security measures are necessary.

15. One of the more frustrating aspects of the film is that its main character seems either incapable of or **uninterested** in conjuring traditional levels of empathy and self-awareness.

Suggested Answers: Connotation (p. 259)

1. Foreign policies are known to change radically from one year to the next; the Cold War is perhaps the greatest testament to the **unstable/uncertain/volatile** nature of international relations and foreign policy.

2. The prospect of free education does sound rather **attractive/appealing/tempting** to students planning to pursue higher education, but college still comes at a price for the government and teachers working for institutions.

3. Since the release of the Common Core State Standards, many issues in education have been called to the public's attention, and great debates have **resulted/emerged**.

4. Because the benefits of free trade **outweigh** its drawbacks, our society would ultimately be better off with free trade.

5. Correct

6. At the beginning of *The Odyssey*, Telemachus is completely unlike his father, but that situation quickly **changes/shifts** when Telemachus begins to become an adult.

7. Correct

8. Some scientists believe there is no adequate alternative to animal testing, but new **advances/breakthroughs** in medical research are providing options that would have been impossible just a few years ago.

9. Correct

10. Contrary to popular opinion, the employment of children in the early Industrial Revolution was not **halted/stopped** by the Factory Acts; rather, they simply sped up a process of technological change that was making child labor obsolete.

Suggested Answers: Informal Language and Clichés (p. 267)

1. Although it is often argued that people can become very successful without a college degree, millionaire college dropouts are actually **extremely** rare.

2. Jhumpa Lahiri's *The Namesake* centers on Gogol Ganguli, the son of immigrant parents who **struggles** with his double identity and desire to rebel against his family.

3. Adrian Peterson, running back for the Minnesota Vikings, is a role model who has continued to show pride and courage, despite the **many personal difficulties** he has faced.

4. The protagonist of *The Great Gatsby* cares only about his dreams; as a result, his life **becomes very** lonely.

5. Too much conformity within a society leads to citizens blindly accepting other people's opinions and **following** unjust laws.

6. Education is a wonderful asset for anyone: with a good one there is no limit to what people can achieve, and without one **people may not have access to important opportunities**.

7. The Middle Ages were a period in which science **flourished** in the Islamic world, particularly in cities on the Iberian Peninsula such as Córdoba.

8. Because physical exercise allows people to calm and clear their minds, many students rely on it to help them manage **their stressful lives**.

9. Human rights organizations work to protect the rights of people all over the world and to **eliminate** abuses such as slavery, child labor, and political persecution.

10. Frederick Douglass's narrative describing his life as a slave allows the reader to experience the suffering of someone who lives in captivity and is unable to **fulfill his potential**.

ABOUT THE AUTHOR

Erica Meltzer earned her B.A. from Wellesley College and spent more than a decade tutoring privately in Boston and New York City, as well as nationally and internationally via Skype. Her experience working with students from a wide range of educational backgrounds and virtually every score level, from the third percentile to the 99th, gave her unique insight into the types of stumbling blocks students often encounter when preparing for standardized reading and writing tests.

She was inspired to begin writing her own test-prep materials in 2007, after visiting a local bookstore in search of additional practice questions for an SAT® Writing student. Unable to find material that replicated the contents of the exam with sufficient accuracy, she decided to write her own. What started as a handful of exercises jotted down on a piece of paper became the basis for her first book, the original *Ultimate Guide to SAT Grammar*, which was published in 2011 and on which this book is based. Since that time, she has authored guides for SAT reading and vocabulary, as well as verbal guides for the ACT®, GRE®, and GMAT®. Her books have sold more than 175,000 copies and are used around the world. She lives in New York City, and you can visit her online at www.thecriticalreader.com.

Made in the USA
Middletown, DE
21 December 2023